D0936670

Literature and Crime
in Augustan England

Literature and Crime in Augustan England

Ian A. Bell

820.9
B413

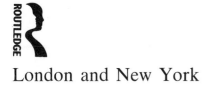

London and New York

First published 1991
by Routledge
11 New Fetter Lane, London EC4P 4EE

Simultaneously published in the USA and Canada
by Routledge
a division of Routledge, Chapman and Hall, Inc.
29 West 35th Street, New York, NY 10001

© 1991 Ian A. Bell

Typeset in 10/12 Times by
Columns Ltd, Reading
Printed in Great Britain by
TJ Press (Padstow) Ltd, Padstow, Cornwall

All rights reserved. No part of this book may be reprinted or
reproduced or utilized in any form or by any electronic,
mechanical, or other means, now known or hereafter
invented, including photocopying and recording, or in any
information storage or retrieval system, without permission
in writing from the publishers.

British Library Cataloguing in Publication Data
Bell, Ian A. (Ian Arthur)
Literature and crime in Augustan England.
1. English literature 1702–1745. Critical studies
I. Title
820.9005

Library of Congress Cataloging in Publication Data

also available

ISBN 0–415–02231–2

For Seona and Lewis

Buttock and Twang, which is walking to be picked up, and, frightening him that does it with her pretended husband, after she has picked his pocket, so that the fool runs gladly away without his watch or money.

Buttock and File, which is the same with the other; only this is the better-natured beast of the two, and performs her stage before she takes her wages, which may be some satisfaction to the ass she carries.

From the *Memoirs of the Right Villainous John Hall*, 1708

Contents

126093

Acknowledgements

I would like to thank a lot of people for their help in writing this book. My knowledge of Augustan writing has been greatly enriched by discussions with Duncan Isles and Shane Flynn, and James Ogden was most helpful in lending me books. Bill Hines and Meirion Derrick of the Law Library, UCW Aberystwyth provided invaluable assistance, above and beyond the call of duty, and my legal advisers include Richard Ireland and Chris Harding of the Law Department, UCW Aberystwyth, and James Meldrum, Deputy Director of the Scottish Courts Administration. My main intellectual obligation is to Philip J. Rawlings, of Brunel University, whose knowledge of the practices of eighteenth-century crime has been as useful to me in preparing this volume as it will prove to be to him in the furtherance of his academic career. But my most profound gratitude must go to my wife and family, who have put up with a distant and distracted figure in their midst while I was thinking this project through, and who were unfailingly positive and supportive throughout. To them, and to all the others mentioned, my heartfelt thanks. Remaining errors or inconsistencies are entirely my responsibility.

Ian A. Bell
Llanbadarn Fawr
Aberystwyth

The photographs of William Hogarth's *Industry and Idleness* sequence are reproduced by courtesy of the Trustees of the British Museum.

Introduction: Buttock and Twang

A crucial dimension for understanding the reaction to deviance both by the public as a whole and by agents of social control, is the nature of the information that is received about the behaviour in question.[1]

This book is a study of information about deviance, and misinformation, and disinformation. It concentrates upon the diverse representations of crime and legality in early eighteenth-century England, on the ways in which the various constituent performers in these cultural practices were portrayed, and on the significance of such representations for their producers and consumers. It is, I hope, an exercise in literary criticism at the service of wider cultural history, where the close reading of works of literature will be informative not just about the internal ordering of those texts or about the workings of their authors' minds, but also about the creation and dissemination of ideology and the diversities of cultural practice. By investigating the kind of information the Augustan public received from its press about deviance and deviants, I want to explore the contemporary ideological potency of the ideas of crime and criminals, the areas of ideological fissure they reveal, and the possible supportive and adversary roles of literature in their distribution. There are obviously a great many areas of uncertainty and trepidation in this endeavour and lest you feel that you have fallen among thieves and swindlers already, I will set out before you at the very beginning the terms of the arrangement.

My original thought for a title for this book was *Buttock and Twang*, as defined by the Right Villainous John Hall in 1708, finding in that evocative phrase an image for the recognised protocols and procedures of this kind of critical study. Following the established patterns of earlier commentators on historical crime, my plan was to attract gullible readers with a lurid catchpenny title and then, having relieved them of their money, scare them off, not with the sudden furious appearance of a pretended husband, but with the predictably alarming intervention of Antonio Gramsci or Louis Althusser. I was sensitive that some tender readers might well find the prospect of the irate E. P. Thompson bursting out from behind a thicket yet again sufficiently intimidating to send them scurrying away elsewhere. But wise caution prompts a more scholarly mode of address and a more sober title, albeit one in which every term is wrapped round a mystery or uncertainty. Let us take these terms individually and see what confusion lies bound within each one.

The opening word 'literature' looks relatively uncontroversial, but still requires some preliminary definition. It would certainly be quite possible to write about this topic from within the traditional 'Eng. Lit.' perspective of the magical and universal powers of identifiable literary value. In such a case, great novels, plays and poems alone would provide the materials, and the conclusion would be restricted to clarifying the views of certain allegedly 'great' authors on these weighty matters. As a project in historical or cultural study, any enterprise of this kind becomes uninformative and highly reductive, and it is by no means my intention to confine myself to this attractively privileged but narrow way of thinking. A more sympathetic and potentially more informative approach to the subject requires a less judgemental attitude to eighteenth-century writing, and I would not wish to have to keep apologising for the unwholesomeness or shabbiness of many of the texts under review. An unthinking attachment to those traditional assumptions about literary merit distorts the otherwise stimulating early essays in this field by F. W. Chandler and others, rendering them now of no more than antique or curiosity value. My scope is of necessity wider than that. I take 'literature' in its least restrictive meaning, requiring it to cover everything written or printed, leaving evaluative notions of literary merit aside, and enthusiastically incorporating unorthodox texts like Hogarth's prints or the Old Bailey Session Papers or Boswell's private journals. And I will be unembarrassed in my use of popular writing. As Raymond Williams has demonstrated, an all-embracing use of the word 'literature', associating it with 'literacy' rather than with 'literariness' is peculiarly appropriate to the publishing and reading practices of the eighteenth century.[2] So although the best-known novels and poems and the like will inevitably be prominent in the following discussion, and the names of the most revered authors will appear frequently, the real focus of attention must be the press as a whole rather than a few tendentiously selected and unrepresentative 'universal' texts.

Similar problems of demarcation and limitation surround my use of the word 'Augustan'. The terminology of a new Augustan Age is most conventionally associated with some of (or all of) the period from 1660 to 1760, from the restoration of Charles II to the accession of George III, and it is such a broad perspective I wish to adopt here. Very precise and narrow definitions can be sought and found, for instance in Oliver Goldsmith's essay in *The Bee* (1759) which limits the period described by the term to the years between 1702 and 1714, but very elastic and imprecise uses can also be located.[3] I have no wish to engage in unfruitful controversy if I can help it, so I may as well lay my cards on the table and declare that I am taking 'Augustan' to include the period from around

1688, the date of the so-called 'Glorious Revolution' that brought William III to the throne, until around 1760, when George III became monarch. However, I would want to emphasise that the monarchical perimeters of the study are only to be seen as a convenience, with the great kings acting as no more than book-ends. On occasions, I may draw on works published prior to this initial date, like Hobbes's *Leviathan*, if they were still significantly in circulation in the period in question, or informative about emergent or disappearing structures of feeling. I may also make use of subsequent writing, like the work of Jonas Hanway or Patrick Colquhoun, as it retrospectively discusses the past. For my present purposes, then, the term is no more than a convenient short-hand, not to be taken as strictly judgemental or over-interpretive, and great precision about when the period began or ended or fastidious discrimination between the term's more delicate shades of meaning should not be sought here.

My use of 'England' is a similar, if rather more reluctant, bow to convention. As a Scot, writing in Wales, I am sensitive to the stealthy imperialist coerciveness of this term (tiresomely over-sensitive, some say). For the purposes of the present study, however, it is probably acceptable enough to use the exclusive noun. After all, Scotland had (and has) retained a separate legal system despite the Act of Union in 1707, and what I say here need not apply to that special case. I have to admit that 'England' here silently incorporates Wales, as it legally did at the time, with due apologies to my colleagues, students, neighbours and children. But at the risk of sounding evasive I will aver that the focus of my current attention is quite properly England, and more specifically London, as the centre of the publishing industry, and as the place where legal practice was most elaborately formalised. Elsewhere in Britain at this time, the ecclesiastical or church courts were still relatively more prominent, prosecuting 'moral' or spiritual offences like adultery or defamation, though even in rural districts they were beginning to lose much of their force and authority by the Augustan period.[4] Also, in the provinces there may have been more prolonged recourse to informal, communally recognised and accepted sanctions, like revenge, or the ritual humiliation variously known as 'rough music' or 'skimmington' or 'charivari' or 'shirrikin'. Although these had not entirely disappeared from the metropolis, as we shall see, they had been incorporated in legal rituals like the elaborate procession to Tyburn, or the ceremonies of the pillory, or else they had become much less authoritative.

London, too, was not only the location of the main courts and prisons, and the venue for the notorious activities of celebrated criminals like Jonathan Wild and Jack Sheppard, it was also the focus of most literary activity. This is obvious in the urbane setting of the developing periodicals like the *Tatler* and *Spectator* and in the declared allegiances of such various relevant texts as *The London Bawd*, *The London Jilt*, *The*

London Spy, *The London Merchant* and *The Whore's Rhetorick Calculated to the Meridian of London*. The metropolis then functioned as a complex cultural sign for contemporary readers, a nexus in which were brought together the seat of government and the dens of criminals, the legislature and the underworld, the triumph of civilisation and the persistence of savagery, the exotic and the mundane, all those dialectical tensions between which the press negotiated, and which in its more lurid forms it exploited. In London, therefore, the agency of law, the role of the press, the tensions between behaviour and its categorisation, and between action and description, are most graphic and most rewarding of study.

The hesitations which have to be introduced when using 'literature', 'Augustan' and 'England' can be acknowledged and dispersed (or suspended) quite easily. The problems involved in talking about 'crime' are much greater, and need more careful examination. In the next chapter, I will linger over the difficulties involved in trying to identify reliable figures for crime and its perpetrators. But at the moment it is important to address an even more basic difficulty: what *is* crime? Anyone presently asked to give a list of crimes is likely to mention uncontentiously illegal violent acts like murder or rape and other obvious cases like larcenies. But even here there are areas of uncertainty, like the killing of enemy troops in wartime or the pilfering of insignificant items from the work-place. And after that, things become even less certain. Since our notions of crime are tangled up with our ideas of wrongful behaviour (an adjacent, but never exactly identical category) and our perception of illegality, our definition of crime is bound to be idiosyncratic.

Also, it is obvious that there is a historical dimension in the definition of crime. Social circumstances have changed so much that the law covers different things at different times. To take a banal example first, the eighteenth century is an unexciting period for the historian of road traffic offences. More interestingly, we no longer criminalise certain activities which were illegal in the earlier period, like the host of offences prosecuted by church courts, including service-dodging or fornication. And conversely, activities largely unremarked in the early eighteenth century, like the maintenance of slaves and the conditions of child labour, were later legally circumscribed. I will return to the fluctuations of legislation and the shifting overlap between law and morality at various points in the ensuing pages. For the moment, the definition of crime which serves my purposes best is one which is historically relative and non-prescriptive. As a result, I am happy to follow J. A. Sharpe in defining crime as 'behaviour which is illegal and which, if detected, would lead to prosecution in a court of law or summarily before an accredited agent of law enforcement'.[5]

There are of course problems involved in this definition, arising from the discretionary nature of the prosecution of certain offences, and the rapid changes in legislation during the Augustan period. These will arise in the body of the argument, and be dealt with where appropriate. However, as a starting point, the broad sweep of Sharpe's definition will suffice. Perhaps, after all these reservations about the identifiability of the subject and the concern with finding appropriate terminology to articulate it, this book should have been called something more elaborate and cautious, something much more scholarly, like *The Press and its Roles in Disseminating and Resisting the Re-Categorisation of Certain Patterns of Legally Stigmatised Behaviour in the Southern Part of Britain at a Fairly Ill-Defined Time Around the Eighteenth Century.* Though that might more accurately describe the drift of the following pages, it is a bit unenticing, and I still yearn for the tabloid simplicity of *Buttock and Twang.* Forewarned then, if not forearmed, let us proceed with appropriate caution and get on with the argument.

1 Literature/crime/society

TALKING ABOUT THE LAW

In 1758, Sir William Blackstone delivered for the first time the series of lectures later published as his *Commentaries on the Laws of England*. Speaking at the University of Oxford, he was addressing an audience drawn exclusively from the privileged and propertied male elite of his society. For their benefit and instruction, Blackstone presented a systematic and easily comprehensible unfolding of the benign principles which, he argued, upheld the whole elaborate fabric of the English legislature. His stated aims could not be simpler, or more obviously partisan – 'I think it is an undeniable position, that a competent knowledge of that society, in which we live, is the proper accomplishment of every gentleman and scholar; an highly useful, I had almost said essential part of liberal and polite education.'[1] With a tone of sustained complacency, Blackstone sought to demonstrate the manifest and manifold felicities of his native constitution. Although it might appear bafflingly complex and incomprehensible to the uninitiated, the body of statute was in fact covertly unified by its concern for the liberty of the propertied oligarchy. Without apology or embarrassment, Blackstone proudly and rhetorically underlined the ways in which the law entitled his listeners to lead lives of unimpeded security and comfort:

> these rights consist, primarily in the free enjoyment of personal security, of personal liberty, and of private property . . . And all of these rights and liberties it is our birthright to enjoy entire; unless where the laws of our country have laid them under necessary restraints. Restraints in themselves so gentle and moderate, as will appear upon farther enquiry, that no man of sense or probity would wish to see them slackened.
>
> (i, 140)

This robustly conservative version of the body of law ('*our* birthright . . . *our* country'), which so outraged Bentham and the later reformers, combines a reverence for the law with a class-based ideology of

Englishness. The overall impression that the speaker was trying to convey is that the landed or propertied Englishman may live more or less unrestrained in a world organised for his benefit. Of course, to advance such an argument, however intelligently or fastidiously, Blackstone had to maintain a discreet silence on the subject of those less generously treated by the laws – the poor, slaves, women, children – and there could be no place whatsoever in his rhetoric for thoughts of agitation or dissent.

Reading his words now, we can hear the voice of mid-eighteenth-century privileged confidence at its most assured and triumphant. Blackstone seems remarkably untroubled by anxiety or apprehension, and encourages his prosperous listeners to have faith in the law, which is designed to support and maintain their cultural dominance. In doing so, he demonstrates the ideological centrality of legislation and enforceable contracts in bourgeois society, which he saw as necessary and wholly desirable. The authoritative chapter and verse which could regulate conduct and arbitrate in the disputes of his audience were not to be found in Holy Scripture, as they might still have been for less comfortable Augustans, but in the statute book.

This was by no means an eccentric or idiosyncratic position. As Adam Smith recognised in *The Wealth of Nations* (1776), an unquestioning belief in the reliability and justice of the laws of contract had been (and still was) the ideological cement which held post-agrarian society together:

> Commerce and manufactures can seldom flourish long in any state which does not enjoy a regular administration of justice, in which the people do not feel themselves secure in the possession of property, in which the faith of contracts is not supported by law, and in which the authority of the state is not supposed to be regularly employed in enforcing the payment of debts from all those who are able to pay. Commerce and manufactures, in short, can seldom flourish in any state in which there is not a certain degree of confidence in the justice of the government.[2]

Smith is here talking about the ways in which the maintenance of the law permits and supports the activities of a mercantile culture, but his language shows a very interesting reliance on ideology rather than on reality. The members of this commercial civilisation must have 'faith' and 'a certain degree of confidence' in things. That is to say, they have to *believe* in the efficacy of the law for their society to function. Whether or not that confidence was entirely justified is a separate, perhaps unnecessary, question, for the belief was sufficiently instrumental to make the law work.

Blackstone's *Commentaries* can be seen as part of the ideological machinery by which this system of belief and confidence is created. His exposition is an elegant, seemingly effortless attempt to bolster belief, to disseminate confidence, to reassure his audience that the laws of England had their best interests at heart. He was demonstrating to them their right to conduct business unhindered, and at the same time instructing them in their future duties as administrators, magistrates and even members of parliament. Furthermore, he was offering the promise that, while the laws of conveyancing, for example, might justly regulate the transaction of property, they would in no way address the fundamental inequities in the prevailing distribution of that property. As well as holding symbolic and ideological importance, the civil law might, on acquaintance, serve certain useful practical purposes in the day-to-day life and business of his listeners – 'the understanding of a few leading principles, relating to estates and conveyancing, may form some check and guard upon a gentleman's inferior agents, and preserve him at least from very gross and notorious imposition' (i, 7).

Some knowledge of the civil law, and attendant confidence in its authority, is thus made to seem like a useful part of a gentleman's social equipment. The statutes could be relied upon to articulate bourgeois hegemony, and to reify the values of the landed classes, and keep 'inferior agents' on their guard. And that, for Blackstone (and his listeners) was the way things should be. However, it is most interesting to notice that even Blackstone becomes much more hesitant in his treatment of contemporary criminal law. Far from demonstrating the felicities of the English constitution, and enabling a gentleman to conduct his business smoothly and legitimately, the criminal statutes seemed to Blackstone to be rather rough and ready:

> The criminal law is in every country of Europe more rude and imperfect than the civil . . . Even with us in England, where our crown-law is with justice supposed to be more nearly advanced to perfection; where crimes are more accurately defined, and penalties less uncertain and arbitrary; where all our accusations are public, and our trials in the face of the world; where torture is unknown, and every delinquent is judged by such of his equals, against whom he can form no exception nor even a personal dislike; – even here we shall occasionally find room to remark some particulars, that seem to want revision and amendment.

(iv, 3)

Blackstone here includes all the features which were regularly cited by patriotic commentators to demonstrate the superiority of English criminal legislation over its continental counterparts – the virtual absence of torture and the alleged impartiality of jurors being two of the most potent and regularly flaunted items. However, after this flag-waving defence of English legislation, Blackstone is required to pause and acknowledge the visible imperfections in the criminal law, and question the necessity for the savage restraints it could impose.

Whereas the earlier, more relaxed and informal system of judge-made law seemed to Blackstone to be well-nigh perfect, the newly developed criminal statute, created by a distant and occasionally ill-informed or partisan Parliament, gave him cause for concern. Blackstone's preferred system was one where magistrates would be local men, well-informed of the particular circumstances of cases, and sufficiently acquainted with the niceties of the law through works like Richard Burn's *The Justice of the Peace and Parish Officer,* Giles Jacob's *The Statute-Law Common-plac'd,* John Mallory's *The Attorney's Pocket Companion,* Michael Dalton's *The Country Justice,* Theodore Barlow's *The Justice of the Peace,* or any of the other digests available in the mid-century. By this method, a magistrate could make appropriate judgements, in keeping with the broad principles set down by Coke, Hale, Stamford and Hawkins, yet responsive to local requirements, and without excessive or pedantic legalistic quibbling.

But as Blackstone saw it, the sensitive and flexible methods so established were being swept away by the growth of rather clumsier centralised legislation. When introducing a discussion of the 'Bloody Code', as it came to be known, his earlier urbanity and confidence begin to disappear. He has to recognise that English criminal law could and did perpetrate grotesque outrages – he mentions that the death sentence could be passed on someone found 'to break down (however maliciously) the mound of a fishpond, whereby any fish shall escape; or cut down a cherry tree in an orchard' (iv, 3) – but he tries to play these down by attributing such severity to a minor bureaucratic inefficiency in supervising and articulating the law.[3] His solution, of course, is to seek for intelligent procedures of 'revision and amendment' rather than to demand any more radical or challenging reforms.

Blackstone's unease here is most interesting. It looks as though he is having to confront a discourse which violates those ideals of gentlemanly conduct which the civil law enshrined and which the tone of his lectures tried to reproduce. Whereas the civil code seemed to weave a fabric of cultured civilisation, the criminal codes could look like the flagrant exercise of power and violence to secure rights and property for a few. Of course, that was not the only function of the criminal law, nor the one that was most widely recognised. The ideological significance of the law was that it managed for much of the time to create the illusion of impartiality and fairness, and it was seen by many as an acceptable tribunal for arbitrating disputes. In most of its operations, the law was not a direct and unmediated articulation of power, but an ideological transfiguration of class values, shrouded in ritual, mystery and ceremony, continually protesting its disinterest. And, as J. M. Beattie puts it, 'to be seen to be serving the interests of the broader community in a fair manner it had indeed to be doing so'.[4] Perhaps it often was doing so, discouraging violence and fraudulent practice by the most drastic of means, and even, now and then, defending the weak against the strong. But yet to the modern commentator there seem to be far too many occasions when the mask of impartiality slipped, and the criminal law seemed to be acting aggressively 'to sustain and legitimize the established social and economic and political arrangements of the society'.[5]

The traditional view of eighteenth-century English criminal legislation is that it represents a kind of Dark Age, lying in wait for the battalion of enlightened reformers like Cesare Beccaria, Jeremy Bentham, John Howard, Sir Samuel Romilly, William Eden, Sir Thomas Fowell Buxton, Sir James Mackintosh and Elizabeth Fry – names almost as well known to the general reader as the names of famous criminals. As Sir Leon Radzinowicz, at his most apologetic and progressivist, famously put it, 'Lord Macaulay's generalisation that the history of England is the history of progress is as true of the criminal law of this country as of the other social institutions of which it is a part.'[6] Such Whiggish confidence in the perfectibility of law has not been borne out by the various more recent studies of the period. Whereas Radzinowicz seems assured that 'the criminal law of England has always been sensitive to the needs and aspirations of the English people',[7] more recent commentators have seen the evolution of the criminal code as reflecting the needs and aspirations more exclusively of certain groups and classes (like those which made up Blackstone's audience) than of some happily amorphous mass called 'the English people'. Although there are very significant differences of emphasis among the most recent commentaries, to which we shall return, they share the perception that throughout the Augustan period many traditional and previously acceptable practices were being criminalised by the introduction of new laws, and that the very rapid growth in statutes (especially in capital statutes) at the time is indicative of 'the aggrandizement of the property rights of the gentry at the expense of common right and customs'.[8] Although the law represented class interests in a mediated and disguised form, shrouded in the majesty of ceremony and the performance of ritual, those class interests were still its central generative force.

It is important to recognise that this version of the ideological function of criminal legislation had a place in the widespread discussion of the law in the eighteenth century itself. There was, as we might expect, intense and sustained discussion of the legal system, even if most of it looked primarily at the practicalities rather than the politics of law. The feature which attracted most attention was that the criminal code in England, while in some respects less atavistic than others to be found in Europe, still relied on a mixture of ceremony and savagery in the form of ritualised executions, transportation, and various violent corporal punishments. Throughout the century, more and more offences, including apparently trivial ones, could be punished by death, although a certain amount of discretion could be exercised in sentencing. The most notorious piece of legislation was the 'Waltham Black Act' (9 Geo. I c.22), which introduced around fifty new capital offences virtually overnight, including the fish-mound example raised by Blackstone. This act has been seen as 'the onset of the flood-tide of eighteenth-century retributive justice' and it served as a focus for discussions of the status of the legal system.[9] For Blackstone, even the discretion which could be employed in the courts did not prevent this act from seeming excessive – 'it is true, that these outrageous penalties, being seldom or never inflicted, are hardly known to be law by the public: but that rather aggravates the mischief, by laying a snare for the unwary' (iv, 4). So although Blackstone is scrupulous in not pointing the finger at anyone for this cruelty, he cannot remain unaware of the potential savagery of at least part of the English constitution.

The problem that the Black Act dramatised and intensified could be seen as a tension within the discourse of law itself. In trying to regularise and legitimise the whole procedure, Blackstone inevitably ran up against the problems of the apparent injustices perpetrated by the legal system itself. He could not help but see that a system for preserving life and property which depended on the sanctions of destroying life and confiscating property was morally complex and might not always be capable of a benign interpretation. Blackstone acknowledged these problems but did not investigate them thoroughly. Other commentators, of a more aggressively ironic temper, could see the paradoxes much more clearly. David Hume, for example, in his *Treatise of Human Nature* (1739), isolated the institutional complexity of the law, and sought to make sense of it:

> When I relieve persons in distress, my natural humanity is my motive; and so far as my succour extends, so far have I promoted the happiness of my fellow-creatures. But if we examine all the questions, that come before any tribunal of justice, we shall find, that, considering each case apart, it wou'd as often be an instance of humanity to decide contrary to the laws of justice as conformable to them. Judges take from a poor man to give to a rich; they bestow on the dissolute the labour of the industrious; and put into the hands of the vicious the means of harming both themselves and others. The whole scheme, however, of law and justice is advantageous to the society; and 'twas with a view to this advantage, that men, by their voluntary conventions, established it.[10]

Hume's argument draws attention to those paradoxes in the operation and purpose of law which many eighteenth-century commentators exploited. On the one hand, it looks as though it was possible to present the institution of law as the public formalisation of a gentlemanly code of good practice, motivated largely by 'natural humanity', as Blackstone does. On the other hand, and with more persuasive support, it could be seen as a powerful, virtually self-regulating institution, very remote from questions of individual conscience, unable to dwell on the minute particulars of individual cases, requiring to act by broad and imprecise principles of social utility as part of a maintained state apparatus of coercion and compulsion. Although the law obviously perpetrated cruelties and defended existing inequalities, it might still be sanctioned as a necessary component in the 'whole scheme' of civilisation. According to many contemporary commentators, the law in practice might inevitably be imperfect, but at the very least it had to be better than the anarchic possibilities of total lawlessness.

Broader questions of the morality of punishment, the role of the state, and the relationship between the law and ethics were widely and frequently discussed throughout the Augustan period, attracting the attention of theologians, philosophers, pamphleteers, poets, politicians, dramatists, novelists, and virtually everyone else with access to print. The legal system and the courts acted as stimuli to discussions of the nature of humanity, the principles of civic organisation, and the possibilities of a rational, just society. In this chorus of commentary, cries for reform vie with cries for consolidation, pleas for mercy alternate with demands for increased severity, respectful praise sits alongside disrespectful hostility, and reverence jostles with contempt. Sir William Blackstone's voice may have been one of the most authoritative and persuasive, but it was by no means the only one talking about the law.

TALKING ABOUT CRIME

The cultural and ideological importance of law in eighteenth-century England ensured that it remained at the centre of public discussion throughout the period. Contemporary commentaries were multi-vocal, and it is hard to provide a consistent or even a fully coherent version of them. With the enviable benefits of hindsight, we might wish to emphasise the rising chorus of cries for reform, as Michael Ignatieff and Sir Leon Radzinowicz do in their different ways, or we might, as Michel Foucault does, try to record a change in the patterns of penal behaviour. In a very stimulating and influential analysis, Foucault compares the grotesquely lingering execution of a French regicide in 1757 with a regimented prison timetable from eighty years later. From these documents, he constructs an elaborate and fascinating argument about changes in 'penal style' and 'the disappearance of torture as a public spectacle'.[11] I have no wish to quarrel with this version of events – indeed, I am much indebted to it – but I feel that both Ignatieff and Foucault (and, from a different perspective, Radzinowicz) overrate the availability of unanimity and coherence. As I hope to show, it is possible to use documents as selectively as Foucault does to present a very different version of the period.

All commentaries on the law, of course, have to be commentaries on crime, and criminal activities in themselves attracted a great deal of intense discussion. From the very beginning of the century, it is possible to find many commentators strenuously declaring that crime was growing all the time. In 1701, an anonymous pamphlet called *Hanging Not Punishment Enough* made an impassioned plea for aggravated forms of the death penalty, like breaking upon the wheel. Mere hanging, it claimed, was too lenient and insufficiently fearsome for the hardened criminals of the day, and as a result it was no longer safe to walk the streets:

> Were it not so, our Roads would not be so pester'd with that wicked Generation of Men, nor our Sessions-Paper Monthly, and the Publick News daily full of so many Relations of Robberies and Murthers, and all the Pleasure and Satisfaction of Travelling destroyed, as it is now, by being so dangerous and unsafe . . . If some Remedy be not found to stop this growing Evil, we will shortly not dare to travel in England, unless, as in the Desarts of Arabia, it be in large Companies, and Arm'd.[12]

This rather hysterical outburst, pointing to the imminence of social collapse and suggesting a very recent deterioration in manners, adopts a rhetorical stance that can be found throughout the eighteenth century and beyond. In fact, as has been pointed out by a number of writers, the bizarre myth of a golden age of law-abiding citizens lurking just within the reaches of memory in the recent past is an essential component of a perennially potent conservative ideology.[13] This particular early eighteenth-century pamphlet is only one of many on similar themes, calling for increased severity in punishment to combat what the writer believes to be a flagrant unchecked growth in crime and lawlessness. Like the similarly intense calls for the introduction of even more elaborate methods of execution in George Ollyffe's *An Essay Humbly Offer'd* (1731), this piece may well have confirmed some temporary anxieties, and reproduced a particular structure of feeling which can still regularly be heard. However, despite the writers' failures to offer persuasive supporting evidence for their claims, their attitudes were so much part of the ideological fabric of their age that virtually no-one questioned or challenged such highly contentious assumptions.

Throughout the century such anxieties about the growth of crime and the dangers it presented to the public appear frequently, and the insistent repetitions can at first sight make the case look persuasive. In 1718, the City Marshal of London announced:

> Now it is the general complaint of the taverns, the coffee-houses, the shop-keepers and others, that their customers are afraid when it is dark to come to their houses and shops for fear that their hats and wigs should be snitched from their heads or their swords taken from their

sides, or that they may be blinded, knocked down, cut or stabbed; nay, the coaches cannot secure them, but they are likewise cut and robbed in the public streets, &c. By which means the traffic of the City is much interrupted.[14]

These fears of the universality and imminence of theft or violence seem to have been strongly felt by many, and they are articulated again and again by contemporary commentators, often involving the anxieties created by the large number of discharged service personnel drifting about after the Peace of Aix-la-Chapelle. In 1751, Henry Fielding's pamphlet, *An Enquiry into the Causes of the Late Increase of Robbers,* opened with a very bleak picture of city life:

The great Increase of Robberies within these few Years, is an Evil which to me appears to deserve some attention; and the rather as it seems (tho' already become so flagrant) not yet to have arrived to that Height of which it is capable, and which it is likely to attain: For Diseases in the Political, as in the Natural Body, seldom fail going on to their Crisis, especially when nourished and encouraged by Faults in the Constitution. In fact, I make no Doubt, but that the Streets of this Town, and the Roads leading to it, will shortly be impassable without the utmost Hazard; nor are we threatned with seeing less dangerous Gangs of Rogues among us, than those which the *Italians* call the Banditi.[15]

It is tempting to see this eloquence as merely a hyperbolic flight of rhetoric, but as the century progressed, the need for a more effective system of policing was made very prominent, and public debate was still provoked by a general feeling that the streets were terrifyingly lawless. In 1775, Jonas Hanway wrote:

I sup with my friend; I cannot return to my home, not even in my chariot, without danger of a pistol being clapt to my breast. I build an elegant villa, ten or twenty miles distant from the capital: I am obliged to provide an armed force to convey me thither, lest I should be attacked on the road with fire and ball.[16]

The most egregiously systematic of these tirades actually appeared as late as 1796. Patrick Colquhoun, a stipendiary magistrate, wrote a *Treatise on the Police of Metropolitan London* in which he claimed that as many as 115,000 people in the city – probably representing something like one in eight of the total population – were 'regularly engaged in criminal pursuits'. He broke these startling figures down into separate categories, the coolness of his statistical procedure contrasting sharply with the sensationalist pitch of his argument. There were, he claimed, at least

8,000 'thieves, pilferers and embezzlers' and 2,000 'Professional Thieves, Burglars, Highway Robbers, Pickpockets and River Pirates'. These are very dramatic figures, made much starker and somehow more authoritative in tone by the remarkable lack of supporting evidence or substantiation offered.[17]

The notion of a widespread criminal class stealthily at work throughout the land, a furtive and nefarious mirror-image of the frightened hardworking citizen, was a very potent idea in the eighteenth-century popular imagination. It can be seen in all these examples I have quoted, and in many others as well. Unfortunately, some influential historians have taken such statements out of their ideological context, and simply reproduced them as incontestable fact. Basil Williams, for instance, in the original *Oxford History of England*, talks blithely of 'a large idle or criminal class who earned a precarious subsistence by their misdirected wits, and whose existence was fostered by the absence of an efficient police-system, the ill-lighted streets, and the horrible rookeries full of brothels'.[18] This very lurid picture seems to hold a peculiar appeal for historians, who mostly lead sheltered and bookish lives, but there is very little to support it other than the iterations of axe-grinding pamphleteers. Of course, it might be tempting to think that something said as often as that has to have some truth in it, but the case for identifying a peculiarly virulent 'crime wave' in the Augustan period would be much more persuasive if there was some more substantial corroboration available to support it. As E. P. Thompson puts it, 'eighteenth-century class prejudice unites here with the anachronistic employment of the (inadequate) terminology of some twentieth-century criminology'.[19] Indeed, on closer examination, the whole notion of 'crime' and attendant groups of organised perpetrators of illegal activity becomes very uncertain.

It is very important to see that these questions about crime lie in the realm of ideological fantasy rather than demonstrable reality. In Adam Smith's model of a mercantile society, the integrity of commerce was maintained by a belief in the reliability and enforceability of contracts. In David Hume's argument, the sporadic inequities of the legal system were eventually excused, as far as possible, by the belief in the necessity of law. So in many other contemporary arguments the whole state apparatus of punishment and restraint is supported and legitimised by the creation of an elaborate scare about growing criminality and an organised criminal class. To put it bluntly, laws would more easily be brought in, and receive more widespread public assent, if they were thought to be in defence of the rights of honest citizens, under threat from the lawless and violent criminal class.

The moral panic about crime which was orchestrated and sustained throughout the eighteenth century seems to have been very effective in maintaining belief in the necessity of the 'Bloody Code'. But was it in any way justified? Despite its obviousness, any such question is remarkably difficult to answer. Alongside the prurient perception of Basil Williams, it is salutary to place the calmer comments of J. A. Sharpe:

> We must therefore conclude that there was little professional crime in our period and, equally, few traces of a 'criminal class' or a 'criminal subculture', at least outside the capital . . . For the most part, whatever the damage to their individual victims, it would seem more sensible to regard the criminal as an irritant to honest people rather than a menace.[20]

This historian's version of events is unlike anything we have encountered so far, and it needs some consideration. If there were no real menaces to society, only irritants, why does the number of offences and executions seem to increase so much? Part of the answer, at least, lies not in the activities of so-called criminals, but in the behaviour of the legislature. It is obvious that the greater the number of laws, and the greater the severity with which they are enforced, the more crimes will seem to have been committed. But to say that without qualification begs the all-important question of whether these new crimes are discovered or created. Does a rise in the number of recorded prosecutions indicate a change in the behaviour of the accusers or the accused, or even both? The traditional view seems to be that criminality was increasing. However, many prominent recent historians, most notably E. P. Thompson and George Rudé, are in broad agreement with Sharpe's view, and have persuasively expressed scepticism about the existence of an active criminal network.

A full discussion and resolution of this issue would require some reliable and incontestable data, and, alas, these cannot be found. The earliest collections of criminal statistics which are of any use (although even these must be treated with caution) are the work of the Statistical Society of London, and date from 1834. In the absence of full documentary information, it might be possible, as J. M. Beattie has shown, to compile lists of actual court cases in given districts at given times, and to use these to speculate on trends. Even this tentative procedure, however, does not avoid important problems. For one thing, it only provides the possibility of seeing crime in its contemporary categories – that is to say, taking the statute as the final arbiter, and unquestioningly accepting the ways it categorises behaviour. More importantly, there is the problem of the so-called 'dark figure' – the number of potential offences which go undetected and unrecorded. Since crime is by its nature furtive, and since criminals understandably invest a great deal of their energy and ingenuity in avoiding capture, the 'dark figure' must always disable the accurate computation of illegal behaviour. A recent study suggests that even today only around 20 per cent of criminal behaviour is discovered and reported, and there is no reason to imagine that eighteenth-century procedures of detection were any more successful.[21]

Any attempts to produce accurate or reliable figures about criminal or illegal activities at any time are thus extremely difficult. For the period in question, some very tentative guesses have been made. Many commentators seem to think that a particular combination of factors in the first half of the century made it seem, at least, as though criminal activity was on the increase. As E. P. Thompson puts it, 'if that unsatisfactory term "crime wave" could ever be used with conviction, it might possibly be applied to the early 1720s'.[22] Thompson's hesitations and uncertainties are unavoidable, and show the precarious, provisional nature of the whole exercise. Although some other writers have been confident enough to talk of a decline in crime after the 1760s, any such estimate must be of necessity unreliable.[23] The paradoxes involved in the venture are clearly illustrated by J. M. Beattie, who quotes the preamble to the 'Murder Act' of 1752 (25 Geo II c.37). This statute tried to increase the severity of the penalty for homicide, on the grounds that it had been 'more frequently perpetrated than formerly and particularly in and near the metropolis'. Despite this stern warning, the available evidence seems to suggest, according to Beattie, that 'the number if anything declined over the century'.[24] What we seem to be confronted with, then, is a sustained chorus of anxiety about crime, about the dangers of living in the metropolis, and about the threat to personal safety, which seems to exist more or less independently of any facts which can be identified.

Of course, even to talk of 'facts' here is misleading. In this area, more obviously than in almost any other one, there can be little possibility of objective data. There can be, for good or ill, no facts, only interpretations, always open to scrutiny and revision. Since positivist historical study is a matter of pragmatism and probability, it is possible to exert pressure on whatever documentary evidence might be available to squeeze out of it as much information as possible, and thereby to construct more or less plausible hypotheses. But even the most optimistic and erudite historians are invariably circumspect when attempting to identify the rate of crime in England in the eighteenth century.

The acknowledged expert in this field is J. M. Beattie, who places what trust he has in records of indictments. He is sensitive to the recognised limitations of archival research, but eventually comes to a surprisingly positive account of the possibilities of quantification. His argument, put very simply, is as follows. Although precise and exact figures even of prosecutions in Britain at this time are unavailable – prosecutions were privately instigated and might not always be scrupulously recorded – there are assize records from specific parishes which can be used to reconstruct a sufficiently complete picture. Fluctuations in the number of indictments can certainly provide a picture of how the legal process operated, and that might well be useful for comparative purposes. However, Beattie argues further that these fluctuations reflect changes in the patterns of crime, and that they can be used to provide reliable evidence for increases and decreases in the number of offences. Beattie here follows Douglas Hay, who investigated the records of the Staffordshire assize for the later part of the century, and tried to correlate the number of offences with identifiable extra-legal factors. Hay's confidence in these figures comes from their accidental nature – they were not recorded for historical purposes – and their proximity to the events. Although Hay recognises that 'control waves' and 'moral panics' cannot be ignored, he sees the private nature of prosecutions as to some extent mitigating the degree of control that could be enforced. Although duly cautious, he concludes that some kind of measurement of fluctuation is possible, even if the base figure of offences committed must always remain elusive.[25]

The confidence exhibited by Beattie and Hay is exhilarating, even if the eventual results seem less exciting. At the very least, though, it can be argued that archival sources can be informative about the mechanics and procedures of the legal system, about how courts conducted themselves, about what punishments were meted out, about what proportion of those indicted were acquitted, and on what grounds. These sources might also yield valuable information about who prosecuted whom, and with what success, and could, at least in theory, offer comparison of trends in indictments and such extra-legal factors as war, or famine. All such information is valuable, and gives us some purchase on the slippery slopes of historical reconstruction. However, what this archival work cannot reveal is the contemporary climate of opinion surrounding the legal system, the pressures it was under to rectify or ignore social abuse, and all the perceptions of legality and illegality that were disseminated and contested throughout the period. To find out what the accusers and the accused thought of the law, and in what standing it was publicly held, we have to leave the historians scrimmaging in the bookstacks and rifling the record offices, and move elsewhere.

READING ABOUT CRIME

The statistical or quantitative approach to crime confidently advocated by many recent historians has thus revealed only a limited amount of information, and it has inevitably turned into a kind of administrative history, revealing much about the way legal institutions have operated but comparatively little about popular perceptions of or attitudes towards illegal behaviour. This apparent failure has led one writer to describe the pursuit of reliable statistics in this field as 'something of a dead end', but that does seem unduly harsh.[26] However, if we are to move away from the archives and record offices in search of more enlightening informa-tion, where should we look? At the risk of provoking hoots of scornful mirth from certain historians, I wish to suggest that suitable sources for the study of crime during this period might be found in the contemporary press. Whatever else may be said of them individually, the law and the press together can be seen as the two central generators of ideology in early eighteenth-century England, twin bodies of commentary on human behaviour, sometimes overlapping, sometimes competing, progressively overtaking the church as the most widely-heeded guides to conduct. The body of statute can be seen as a sustained and elaborate commentary on human activity, which is of necessity categorical, explicit, univocal. The press, on the other hand, provides a body of commentary which can be multi-vocal, inexplicit, suggestive and ambiguous, exploiting the pos- sibilities of human absurdity and the inability to be exactly precise. And we must remember that both the press and the law, of course, can be equally misleading and unreliable guides to the actual behaviour of contemporary people.

Throughout this period the press was instrumental in creating a repository of ways of thinking about social issues, including crime and the law, and, even if the views it presented were inevitably contested and various, it still set the agenda for public discussion. According to some recent critics, the press alternately took on a 'static' and a 'dynamic' role in early eighteenth-century culture:

> The newspaper continued to help define and integrate communities around the dominant social and economic groups and in this respect emphasized the primarily 'static' position of the press . . . Paradoxi- cally, this integrative role was combined with a more 'dynamic', even a potentially more radical, approach developed through the consistent involvement of sections of the English press in the workings of the political system . . . Throughout the eighteenth century sections of the English press offered readers a torrent of abuse and criticism leveled at those in authority.[27]

Such a vociferous press, variously supportive and subversive of es- tablished authority, did much to create and disseminate ideas of and attitudes to crime and legality in early eighteenth-century England. Since crime was one of the pressure points of ideology, if I may put it that way, the press can give us access to both the conservative and the more radical arguments at their most fully developed and articulate. And although contemporary newspapers and journals are perhaps the most immediate forms of commentary, attention should also be paid to more ruminative and reflective styles, like diaries, biographies, pamphlets, poems, novels and plays.

Although this seems an eminently sensible position to me, the merest mention of 'literary sources' is enough to set the archivists roaring and falling about. J. A. Sharpe, for instance, puts the case against the use of literature in historical research as forcefully as anyone:

> we are confronted with a refusal to take social history seriously, and

the limitations of what might be termed the *Belles-Lettres* approach to the study of the subject are all too apparent. It is indicative of the priorities of English historical writing that historians who would otherwise have prided themselves on their scholarship, intellectual rigour, and talent for source-criticism should become slack, lazy, and uncritical when using literary sources to discuss historical subjects, crime included . . . Unfortunately, the familiarity, the vividness, and accessibility of literary sources makes them very attractive, and a number of writers, professional English scholars among them, have thrown these sources together to form easily palatable if hopelessly inadequate books.[28]

It seems that when faced with the blowsy charms of literature, dignified historians go all to pieces, and start behaving like Professor Unrat in *The Blue Angel*. Professional English scholars, on the other hand, a less scrupulous bunch to begin with, see the same material as an opportunity for a kind of smash-and-grab exercise, acting like what the Right Villainous John Hall would call 'running-smoblers'.

There may be something in what Sharpe says, for there are certainly some pretty feeble books on Shakespeare's England and the Elizabethan underworld and Dickens's London and so on, written as though the literary text was a direct and uncontroversial source of reliable information. Similarly, there are plenty of examples of historians being bamboozled by 'imaginative' writing, blithely lifting citations from plays and novels to illustrate the issues they are researching. James Heath, for example, makes surprisingly casual use of *Bartholomew Fair*, *Tom Jones* and *Measure for Measure* in discussing the theories of punishment in eighteenth-century England.[29] Previous generations of historians were even less inhibited in their reliance on such sources, following Macaulay's famous discussion of the eighteenth-century country gentleman in his *History of England,* which he admitted was derived entirely from 'the lighter literature of that age'.[30] It would be startling to come across anything as sweeping as that today, but surprisingly enough it is still possible to find one of the most dogged of modern archivists referring to that load of preposterous tomfoolery known as *The English Rogue* by Richard Head and Francis Kirkman as 'descriptive'.[31]

The attractiveness of literary sources is obvious, but so are the dangers. What seems to get in the way of serious study here is a persistent uncertainty about the cognitive functions of literature. The traditional Aristotelian idea that literature is somehow *more* true than history still lingers on despite all the efforts of modern literary theorists to dislodge it. For some traditionalist and high-minded literary critics, historians may make agreeable colleagues, but they can at best provide backgrounds to help us understand the more important transcendent activities of the great imaginative writers. If there is any basis for the belief that literature somehow encapsulates the essential truth, the *real* truth about things, as Shelley argued, then history can only be a shabby second-hand thing in comparison. But surely literary and historical study need not be forced into such a hierarchical relationship, nor need they be inscribed in such an impasse. It is perfectly possible to re-insert literature in its social and historical context, and talk about the written word as something other than the unsullied product of a singular imagination, without behaving in the way that Sharpe caricatures. Literary works are quite obviously informed by history, and the problem for historically-oriented critics is finding a language adequate to express the very complex relationship between texts and their various contexts without being reductive or over-emphatic.

Since history surrounds and infiltrates literature, and literature intervenes in history, how is their mutual relationship to be described? The first and most naïve assumption is that they are inseparable, that literature is a kind of window on the past, offering reliable access to lost worlds. Such an attitude lies silently behind the crudest historical uses of literature, like Macaulay's, and is clearly misguided. The notion that literature can be impartial, non-partisan, or even simply referential cannot be sustained beyond the simplest inspection. Anyone who used, say, the eighteenth-century novel as a source of unproblematic information about eighteenth-century society could only end up with a bizarre caricature of the individuals and institutions concerned, since literature so often dramatises the exceptional in preference to the mundane, the remarkable in preference to the ordinary. And the whole system of selection, omission and deliberate or inadvertent distortion that goes into the construction of any piece of writing (including this one, of course) means that an unproblematic access to truth and reliability can never be found. Many examples could be offered to substantiate this argument – to assume that, say, Smollett's picture of naval life in *Roderick Random* is in any way accurate or representative is clearly misguided, and can lead to great misconceptions, as recent scholarship has shown.[32]

A more subtle suggestion is that literature reflects society, with a greater or lesser degree of distortion perhaps, but with sufficient accuracy for the skilled viewer to discover the true picture. The theory of reflection has a long history, and in the eighteenth century it surfaced most powerfully in Dr Johnson's defence of Shakespeare as 'the poet that holds up to his readers a faithful mirror of manners and of life'.[33] In discussion of the novel, in particular, the image of the mirror has repeatedly been used, in the service of the idea of 'realism'. Any notion of verisimilitude must have somewhere behind it the enabling belief that literature can accurately portray life or reality or whatever. As is well known, these arguments were most strongly put in the nineteenth century by George Eliot in Britain, and by Balzac, Flaubert and Zola in France, and they are still occasionally heard today. If this belief in the accuracy and reliability of literature were true, fortunate historians would be able to use imaginative texts as unproblematic source material. Unfortunately, of course, it is not.

The problem is always the inevitable partisanship and tendentiousness of literature, be it conscious or unconscious. After all, even what you see when you look in a mirror is a kind of construction, and the notion of writing being a special sort of mirror is full of hidden problems and complexities. For one thing, this way of thinking makes literature seem very passive, simply receiving and transmitting (to change the metaphor) the signals which society puts out. But all writing is by its very nature interventionist and partial, involving the selection of details, the relative positioning and prioritising of individual elements, and the omission of features thought to be irrelevant or accidental. Literature, that is to say, is always a construction, not just a revelation, a more or less deliberate act of shaping and forming, which is under no compulsion to give the whole picture, or even an accurate part of it. Writers do not invariably act as faithful amanuenses, but as ardent reactionaries or *agents provocateurs,* their works being relatively nostalgic or progressive as they articulate disappearing or emergent structures of feeling. In the early eighteenth century, when the scratching of pens so often coincided with the grinding of axes, any protestation of disinterest by an author should be treated with the utmost suspicion. Our knowledge of the political role of the Augustan press shows that it was inherently ideological, both in its 'static' and its 'dynamic' roles, disseminating false consciousness and illusion, offering allegiances to different constructions of the past, present or future, rather than determining truth in a disinterested way. Perhaps that is always the way writing works in societies, and, if so, the historian's job in interpreting it is made no easier.

Given that writing is so inherently ideological, might it offer a way for us to gain privileged access to important eighteenth-century ideologies? Or at least, might reading imaginative literature allow us to retrieve those particular issues to which the eighteenth century gave special priority? R. W. Malcolmson attempts to use literature in this way in his discussion of foundlings:

> In England they have appeared periodically in the annals of the poor law, and more memorably, in works of the literary imagination: Fielding's *Tom Jones,* Eppie in George Eliot's *Silas Marner,* and the central character in Oscar Wilde's *The Importance of Being Earnest.* Such recognition attests, perhaps, to the prominence of abandoned infants in everyday experience, but details of those fictional careers should not be accepted too literally.[34]

No, indeed not. It is a sad fact that the plays of Oscar Wilde cannot be taken as wholly reliable historical documents, unless we wish to argue that nineteenth-century railway stations functioned as surrogate maternity wards. But even on a more serious level, the casual use of imaginative writing here weakens rather than strengthens Malcolmson's case. Can the appearance of foundlings in only *three* books, written between 1749 and 1895, really attest to 'the prominence of abandoned infants in everyday experience'? The case would be more convincing if Malcolmson produced whole torrents of novels, plays and poems with foundlings in them (*Oedipus Rex? The Winter's Tale? The Bundle?*). But to produce only three, from such different periods, looks mightily unimpressive. By a similar argument, the selective deployment of *Evelina*, *The Murders in the Rue Morgue* and *King Kong* would allow the interested historian to remark on the frequent appearance of variously-sized rampaging apes in everyday bourgeois social experience.

A different, and more useful perspective on literature is adopted by W. A. Speck, who has a more flexible version of its historical functions. While acknowledging that 'if . . . we use it to try to document social realities, we shall be seriously misled', Speck remains confident that 'it can become a prime source for the ideologies of the period 1700–60'.[35] Throughout his study of literature in society, Speck takes it as axiomatic that the written word documents or records or reflects ideologies. Although this is broadly incontestable, and provides him with a very fruitful way of contextualising literature, Speck concentrates almost exclusively on the 'static' role of the press. However, as we shall see, literature was a forum in which ideologies were contested as well as disseminated, and it is this ability to challenge and subvert which is particularly interesting when dealing with legislation and crime.

Many of the 'criminal' texts which I shall go on to discuss do not simply reproduce in a more decorative way an ideological position which can be isolated and identified elsewhere. Rather, they disrupt the protestations of ideologies to be something other than themselves. Most ideological writing adopts a disguise, disowning its ideological status, and pretending to be something else, objective or impartial: the voice of moderation, the space beyond ideology. What a great many eighteenth-century texts do is contest the authority of other texts, to show that finality and fixity must be sought but cannot be found. I will go into this in more detail later, but for the moment we need to ask if a study of literature can ever be anything other than the exploration of disappointingly uninformative fantasies and rhetoric. To put it another way, can literature ever inform its readers of anything, other than the principles of its own construction?

To reverse the usual terms of discussion, the question is: how can we turn the base metals of literary works into the pure gold of historical information? In alchemy, this magical transformation is achieved by the philosopher's stone. In recent historiography, it is just as magically achieved by Lawrence Stone. Professor Stone's remarkable work on popular attitudes and behaviour draws heavily on literary sources, and shows all the challenging and attractive possibilities and impediments of this method. At times, he is at pains to sound even-handed and judicious, using selected literary examples to indicate only areas of uncertainty and controversy:

> This literary evidence shows that there was a prolonged public argument during the late seventeenth and eighteenth centuries about a child's freedom of choice of a marriage partner, with more liberal views becoming more common among authors catering both to the middling ranks of commercial and professional people, and also to the wealthy landed classes.[36]

It is hard to argue with Stone's conclusion: if there is indeed a body of literature in which such a question is prominent, then it is reasonable to assume that many people were concerned by it. If the focus of the discussion changes, then it is reasonable to assume that the audience's interests similarly change (though it remains a matter of debate whether the writing responds to a re-orientation or helps to initiate one). Elsewhere, Stone presses his information a little harder, and tries to get more evidence from it. In his discussion of conventional marriage practices, he quotes a passage from George Crabbe, which suggests that successful marriage partners need not be romantic lovers. Stone concludes:

> The urban tradesmen and artisans and the rural smallholders of the late eighteenth century were *thus* probably largely unaffected by the new demands of love, generated among their betters by the romantic movement of the age.[37]

Although Stone supports his conclusion with a few contemporary diary entries as well, the burden of proof is still almost exclusively carried by the isolated and possibly unrepresentative Crabbe passage.

Perhaps, in a rough and ready sort of way, the lack of rigour in Stone's procedure is acceptable. In this context, Crabbe is probably a reliable enough witness, but it would be reassuring to see some more tangible support for his isolated remarks. Where Stone goes completely to pieces, however, is when he starts seeing not only his various authors as reliable informants, but their characters as well. And what characters! In his lengthy discussion of mating arrangements, an area of obvious difficulty, Stone calls upon some pretty unlikely witnesses:

> In lower middle-class circles, where capital was a critical factor in getting a start in life by buying a shop or starting a business, it was inevitable that financial considerations should continue to play a very large part in marriage plans . . . Defoe's Moll Flanders, who moved in these circles, soon came to the sad conclusion that 'marriages here are the consequence of politic schemes, for forming interests, carrying on

business', and that love had no share or very little in the matter. After a bitter experience she decided that 'money only made a woman agreeable . . . the money was the thing'. In other words, in terms of marriage, a woman in the late seventeenth and eighteenth centuries was still regarded in these circles less as a companion or a sex object than as property, and to some extent also as a status object.[38]

To suggest that financial arrangements are central to Moll's wedding plans is a perfectly plausible and orthodox reading of Defoe's fictional narrative. But to what extent can the behaviour of this character, however meticulously imagined, fairly be seen as typical? After all, Moll does not really move 'in these circles' at all, but inhabits instead the shady and mendacious realm of a work of prose fiction. If her views on money and marriage are to be taken as typical, which features of her experience are to be seen as idiosyncratic, and by what criteria are they distinguishable? Stone seems impelled by the logic of his argument to accept all of Moll's experiences as representative, and a glance at the book's title-page, with its hectic promise of the most extraordinary adventures, makes this look rather unlikely.

In this instance, Stone seems seduced by the plain style of the narrative into accepting it as a factual record, a genuine confession acceptable in a court of law. A similar, and even more unlikely reading involves his search for evidence of preferred styles of love-making in different social groups. The clinching evidence appears when he argues that sexual modesty was peculiar to the lower-middle classes: 'James [*sic*] Cleland's Fanny Hill, a respectable country girl, was genuinely shocked to discover that some men and women took all their clothes off in daylight to make love.'[39] While it is hard to avoid the suspicion that any case supported by Moll Flanders and Fanny Hill is struggling to persuade, this particular example is especially interesting in the way it raises all the problems of irony. What if this point was introduced by Cleland to reveal Fanny's entertaining and incongruous innocence? After all, there is no intrinsic reason to assume that the story-teller has to represent the voice of authority within the tale. As anyone familiar with *Gulliver's Travels* or *Tristram Shandy* can testify, unreliable narrators are not exactly unknown in eighteenth-century fiction. If Cleland expected his audience to be amused by Fanny's surprise, we could read the episode as evidence of the prevalence of daytime sexual disrobing. Maybe everybody *except* Fanny Hill knew all about it.

Areas of well-trodden difficulty are coming into view here, and need not be further explored at the moment. The single point to make now is that it can only be a high-risk strategy to rely on the evidential authority of literary characters. Any individual episode within a work of fiction might be an idiosyncratic feature of the character's personality, or there might be some overall ironic structure controlled by the author which could make isolated extracts unrepresentative. One promising way of trying to avoid this problem, and arrive at a compromise between the requirements of literary and historical study, is to move beyond individualised or idiosyncratic characters and concentrate on the representative character. If it is possible to read across a range of texts and find similar figures presented in similar ways, it might be possible to identify a stereotype, which might be evidence of a widely-shared perception of some group or profession.

This is another method employed by W. A. Speck, following the work done by John Loftis on dramatic characters.[40] In a more recent work, Lawrence Stone too deals with 'the stereotypes of fiction, the theatre, and popular imagination'.[41] I have argued elsewhere that this kind of supervised, typological reading, where the meaning of specific texts accrues from similarities to, and differences from, acknowledged generic forms is particularly appropriate for the popular writing of this period.[42] And it is clearly possible to find suitable stereotypes permeating the presentation of legal affairs in eighteenth-century writing, which may be taken as symptomatic of widely-held attitudes. In particular, the character of the lawyer is treated with almost universal contempt by writers who might disagree about virtually everything else. In a host of graphic representations, lawyers are figured as avaricious leeches, unscrupulous and unprincipled, much more concerned with fees than with verdicts. In narratives as diverse as the *Memoirs of Martinus Scriblerus*, *The Whore's Rhetorick* and *Tom Jones*, lawyers may be represented with differing emphases, but to much the same vitriolic end. And not only lawyers were treated this way. As Speck puts it, 'the subjects of Queen Anne seem to have pretty well agreed that all lawyers were pettifoggers who deliberately bamboozled their clients, all doctors were ignorant quacks who bilked their patients, and all clergymen were timeserving careerists bent on ascending the ladder of preferment at all costs'.[43] I shall deal more fully with this later, but for the moment it is only necessary to point out that as lawyers became more prominent in legal proceedings throughout the century, their popularity seems to have remained consistently low, despite their strenuous efforts to adopt the legitimising mantle of professionalisation. If, that is, this kind of literary evidence can be trusted.

The treatment of lawyers and other professions is unusually unanimous, and it is hard to present a repertoire of other images of equal stability and consistency. Although it might be possible to identify at least a few other obvious stereotypes – cuckolded husbands are more frequently presented as figures of scorn rather than sympathy, for example – most representations are contested and polarised. And there remains the vexing question of how many repetitions it takes to create a stereotype. In fact, analysis of the literary evidence almost invariably reveals doubts and uncertainties instead of unanimity and confidence.

Literature seems to draw attention to the pressure points in ideology, those places where a culture is less confident of itself, where the greatest contestation of images can occur. To say this is partly to repeat the traditional view, scarcely unfamiliar in late twentieth-century Britain, that the press in all its forms encourages controversy while playing on shared prejudices, but it is also to say that literature both disseminates and resists ideology. In the case of crime, for instance, the representations of the criminal are fascinatingly diverse rather than unanimous. Criminals are sometimes presented as menaces to society, sometimes as mere irritants, sometimes as a social problem to be solved, and even sometimes as romantic brigands and outlaws. Images of demonic cruelty alternate with images of heroic banditry. Opprobrium alternates with admiration, admonition with panegyric, until it becomes virtually impossible to find any consensus which might allow easy speculation about a general or universal attitude towards crime.

This diversity of response is apparent not only in the literary incarnation of criminals, but, as far as we can tell, in their public appearances as well. When criminals were put on display in the pillory or at Tyburn, they could receive cheers or jeers. Fernand Braudel claims that 'the crowd that milled around scaffolds and gibbets out of morbid curiosity was never on the side of the victim'.[44] There is certainly some evidence to support this view, in the records of the very violent and abusive treatment of condemned homosexuals, or other especially unpopular individuals, who were sometimes stoned to death or very badly injured in the pillory.[45] However, alongside these there are well-known counter-examples where the crowd refused to endorse the sentence passed on the victim, and responded much more positively, as most famously in the triumphant appearance of Daniel Defoe in the pillory and the popular success of Jack Sheppard.[46]

By looking at the whole body of writing concerned with crime, it is possible to see parallels to this unpredictable public response, which, we must remember, is in itself only available to us through mediated written accounts. The literary testimony is exceptionally various, and shows that the conceptual structure surrounding the ideological notion of crime was volatile and unstable. A number of recent writers, particularly those associated with *Albion's Fatal Tree*, have discussed those cases where the criminalisation of previously acceptable practices met with concerted resistance. I want to range more widely than that, and look at the ways in which literature intermittently explored the mismatching of law and morality, isolating and exploiting paradoxes and ironies which the univocal body of statute sought to ignore or suppress. By looking at the different ways that criminals were treated in the parallel discourses of law and letters it may be possible to identify some of the ideological tensions of early eighteenth-century English culture. It is unlikely that such examination will result in the identification of anything as unanimous as an attitude to crime shared by many, or a fugitive alternative system of ideology. The law, by its ideological centrality, provided the focus for a whole range of expressions, both supportive and adversary, static and dynamic, and it is these which will be explored, in the hope of clarifying the social function of literature and revealing the contested status of legislation.

INDUSTRY AND IDLENESS

My argument so far has been of necessity a predominantly negative one, illustrating the many ways in which it is possible to misappropriate and misuse Augustan literature in a process of historical analysis. It seems proper, and perhaps essential, to conclude this introduction by looking closely at one specific document from the time to see what kind of historical information, if any, it might properly yield. Before embarking on a study of the written word, therefore, I have chosen to re-examine one of the best-known pictorial representations of an eighteenth-century execution, the penultimate print in William Hogarth's sequence of engravings known as *Industry and Idleness,* produced in 1747, the particular print being 'The Idle 'Prentice Executed at Tyburn' (see Plate 11).[47]

The scene is a familiar one. After a career of sustained lassitude, vividly portrayed in the preceding sequence of prints, Tom Idle is being led in a cart towards the gallows at Tyburn, travelling through a boisterous holiday crowd of eager spectators. He is sharing his conveyance with a religious enthusiast, who is pointing at the sky (which occupies about half of Hogarth's composition). He is attended by some rather indifferent-looking soldiers. The waiting executioner calmly puffs a pipe on top of the gibbet. A clergyman rides ahead in stately procession. The officers of justice and representatives of divine mercy are thus unexcited by the whole business, but the bystanders, who occupy much the greater part of the composition, are significantly more animated. A jostling throng is occupied in shouting, scrapping, throwing fruit (and in one case a small dog) and struggling against restraint. Far off to the right of the picture as we look is the figure of Tom's mother, recognisable from the earlier prints, hiding her face from the scene. Near her is a recognisable caricature of one 'Mother Douglas', a notorious bawd, surrounded by her ladies, drinking. Given great prominence in the centre of the scene is a dishevelled woman clutching a small child and shouting, prematurely offering for sale a broadsheet called *The Last Dying Speech and Confession of Tho. Idle.* The eponymous Mr Idle himself, as his name suggests, may be the occasion of this exuberance, but he is only a small and relatively insignificant figure in the picture, doing very little except look distraught.

On one level, then, the print is an ironic juxtaposition of the intended

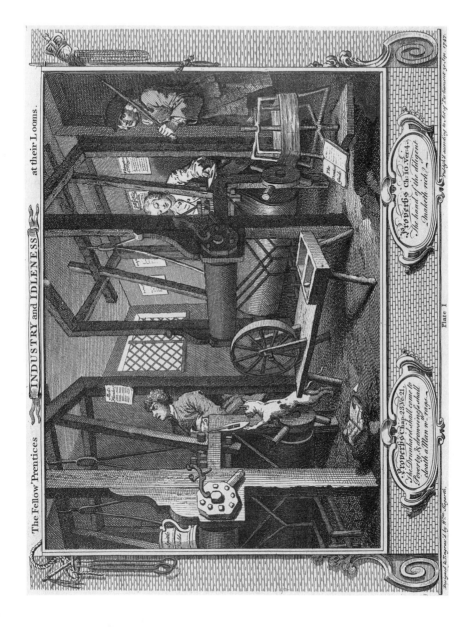

The Fellow 'Prentices INDUSTRY and IDLENESS at their Looms.

Proverbs Chap. 23 Ver. 21
The Drunkard shall come to
Poverty, & the man that is slothful
shall be cloath'd with raggs.

Proverbs Ch. 10 Ver. 4.
The hand of the diligent
maketh rich.

Plate I

Designed & Engraved by Wm. Hogarth.

Publish'd according to Act of Parliament 30 Sepr. 1747.

The INDUSTRIOUS' PRENTICE performing the Duty of a Christian.

Pſalm cxix ver: 97.
O! How I love thy Law it is my
meditation all the day.

Deſign'd & Engrav'd by W.ᵐ Hogarth

Publiſh'd according to the Act of Parliament. June 30.ᵗʰ

Plate 2

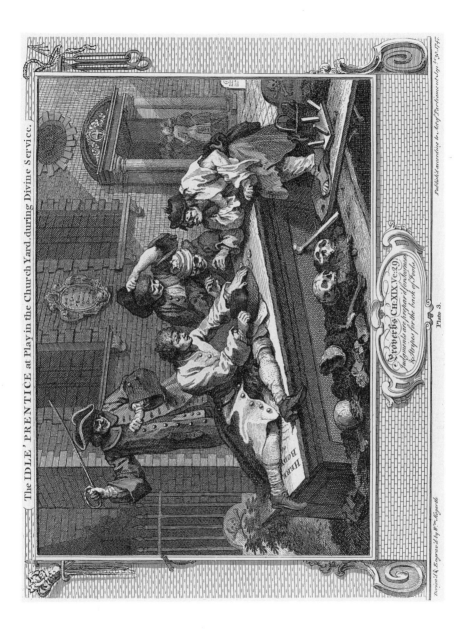

The IDLE 'PRENTICE at Play in the Church Yard, during Divine Service.

Proverbs Ch: XIX Ve: 29
Judgments are prepared for scorners &
Stripes for the back of Fools.

Designed & Engrav'd by W.m Hogarth.

Published according to Act of Parliament Sep.t 30. 1747.

Plate 3.

The INDUSTRIOUS 'PRENTICE a Favourite, and entrusted by his Master.

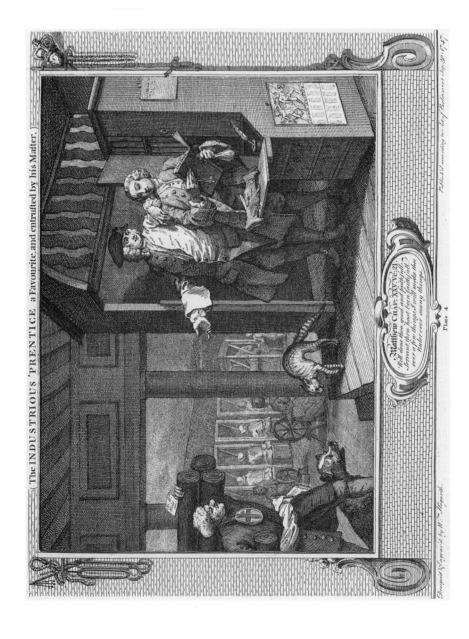

Matthew Chap: XXV. v. 21.
Well done thou good and faithfull
Servant; thou hast been faithful
over a few things, I will make thee
Ruler over many things.

Plate 4.

Designd & engravd by Wm. Hogarth.

Publishd according to Act of Parliament Sepr. 30th. 1747.

The IDLE 'PRENTICE turn'd away, and sent to Sea.

Proverbs CHAP: X. Ve: 1.
A foolish son is the heaviness
of his Mother.

Plate 5.

Design'd & Engrav'd by W.m Hogarth.

Publish'd according to Act of Parliam.t Sep.r 30.t 1747.

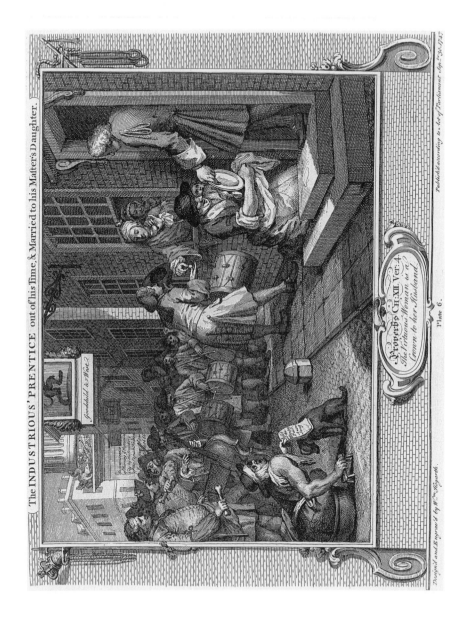

The INDUSTRIOUS PRENTICE out of his time, & Married to his Master's Daughter.

Goodchild & White?

Proverbs Ch. XII. Ver: 4.
The Virtuous Woman is a
Crown to her Husband.

Plate 6.

Designed and Engraved by Wm. Hogarth.

Published according to Act of Parliament Sepr. 30. 1747.

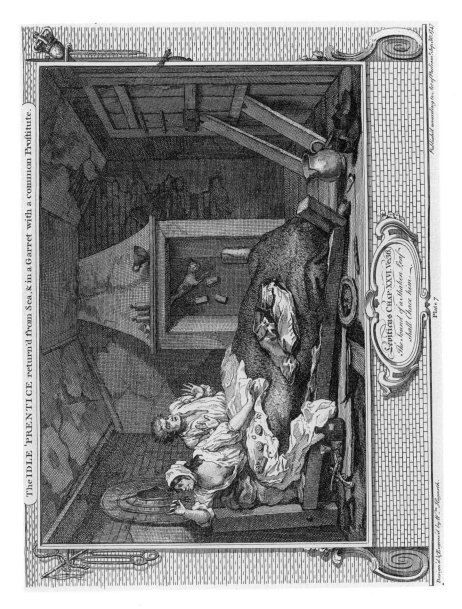

The IDLE 'PRENTICE return'd from Sea, & in a Garret with a common Proftitute.

Leviticus CHAP: XXVI. Vo 36.
The found of a fhaken leaf
fhall chace him.—

Plate 7

Defign'd & Engrav'd by Wᵐ. Hogarth.

Publifhed according to Act of Parliam Sepʳ 30. 1747.

The INDUSTRIOUS 'PRENTICE grown rich, & Sheriff of London.

Proverbs Ch: IV: Ver: 7, 8.
With all thy getting, get understanding.
Exalt her, & she shall promote thee: she
shall bring thee to honour, when
thou dost embrace her.

Plate 8.

Designd & Engraved by Wm Hogarth

Publish'd according to Act of Parliam.t Sep.tr 30. 1747.

The IDLE 'PRENTICE betray'd by his Whore, & taken in a Night Cellar with his Accomplice.

Designd & Engravd by W.ᵐ Hogarth.

Publishd according to Act of Parliament April 1.ˢᵗ 1747.

Proverbs Chap: VI.v.26.
The Adulterefs will hunt for
the precious life.—

Plate 9

The INDUSTRIOUS 'PRENTICE Alderman of London, the Idle one brought before him & Impeach'd by his Accomplice.

Psalm IX Ver: 16.
The Wicked is snar'd in the
work of his own hands.

Leviticus Ch: XIX Ve.15.
Thou shalt do no unrighteous
ness in Judgment.

Design'd & Engrav'd by W.m Hogarth.

Plate 10.

Publish'd according to Act of Parliament Sep.t 17.

The IDLE PRENTICE Executed at Tyburn.

Published according to Act of Parliament — Hogarth

Proverbs Chap: I. Ver: 27, 28.
When fear cometh as desolation, and their
destruction cometh as a whirlwind, when
distress cometh upon them, then they shall
call upon God, but he will not answer.

Invented & Engraved by W. Hogarth

Plate II

The INDUSTRIOUS 'PRENTICE Lord-Mayor of London.

Proverbs CHAP: III Ver: 16.
Length of days is in her right hand, and
in her left hand Riches and Honour.

Plate 12.

majesty and solemnity of capital punishment with the actuality of carnivalesque mayhem its performance seems to encourage in onlookers. The enactment of the awful process of legal execution is attended by all the due figures of authority, ready to carry out their legitimate duties, but also, and more prominently, the scene is composed of pickpockets, ruffians, prostitutes, drunks and various other delinquents, all remarkably untouched by the gravity of the occasion or its potential relevance to themselves. So in the climactic prints in this didactic sequence we see the idle apprentice coming to his inevitably sorry end, and, what is perhaps worse, to a grotesquely undignified and pointless one.

Taken in isolation, this picture seems to illustrate the turbulent and violent nature of justice upon earth. Although the scene includes various clerical figures, and has a portentous quotation from the Book of Proverbs appended below, and is played out below the broad sweep of the sky, the whole episode remains stubbornly terrestrial. The overall impression created is one of bustle, of disorder, of a macabre and disturbingly exploitative kind of celebration. As we shall see, many contemporary commentators were concerned by the holiday atmosphere which had come to surround the appointed days for executions, with all the celebratory paraphernalia of speeches and processions, and the whole elaborate ritual of the gallows scene, the most notable being Bernard Mandeville in *An Enquiry into the Causes of the Frequent Executions at Tyburn* (1725) and Henry Fielding in *An Enquiry into the Causes of the Late Increase of Robbers* (1751). Hogarth's print seems to complement these arguments by miniaturising its alleged subject in favour of a more expansive treatment of the 'mob'. In what looks more like the engraver's characteristic technique of bathos than tragedy, Idle's indolence has led him through a series of lacklustre postures to this lackadaisical final scene. Even on the day of his execution, his positively final appearance, he seems remarkably reluctant to impose himself forcefully on his surroundings.

It is possible to examine this print in isolation, as above, in the hope of discovering some details about the procedures of Tyburn days, but if we wish to ask more telling questions about the dynamic nature of Hogarth's interpretation of these events, its immediate context is extremely important. It appears as the eleventh of the series of twelve prints collectively called *Industry and Idleness*, in which the relative fates of the idle apprentice (Thomas Idle) and the industrious apprentice (Francis Goodchild) are episodically contrasted. From the opening print, where we see them side by side, the one working attentively, the other dreaming, their paths diverge. Goodchild marries his master's daughter, takes over the business, becomes Sheriff of London, and, climactically, Lord Mayor. In dramatic contrast, Idle goes off to sea, falls in with prostitutes and shady characters back in London, and is betrayed into the hands of the law. The only point where the two figures again converge is when Idle, as indicted criminal, has to be sentenced by Goodchild, as magistrate. After this, Idle goes off to Tyburn, and Goodchild to the Guildhall.

When presented in this simple way, the moral scheme of the engravings thus looks unquestionably clear and emphatic: the industrious shall be rewarded by the horn of plenty, the idle can only look forward to squalor, ignominy and death. The narrative elaborates and reiterates this fundamental idea through various stylised contrasts, as intense as those in Hogarth's other representations of antithetical conditions, like *Gin Lane* and *Beer Street*. These didactic sequences were, of course, designed for a popular audience and they look as though they contain very deliberate messages represented in a comprehensible parable form, most suitable for the instruction of apprentices and others thought to be in danger of falling into wicked ways. The contrasts are worked out by elaborate and easily-followed images of felicity and infelicity, climaxing in the explicit final contrast between Goodchild's triumphant success and Idle's abject failure.

Read in this way, *Industry and Idleness* fits into the established and traditional ideological pattern in which crime was seen as an expression of moral weakness or corruption, and in which the legal system was seen as the incarnation of justice. Hogarth's prints would then take their place alongside Defoe's *Complete English Tradesman* (1732), Richardson's *Apprentice's Vade Mecum* (1734) and Fielding's *Enquiry* (1751) as admonitory guides to the behaviour of the lower classes. By mythologising and polarising the twin paths, Hogarth seems to be articulating the mercantile sensibilities expressed elsewhere by George Lillo, whose play *The London Merchant* (1731) inhabits a similar structure of feeling. At the end of that play, the idle apprentice, George Barnwell, has committed terrible deeds, and is about to be executed. Partly to his virtuous counterpart, Trueman, and partly to the audience, he acknowledges the propriety of his fate: 'Thus justice, in compassion to mankind, cuts off a wretch like me, by one such example to secure thousands from future ruin.'[48] The admonitory role of the play really needs no further comment, and its dour bourgeois protestantism, and its valorisation of work and industry make it seem like a sympathetic antecedent of this feature of Hogarth's work.

But was Hogarth (or Lillo, for that matter) really such an abject apologist for his enterprise culture? Was he really so immersed in its assumptions that he wholly endorsed the moral value of hard work and the unquestionable authority of the law? Given the events of his own career, which was a lot more like Goodchild's than like Idle's, there might be reason to think he was as clear-sighted and complacent as the sequence suggests. However, it is possible, on closer examination, to find tensions and ironies in the pictorial narrative which bring the artist significantly closer to Hume's scepticism than to Blackstone's assurance.

As Ronald Paulson puts it, 'the effect of Hogarth's series is somewhere between a pun and an ambiguity'.[49] Paulson has found a hidden, subordinate argument in the pictures, which puts in doubt the overt and clear message about the rewards of industry. In fact, it becomes possible on examination to find all sorts of extraordinary uncertainties and complications in the series, which seem to provide an antithetical and critical system of meaning, in covert but dramatic dialectical opposition to the more obvious one.

My own scepticism was raised when I noticed the difference in the tone of Hogarth's ending compared with Lillo's. Since Idle's fate is not attended by the gravity and solemnity of Barnwell's self-recrimination, it is possible to think of the print outside the strict confines of didactic purpose. That is to say, the energy in Hogarth's pictures does not just go into decorating a simple message, but complicating and problematising that message. His scheme is made more complex, for instance, by the way the prints are ordered. After the first, where Idle and Goodchild are both included, the numbering puts Goodchild first, and Idle second. In Plate 10, they are brought together again, in the courtroom scene. After that, the order is reversed, and Goodchild comes *after* Idle – for once the farce precedes the Lord Mayor's show. Though this looks as though it is designed to facilitate the triumphal ending, it also involves curious shifts of emphasis. For one thing, the left-to-right movement of the procession to Tyburn is matched by the right-to-left movement of the new Lord Mayor, which ideographically suggests that the two figures are converging rather than diverging. Had the order of the previous sequence been continued, the suggestion would have been that the two symbolic figures were moving to fates as far apart as possible. Or Hogarth could have reversed the sequence, and still suggested this by having Idle move from right to left, and Goodchild from left to right. Yet he contrived the sequence to evoke unmistakable visual images of convergence, to imply that Idle and Goodchild are about to confront each other once again in a grand bathetic ending.

Once scepticism about the 'message' of the pictures breaks out, more and more disquieting features start to become apparent. Goodchild's companions in prosperity are particularly interesting. When he is shown in church (Plate 2), he is a model of pious behaviour, but everyone around him is either indifferent to the proceedings or fast asleep. When he is being entrusted by his master (Plate 4), there is a rather surly-looking man bringing in rolls of cloth and we can make out the shadowy figures of people working in the background. Right in the centre of the composition, a cat is arching its back and hissing at a dog. An unimportant detail, perhaps, given unusual prominence for no good reason, unless to suggest an antipathy of species between masters and men, rather than a simple difference in industriousness. And although you may feel that an academic has little right to accuse, Goodchild does not really seem to be working terribly hard. His actual 'industrious' character is scarcely represented in the sequence, which illustrates instead moments of festivity and respite from work. In Goodchild's next picture (Plate 6), he is seen giving money to the musicians who have played at his marriage to his master's daughter. The players are squabbling among themselves, and nearby a grotesquely deformed beggar is offering an epithalamion for sale. On the right of the picture, a servant is covertly giving a plate to a kneeling woman, presumably pilfering from Goodchild. Of course, it is appropriate that the industrious man be seen in a public act of philanthropy like this, associated with money and commerce, but his bounty here seems to be creating discord rather than harmony, and the beggar (to whom he is paying no attention) is an overlooked reminder of the limits of his bounty.

In Goodchild's next appearance (Plate 8), he is seen at a civic banquet in his new role as Sheriff of London. But you have to look at the picture very closely to identify him. He is represented in the background, oddly miniaturised and peripheral. Much more prominence is given to the other diners, presumably meant to represent wealthy figures in London commerce, and they are made to appear as hideous caricatures, gorging themselves in a grotesque way. The commercial worthies of the city of London seem no more appealing than the shabby band of crooks and prostitutes Idle is seen to hang around with. And if Idle is morally diminished by his choice of companions, can Goodchild remain superior to his? What seems to be happening is that the overall composition of and the meticulous details incorporated in the plates complicate our initial responses, and undermine the certainty and confidence of the mottoes underneath. The simple clarity of good rewarded and indolence punished begins to get clouded over by the more complex world of money and duplicity figured in the prints.

When the two protagonists are brought together in court (Plate 10), it is obvious that the trial is unjust. Although the motto under Goodchild is an unambiguous one – 'Thou shall do no unrighteousness in Judgement' – the practice of the courtroom is more devious. The main witness is swearing on the Bible with his left hand, thereby invalidating his evidence, and the clerk of the court is being slyly bribed to keep quiet about it. Goodchild as magistrate adopts a very interesting posture – he is looking away from it all, shielding his eyes and making a gesture of refusal. Just as he failed to notice the poor and the needy in earlier scenes, in court he refuses to recognise anything, and pays no attention to the supplications of Idle or of his weeping mother. And it is not even clear exactly what Idle has done to warrant his court appearance. In the preceding plates, he has fallen in with a bad crowd, certainly, but he himself has also been robbed and betrayed. He has gambled, and is seen splitting the spoils of what is probably a robbery while a body is disposed of nearby, but the evidence of Idle's complicity is left wholly circumstantial by Hogarth, and there is no clear indication, beyond reasonable doubt, that Idle has indeed committed a capital offence. Unfortunately for him, justice, in the shape of his old colleague Alderman Goodchild, is blind.

The simple moral homily about the value of honesty and hard work which looked like the basis of *Industry and Idleness* has now started to look more complex, and its meaning seems much less emphatic. In a world typified by bustle and disorder, the simple clarity of this moral structure looks far too naïve. What Hogarth has done has been to infiltrate an insidious distinction between money and poverty which overrides the overt moral distinction between industry and idleness. In a commercial world, wealth and success take on a momentum of their own, and so do poverty and failure. As a result, the wealthy get wealthier, and the poor get poorer. The law does not function as a disinterested arbiter of disputes and instrument of higher justice. The world as we see it in Hogarth's work is just too messy for that. Rather, the courts are part of the social apparatus by which the distinction between rich and poor is maintained, almost irrespective of the moral distinction between good and evil.

For these demonstrable reasons, we may reclaim the sequence from its overt morality, and the appropriateness of such a revision is even reinforced by the surprising similarity of Idle's face and Hogarth's own. Hogarth seems to be illustrating what might have been his own fate, a path which might have been followed by a more naïve version of himself. An alert reader of the prints must come to realise that the world is not organised by moral properties, but by luck and by money. The stark contrast between good and evil conventionally represented by the Guildhall and Tyburn is at best a façade, for the public in the two prints is simply enjoying the pageantry in each case. Even as Goodchild makes his triumphal procession, a small boy tucked away in a corner of the picture is reading the story of Idle. Goodchild's pomp is leading to another kind of bathos, and the series overall deliberately gives a tabloid, sensationalised version of the two careers, couched in an entirely inappropriate religious rhetoric.

So, now that the complexities of the prints have been teased out, what can they indicate about the relationship between literature and crime at this time? It would, of course, be quite wrong to assume that Hogarth accurately preserved the details of actual events, providing us with reliable documentary evidence of existing practices. Spectators at Tyburn may or may not have thrown small dogs at condemned men, but Hogarth's inclusion of such a puppy projectile will neither confirm nor deny the possibility. Rather than offering an unambiguous record of one point of view, Hogarth's prints are essentially multi-vocal. They may be seen as homiletic or ironic, but these meanings do not explicitly contend for authority – they are simply *both* there. Unlike more restricted commentators, Hogarth can avoid overt partisanship, and can suspend these two systems of meaning, delighting in the ambiguities and contradictions that are thereby created.

It is this festive and subversive technique, which may even become anarchic, that I find most interesting. Many creative writers, acknowledging the necessity of the law, went on to explore its practical inadequacies and inconsistencies. Fiction, then as now, regularly provided parodic and ironic versions of ideology, disclaiming the possibilities of certainty or assurance which are inscribed in the discourse of law. So, for better or for worse, literature cannot merely give us access to legal procedures or some things loosely called 'attitudes' to law. What it does provide, however, is a fascinating panorama of critiques and interrogations, where the assumptions behind legality and criminality are vigorously scrutinised and analysed. These critiques may range from the admonitory and practical, like Mandeville's or Fielding's, to the radical and disturbing, like Swift's. Although much literature, as we shall see, was obviously used to disseminate and reinforce the prevailing ideology of law, often creating and directing fears about criminality, other writers played on different uncertainties, and took the opportunity to unveil ideology. Hogarth's *Industry and Idleness* seems to me to show how the more subversive and critical project can be carried on under a disguise, how a document which looks to be supportive of simple ideas about criminality can also be radically critical of the assumptions which legitimise and sustain that criminality. Such 'doubleness' of focus will be seen again later, and for now it is necessary to concentrate on that most notorious ideological mechanism, repeatedly constructed and deconstructed on the printed page: the criminal.

2   Representing the criminal

RELENTLESS RUFFIANS

A single Jail, in Alfred's golden Reign,
Could half the Nation's Criminals contain;
Fair Justice then, without Constraint ador'd
Held high the steady Scale, but sheath'd the sword;
No Spies were paid, no *Special Juries* known,
Blest Age! but ah! how diff'rent from our own![1]

These are a few of the valedictory words of 'injur'd Thales' in Samuel
Johnson's powerful satiric poem *London*, written and published in 1738.
With unusually controlled acerbity and vigour, they bring together a
number of the accusations regularly levelled at Augustan society and at
its legal system by those many contemporary commentators less
infatuated with the benignity of the statute than Blackstone or his
eminent legalist predecessors. Johnson chooses to speak through the
voice of Thales, an individual so horrified by the depravity and barbarity
of London life that he can even contemplate the extreme gesture of
departing for 'Cambria's solitary Shore'. In doing so, the poet allows
himself sufficient room to create an elaborate and sustained critique of
metropolitan life under Walpole, without necessarily being seen to
endorse fully or wholeheartedly the views put forward. Although the
encompassing authorial presence never entirely disowns or ridicules the
denunciatory words of Thales, it never simply reiterates them either. By
this means, the poem exploits the interaction of its two constituent
personalities to construct a self-examining double perspective, articulating
a complex mixture of detailed fascination with the hectic experience of
the city juxtaposed with virulent dismissive contempt for the flagrant
iniquities of urban life.

In effect, Johnson creates a subtle and astutely handled dialectic which
advocates, on the one hand, the desirability of immediate retreat from
the contagion and fears of the sordid city, and, on the other, the equally
pressing necessity for continuing confrontation with the variousness and

excitement of metropolitan life. However, although the passage quoted above, like the poem as a whole, is not wholly innocent of controlled ironic exaggeration and stylised self-mockery, we may notice for the present purposes how it articulates and directs through both its voices a particular jaundiced attitude towards the perceived recent increase in urban crime and criminality. For all their obvious differences of emphasis, Johnson and Thales both articulate and share a commitment to an important structure of feeling which was becoming more prevalent and recurrent in a great deal of conservative cultural commentary and diagnosis throughout the earlier eighteenth century. For both speakers, London is at once the centre of the most developed modern civilisation, and the baffling apogee of proliferating crime and corruption.

For the disenchanted Thales, who stands as a metaphorical equivalent for and naturalisation of Juvenal's even more disillusioned Umbricius, British culture had fallen into gradual but apparently irrecoverable decline since 'Alfred's golden Reign' (871–899). From Thales's point of view, the distant days under the relaxed rule of Alfred the Great represented the mid-point peak of recorded native history and the golden mean between the extremes of barbarity and civilisation. In contrast to Alfred, and even to the relatively glorious monarchs of previous years who retained some vestiges of earlier nobility – Elizabeth, Henry and Edward are mentioned – the ignoble rulers of contemporary London are treated with the utmost contempt and hostility. Seen largely through what we can recognise to be Johnson's oppositional Tory perspective, the governing authorities are presented as no more than shabby time-servers, self-interested and overtly partisan politicians, presiding incompetently and uncaringly over the collapse of an empire, relying on crude and inefficient legal measures.

Since those far-off happy times when no more than two jails were necessary to accommodate all the criminals in the land, moreover, the demonstrable development of the law and growth of the statute need not represent a continuous process of sophistication or civilisation. The Enlightenment optimism which permeates contemporary Whiggish and progressivist rhetoric, perhaps most famously and forcefully expressed in David Hume's essay 'Of the Study of History' (1742) and in Blackstone's *Commentaries*, is wholly absent from this poem. Rather, as far as Johnson and Thales are concerned, the flagrant increase in crime reveals a peculiar atavistic savagery in the proliferating criminals and persistent ruthlessness and corruption in their incompetent judges. That is to say, both Johnson and Thales agree on a diagnosis, even though they may yet differ on the possibilities of a remedy. If the number and the nature of apprehended criminals could be taken as indicative of the nation's moral well-being, as conservative thinkers claimed, then Augustan England seemed to Thales, to Johnson, and to many others to be very sick indeed. For the most pessimistic commentators, it was perhaps even terminally ill.

The poem is densely textured throughout by persistently disparaging references to the operations of the law and by insistent recognitions of the pervasive social possibilities of crime. Within the discursive and argumentative structure of the satire, Johnson and Thales intermittently contrive to incorporate mentions of 'relentless Ruffians', 'the fell Attorney', 'Pirates', 'publick Crimes', 'Theft', 'Perjury', 'bribe', 'Guilt', 'Villainy', 'steal', 'Gibbet', 'ransack', 'the rigid Law', 'Plunder', 'Dungeons', 'Death', 'Will', 'fiery Fop', 'kills', 'stabs', 'the midnight Murd'rer', 'Dagger', 'Tyburn' and 'Gallows'. The dramatic accumulation and disquieting reiteration of these terms are designed to create the impression that the metropolis is the most intensely criminal part of the contemporary world, virtually infested with all of the varieties of villainy, and the poem does as much as it can to suggest that the experience of living there is constantly fraught with manifold anxieties and terrors. In London, it seems, exemplifying and intensifying Johnson's understanding of the course of life in general, there is much to be endured and little to be enjoyed. And rather than helping to combat or disperse these many terrors, the operation of the law seems only to be adding further anxieties to them. The author is quite deliberately offering as bleak a presentation of the contemporary urban scene as possible, and, as in so much Augustan satire, there is a certain dark and sardonic inventive glee lurking within the gloom of his catalogue. Although the analysis is partly distanced by the use of the speaking persona, it is still not in any substantial way disavowed or contradicted, and indeed it offers in concentrated and compressed form a dialectic commentary on crime which could also be found in many contemporary newspapers, journals and pamphlets.

For the present discussion, it is most interesting to notice the way Johnson centralises the interaction of the law and criminality as the most fraught point of inner tension in his culture, the point of contact between the civilised and the barbaric. The ubiquity of crime is presented as the most obvious way in which the inhabitants of London could recognise the severity of the problems that beset their culture. Although the overall tone of the poem is characteristically very sombre and pessimistic, the dialectical and antithetical structure of the piece offers simultaneous moments of accommodation and even some fleeting hints that things still might not be entirely beyond improvement or at least reconciliation. On the one hand, Thales seems to be describing a society on the point of imminent collapse, tearing itself apart by intractable internal problems. Immediate flight becomes the only sensible response. On the other hand, though, the insinuated and encompassing voice of Johnson himself holds up at least the possibility of therapeutic legislative intervention through a more properly managed statute, and he identifies the rapacity of 'criminals' and the failings in the operations of the legal system as the main guilty parties in bringing about the obvious chaos of the urban scene. If the legal system could be improved, and the city made safer, then there might be no need for Thales's flight.

Although the contemporary situation in London is presented as frighteningly bleak, and clearly beyond the tolerance of Thales, it is still not entirely without more hopeful possibilities for Johnson. The fatalistic moral and economic analysis that is rhetorically flourished within the poem – 'Slow rises Worth, by Poverty deprest' (l. 177) – is powerfully expressed, but its significance is overwhelmed by the reiteration and diversification of the stigmatising language of criminality. Such sustained attention to the dangers posed by the criminal creates the notion that the way to bring matters into line is not by addressing fundamental and apparently insoluble inequities in the distribution of wealth or property, but by improving and redirecting the effective vigilance of the legal system, and by bringing genuine criminals before proper justice. The civic culture and economy of London inevitably relies on mercantile transactions and on money, and, given the natural human propensity to corruption, that leads just as inevitably to criminality. Things would certainly be improved if the worthy poor were 'decriminalised', as it were, but the statute should be (and could be) more adroitly and intelligently used to bring all the other flagrant evils under stricter and more authoritative legislative control.

At the time of writing the poem, according to the main speaker, 'All Crimes are safe, but hated Poverty' (l. 159). However, for Johnson, if not for Thales, there remains the possibility that revealing such institutionalised injustices might yet lead to some improvements. Even a more intelligent use of the statute would not make things perfect, of course, but the employment of such a policy might begin to make them slightly better. In this argument, Johnson provides his own idiosyncratic version of what we shall see to be one of the central perceptions of Augustan satire: the idea that the law regularly fails in its duty to identify and apprehend the worst criminals of the day, who remain at large in their positions of power and influence. According to most of the oppositional satirists, the law was enfeebled by preferring to content itself with the arraigning of relatively insignificant and petty offenders, whose excessive punishment served no useful social function.

By constructing its dialectic in this way, Johnson's poem is one of a great many Augustan texts at the service of the prevailing 'myth' (or 'myths') of criminality.[2] As well as offering intense descriptions of crime in formal and deliberately complex poems like *London*, the Augustan press poured out a torrent of criminal biographies, court reports, dying speeches, ballads, broadsheets, case histories and all sorts of writing about the law and law-breakers. Crime reports, designed mainly to warn the public of the dangers of known criminals, figured prominently in nearly all available newspapers at this time, and some, like *Applebee's*

Original Weekly Journal, were virtually dominated by this type of coverage.[3] Alongside the most sensational crime stories were more ephemeral recognitions of law-breaking like the private advertisements for the recovery of stolen property which appeared in most papers. At the same time, the press directed and exploited the public's interest in such affairs through a great many cheap and easily distributed broadsheets, which claimed to be authoritative and informative of well-known recent cases. A typical broadsheet, showing the orthodox contents and the narrative priorities which conventionally governed them, is *A Full and True Account of the Apprehending, taking and Examination of one Mr. Harris, and carried before Justice Tully, Sworn against by Mr. Stagg, to be that Notorious Highwayman that used to Rob on the Black Mare on Hounslow-Heath: then Committed to the Gatehouse, August the 11th, 1704*, published in London within a few days of the incidents it records.

In these cheap and popular productions, the press was seeking to exploit topical interest as quickly as possible. On other occasions, the press's concern with crime was articulated through more expensive, and more leisurely productions like the frequently republished three volumes of Captain Alexander Smith's *A Complete History of the Lives and Robberies of the Most Notorious Highway-Men, Footpads, Shop-Lifts, and Cheats of both Sexes, in and about London, Westminster, and all Parts of Great Britain, for above an Hundred Years Past, Continu'd to the Present Time* (1713–14). All degrees of literacy were catered for by the emergent book trade, and crime writing of some kind could be had for all ranges of possible expenditure. Stylised discussions of contemporary and recent crime in some suitably palatable form were available to virtually anyone, and the reproducibility and accessibility of these records helped create the widespread belief in the proliferation and virulence of criminals.[4] Still, to talk of this energetic publishing activity in terms of something as broad and ill-defined as 'myth' clearly needs some explanation, and I place the term in parentheses to indicate my trepidation. The snares and complexities of social anthropology have, after all, claimed many victims among wide-eyed literary critics tempted to stray from their more familiar paths.

By using the rather ambiguous term 'myth' I do not want to suggest, of course, that the representation of criminality in Augustan England was some kind of elaborate hoax. The reporting of crime was not a practical joke constructed entirely through the press – a grotesque magnification of Swift's *Bickerstaffe Papers*, say – nor was it simply a pervasive distopian fantasy, nor a universally shared delusion. Crimes and criminals were recognisable and important features of the real social experience of the Augustan public. It has already been mentioned that contemporary newspapers were full of reports of recent crimes, and even if there is clear justification for some scepticism about their complete accuracy or veracity, it would still be impossible to deny that they described and represented certain known features of the Augustan world. Tyburn and Newgate and the Old Bailey were real places in Augustan London, albeit ones which carried many symbolic meanings and significances. And amongst the host of recorded and documented criminals, widely disseminated through individual pamphlet biographies, published trial reports and such popular pieces as the Ordinary of Newgate's various accounts of prisoners awaiting execution, even the remarkable Jonathan Wild was not exclusively an invention of over-imaginative authors, however much his career was subsequently made and remade on the printed page. Throughout the Augustan period, criminals and crimes certainly did exist, although perhaps that fact alone did not absolve writers from the responsibility of inventing them.

But even if the representations of criminality in Augustan England were often attached to a genuine experiential history, it remains clear, as I argued in the last chapter, that the press did not and does not simply record or reproduce these social facts and events in any uncontentious or non-interpretive way. To take one interesting example from this period, the fact that the famous and notorious Dick Turpin existed, and was undoubtedly hanged for horse-stealing in York on 7 April 1739, does not mean that the various documents devoted to his life were required to tell the truth, the whole truth and nothing but the truth about him, disinterestedly or informatively. Indeed, something of the curious unreliability of criminal biography could be seen by looking at two contemporary pamphlets devoted to presenting accounts of this particular villain, *The Genuine History of the Life of Richard Turpin, The Noted Highwayman* and *The Trial of the Notorious Highwayman Richard Turpin*. Although both of these short pieces were published relatively soon after the events they purport to recount in 1739, the two versions are inconsistent and even mutually contradictory, with the second pamphlet spending much of its time attacking the inaccuracies and distortions of the first. And of course, this veridical uncertainty was further complicated later on by the great wave of Turpin fictions and gallant highwayman novels which started to swell in the early nineteenth century after the highly successful publication of *Rookwood* and which can still be found today in print and on film. Dick Turpin might have been a 'real' Augustan criminal, but, like John Sheppard, Jonathan Wild, Mary Carleton, Eugene Aram, Mary Blandy, Captain Kidd, Jenny Diver, Sawney Beane, Moll King and so many others, he was quickly transformed into a semi-fictional, legendary or mythical figure by the intervention of the press.

Another indication of the obliquity and indirectness (to put it most neutrally) of eighteenth-century reports of crime might come from recognising the ways certain ingenious criminals seem to have exploited the developments in the press to their own ends. Part of Jonathan Wild's success came from his startling ability to communicate with his potential victims through the pages of legitimate newspapers. In the *Daily Post* in 1724, for example, Wild advertised an item, apparently lost:

> Lost, the 1st of October, a black shagreen Pocket-Book, edged with Silver, with some Notes of Hand. The said Book was lost in the Strand, near the Fountain Tavern, about 7 or 8 o'clock at Night. If any person will bring the aforesaid Book to Mr. Jonathan Wild, in the Old Bailey, he shall have a Guinea Reward.[5]

In this egregious way, Wild was offering to sell the stolen pocket-book back to its rightful owner for a guinea, with the suggested threat of blackmail contained in the references to its discovery near a notorious brothel, the Fountain Tavern. The owner is being told to pay up for the recovery of his property, or face exposure, in an elaborately coded way made possible by the development of the press.

The other role played by the periodical press, as we have already seen, was in creating powerful and effective scares about the dangers of criminality. Perhaps the best example of this is the discussion of the 'Mohocks' in the *Spectator* in 1712. In a letter given over to the history of clubs from 'Philanthropos' (Richard Steele), there is a dramatic and frightening description of a recent misanthropic addition to the nocturnal ramblers in London:

> they take Care to drink themselves to a Pitch, that is, beyond the Possibility of attending to any Motions of Reason or Humanity; then make a general Sally, and attack all that are so unfortunate as to walk the Streets thro' which they patroll. Some are knock'd down, others stabb'd, others cut and carbonado'd.[6]

The aristocratic individuals in this gang are distinguished by their expertise in different forms of violence and mutilation, and the whole portrait is rendered grisly and disquieting. It was supplemented by widespread rumours about such scandalous outrages, with a list of people claiming to be thus assaulted being published in the *London Gazette* on 19 April 1712. Further discussion of these scary figures appeared around this time in Defoe's *Review*, in a number of independent poems, satires, pamphlets, like *The Town-Rakes: or, The Frolicks of the Mohocks or Hawkubites* and *The Mohocks: A Poem, in Miltonic Verse: Address'd to the Spectator*, as well as in John Gay's little-known first play *The Mohocks*, published a month later. Seeing an opportunity for political gain, the Tory government tried to smear the opposition with responsibility for the deeds, and in the *Observator* for 15 March 1712, Whig writers retaliated by accusing the Tories of being unable to ensure that the streets were safe at night. The whole issue of the Mohocks became so complex and intricate that, as Swift wrote to Stella on the day the first *Spectator* essay appeared, 'Grubstreet Papers about them fly like Lightning'.[7]

Such an accumulation of evidence looks very persuasive: here is the press at its most active, giving us copious information about the fugitive night life of Augustan London which we could not otherwise come by. However, although the press generated a great deal of smoke about the Mohocks, there is surprisingly little evidence of the original fire. Despite rumours of aristocratic arrests, no-one actually ended up before a court for these particular misdeeds, and, although there were regular outbreaks of upper-class boisterousness and hooliganism, and there undoubtedly were groups of wealthy young men who called themselves Mohocks (or Mohawks), these groups began to appear after the wave of publicity, and seem to have restricted themselves to the more traditional male aristocratic vices of excessive drinking and wenching, rather than showing any fondness for casual violence. The *London Chronicle* in 1764 (fifty-two years after the original reports in the *Spectator*) gave an account of an enormous debauch by some 'Mohawks', but there is no suggestion of any real criminal activity. The orthodox historical view, as expressed by John Oldmixon in his *History of England* (1735) and William Maitland in his *History and Survey of London* (1756), was that the stories were unsubstantiated and that the whole thing was unfounded. So there seems no reason to take the press at face value in this case, or in earlier cases when it had raised similar fears about the activities of gangs called the Roaring Boys, the Bugles, the Hectors, the Scourers or the Nickers. There undoubtedly was violence in the dark and unpatrolled streets of Augustan London, but that is insufficient reason to accept the press's interpretation of events, and it is surely better to see the various journals as creating and encouraging controversies, generating rumours, and developing appropriate contemporary 'myths' based on the unknown terrors of urban night life.

In the face of these obvious unreliabilities and distortions, it might be tempting to see all literary representations of crime as no more than conventionally disguised fictions, and to treat them as entirely unconnected to their original sources or material stimuli. However, such an approach seems unnecessarily formalist and defeatist, severing the ties between literature and the surrounding culture far too cleanly and finally. By appropriating the anthropological terminology of 'myth', there is a more suggestive method of articulating some of the connections between writing and society, which avoids the obvious dangers of being over-reductive or excessively tendentious. In his construction of *London*, I believe, Johnson is typical of a great many Augustan writers in using the representation of crime in what the British anthropologist A. R. Radcliffe-Brown called a functionalist way, as an aetiological fabrication, exploited to secure a comprehensible causal explanation for the complex inner tensions of his society, and to address obliquely all the seemingly intractable problems of urbanisation. Like Hogarth, the satiric poet does not simply reproduce the identifiable facts of contemporary criminal behaviour, preferring instead to manipulate and direct his presentation towards the ends he thinks appropriate in this particular case. The problems of living in Augustan London, according to the poem, arise from the government's failure to criminalise and prosecute the most harmful behaviour, as well as from its concomitant failure to identify and reward true merit.

The socially-defined category of 'crime' then provides Johnson and a great many other Augustan writers with a powerful diagnostic tool. The representation of 'crime' is designed to make social experience comprehensible, albeit in different ways in different texts, to give meaning to and provide possibly contending explanations for the disconcerting bustle and apparent chaos of urban life. At the same time, the published discussion of crime offers authors the opportunity to comment on or interrogate the increasingly interventionist penal code, and pass judgements on its legislators. Crime and the law operate at the point of intersection of social and political life, with the consequence that the formulation of these notions in literature may be peculiarly potent, and capable of many different social and political nuances. As Claude Lévi-Strauss famously put it, 'the purpose of myth is to provide a logical model capable of overcoming a (real) contradiction'.[8] The contradiction in this case lies in the puzzling relationship between the orderly statute and rituals of legal procedure, and the apparent chaos of everyday experience, or in broader terms, in the persistent conflict between civilisation and anarchy. The negotiating myth is that of crime, a volatile and unstable category, interpreted, as we shall see, in widely differing ways and performing significantly different aetiological functions for different writers. Despite the extensive statute, many argued, experience remained chaotic and society disorderly because of the recidivism of criminals, inadequately controlled by the contemporary legal institutions.

There are, of course, many different possible literary uses and formulations of the 'myth' of crime, and the contending versions transmitted through Augustan writing are by no means the only ones to have achieved literary prominence. In 'Golden Age' British crime fiction, for instance, crime is conventionally presented as an interruption of more settled and orderly patterns of existence, often attributed to the corrupting influence of the city being imported to the relative tranquillity and order of the country. Moreover, crime is presented in these soothing fictions as a disruption which can be made less significant and eventually less frightening within the small world of the text by the mediating offices of the intuitive and deductive sleuth, like Dorothy Sayers's Lord Peter Wimsey or Agatha Christie's Poirot and Marple, whose investigative powers lead eventually to a proper redistribution of reward and punishment. In this case, the press is disseminating the charming pastoral myths that crime is eradicable within the confines of the fictional universe, that a clear and effective motive for such a breach of decorum can be found, and that fastidious detection can lead to satisfactory solutions. Although the authorised officers of justice are plainly as incompetent as their Augustan counterparts, the books reassuringly provide eccentric but effective problem-solvers, from Sherlock Holmes onwards. In other, darker styles of crime fiction, and in the style of Augustan anti-pastoral writing exemplified by Johnson's poem, no such comforting confidences are offered, and the prevailing myth is that the reader's experience seems threatening and chaotic because of the ubiquity and virulence of crime. Although crime is then used to explain this confusion, it remains enigmatic and resistant to explanation in itself, as Lincoln Faller's exhaustive study of the varieties of criminal biography shows, appearing as an unchecked, possibly inexplicable, and perhaps fundamentally ineradicable feature of urban life.[9]

Although I think this contrast between pastoral and anti-pastoral mythical formulations of 'crime' is an interesting one, I do not wish to lay more emphasis than is necessary on the term 'myth', as it clearly overlaps with my definition of the cognate term 'ideology'. Furthermore, 'myth' has been more carefully developed for use in this particular context in stimulating works by John J. Richetti and Lincoln Faller, as we shall see. Nor do I wish to take on board all the well-rehearsed complexities of Lévi-Strauss's more idealist and universalist arguments. To put it briefly, however, tentatively appropriating Lévi-Strauss's terms once again, ideas of crime and the law as they were represented and disseminated through the Augustan press served primarily to negotiate between the otherwise intractable dialectic of 'Nature' and 'Culture'. These rather imposing oppositional binary categories were variously defined throughout the period, as the subsequent discussion of Hobbes and Locke will illustrate, and carried different political and theological inflections. In the particular case of the poem *London*, the categories are metaphorically localised, given contrasting historical locations in the Alfredian Golden Age and the present day, and offered simultaneous geographical locations in the Celtic fringes and the metropolis respectively.[10]

What is so striking about Johnson's poem, as about so many similar contemporary satiric or descriptive pieces, like Ned Ward's *London-Spy* or John Dunton's *Night Walker*, is the way it represents indiscriminate crime as the single most characteristic feature of the immediate and familiar Augustan city (culture), defined in opposition to a distant and fantasised version of the country (nature):

> For who would leave, unbrib'd, *Hibernia's* Land,
> Or change the rocks of *Scotland* for the *Strand*?
> There none are swept by sudden Fate away,
> But all whom Hunger spares, with Age decay:
> Here Malice, Rapine, Accident, conspire,

And now a Rabble rages, now a Fire;
Their Ambush here relentless Ruffians lay,
And here the fell Attorney prowls for Prey;
Here falling Houses thunder on your Head,
And here a female Atheist talks you dead.

(ll. 9–18)

While the brief representation of the remote country in this passage is by no means gently pastoral or even particularly attractive ('with Age decay'), nature is at least offered as following its own internal logic, superior to the volatile, rapacious world of culture, where things are demonstrably falling apart, and where the worst are full of their usual passionate intensity. Alongside the corrupting influence of money, the law and crime serve to identify the most fundamental feature of this paradoxically uncivilised cultural world, where the human capacity for evil is officially encouraged and developed.

Such an apparently widespread belief in the ubiquity and centrality of 'relentless Ruffians' in Augustan culture was engineered for the most part in the contemporary press, and articulated through its various channels. By exploiting a whole range of different forms, the press helped to confirm and reinforce Johnson's perception that crime was everywhere increasing, and that the law was struggling rather ineptly to maintain order. In fact, the catalogue of criminal terms in this particular poem can be seen as a metonymic version of the activities of the press in general, which, by the extraordinary range of criminal writing it produced, accumulated contending and confusing images of criminality in the aetiological pursuit of plausible explanations for urban social disorder. Interpretations of the growth in crime could vary greatly in emphasis, from blaming politicians for failing to control properly the more aggressive members of the community (as in Johnson and Pope), to blaming the more volatile citizens for refusing to be properly controlled by their betters (as in the individuated Newgate accounts and most official court reports). Those remarkable criminals who were thought worthy of the individualised attention of the press offered challenges to conventional explanations of criminality, rather than convenient answers, leaving plenty of space for specific ideological interpretations.

However, the point to make most strongly is that the apparently widespread belief in the contemporary growth of crime in Augustan England, which was such a potent political force in creating and directing public anxieties and in facilitating the centralisation of legislative authority, was created at least as much by developments in the reporting of crime and in imaginative invigorations of the criminal, as by any actual and detectable changes in the behaviour and practices of law-breakers. By an extensive, diverse and well-orchestrated campaign of publicity, the Augustan criminal became installed as an intrinsic and potent figure in the imagining of Augustan urban life, more highly visible than criminals ever before, and more easily identifiable by readers of all classes, even if still fundamentally enigmatic in terms of motivation or purpose.

Of course, we should not forget that there had been a substantial body of criminal literature in English extensively distributed and widely familiar before the Augustan period. As well as the notorious regicides, traitors and poisoners of Jacobean tragedy, there were the more workaday rogues and cutpurses of the various city comedies and the numerous conny-catching pamphlets. Flourishing throughout the late sixteenth and early seventeenth centuries, these entertaining pieces resemble subsequent criminal writing in their association of crime and the city, even if they differ from the Augustan works in their avoidance of any developed sense of threat and in their inability to construct any elaborate legal context, as well as in their frequent preference for conducting their narratives in a more boisterous jest-book style. Although they might seem to anticipate such later performances as the *Memoirs of the Right Villainous John Hall*, they seek to amuse more than admonish or frighten by concentrating on confidence tricks and pranks rather than the more straightforward threats of physical violence, and by ironically presenting the criminal world as a revelatory mirror of the dog-eat-dog world of allegedly more upright Elizabethan life.

Such a Jonsonian notion that life is inherently competitive, and that the trickster serves to reveal the knaveries and hypocrisies of those he or she encounters, appears also in the various English translations of the European picaresque novels available throughout the seventeenth century. These were sometimes fairly straightforward adaptations, like the many translations of *Lazarillo de Tormes*, retaining the essential foreignness of the action. However, the original texts were also sometimes interestingly naturalised as versions of the lives of known English criminals, like George Fidge's *The English Gusman* (1652), declared to be based on the life of the genuine highwayman Captain James Hind, but in its structure and narrative drawing heavily on the popular translation of Mateo Alemán's *Guzmán de Alfarache* by James Mabbe (1622). The title-page of Fidge's book promises 'a full Relation of all the severall Robberies, madd Pranks, and handsome Jests done by him' and many other mid-seventeenth-century criminal biographies also exhibit the pervasive influence of this boisterous comic style.[11]

A similar jest-book spirit informs the most successful of these earlier native works, *The English Rogue: Described in the Life of Meriton Latroon, a Witty Extravagant*, by Francis Kirkman and Richard Head (1665). This amazingly extensive compendium of japes and frolics, almost forgotten since the seventeenth century, and held in contempt by more high-minded critics like F. W. Chandler, unashamedly draws together most of the best-known tricks available in the conny-catching pamphlets and the translated picaresque novels. The meaning and significance of

Meriton Latroon's seamy adventures are accurately, if a shade solemnly, summed up by Richard Bjornson, when he says 'in *The English Rogue*, the social world is a battlefield where everyone is competing against everyone else . . . acquisitiveness and mask-wearing are the natural concomitants of his and every person's struggle for survival and success'.[12] By his campaign of trickery, the eponymous witty extravagant shows up society as an elaborate charade, a hypocritical conspiracy to disguise the inherent assertiveness and rapacity of all human beings.

In terms of disseminating a 'myth' of crime, these adaptations and compilations present a specific understanding of nature and culture, rather different in emphasis from most comparable Augustan works. In the body of this seventeenth-century writing, the most characteristic signifying practice is indicated in the title of Francis Kirkman's *The Counterfeit Lady Unveiled* (1673). The criminal (or rogue or trickster, since the central figure rarely appears before a formal court for sentencing) is revealed in the texts, but in turn that figure serves to reveal more by his or her presence. The function of the narrative may be primarily to unmask and display the criminal: but the function of the criminal is to unmask and display the pretensions of society to be anything other than a grimly competitive Hobbesian arena where survival is the only thing that really counts, and where the law is an insignificant force. The technique of criminal biography, at least as articulated in this particular fantasised form, is thus fundamentally satiric and revelatory, designed to show that the ceremony of Culture is only a façade, and that the version of Nature it strives vainly to conceal is no more than that continuing no-holds-barred struggle for personal survival which drives the trickster to perform his or her feats.

It is very important to pay attention to this change in the use of crime in literary works over the period. Too many literary critics have recognised crime as a formal ingredient of much writing, without recognising that it need not always have the same significance, or be used to perform the same ideological or mythic functions. To see the absence of nuance and etiolations of meaning this oversight can lead to, it is worth looking at the extraordinarily autonomous version of aesthetic development offered in this interpretation of English literary history:

In England, although Nashe's *Unfortunate Traveller* (1594) gave early promise of an independent realism, the French heroic romances held sway for the greater part of the seventeenth century. Mabbe's translation of *Guzmán de Alfarache*, under the title of *The Rogue* (1622), was followed by *The English Rogue* of Head and Kirkman, in three parts (1665, 1668, and 1671). Biographies, real or fictitious, of members of the criminal class became popular, and Defoe then emerged. *Colonel Jack* and *Moll Flanders* both appeared in 1722; the latter is generally considered the best of Defoe's novels of delinquency and marks the peak of the picaresque tradition in England, almost exactly contemporaneous with *Gil Blas* in France. Smollett is still within the tradition with *Roderick Random* (1748) and *Ferdinand Count Fathom* (1753).[13]

This critic is eager to identify a clear line of progressivist literary development which can be independently charted, making the connections between Nashe and Smollett via Head and Kirkman and some unnamed biographies, producing a diagrammatic version of literary history which may be dignified with the title of a 'tradition'. The discovered (or, more accurately, invented) tradition is sufficiently loose to accommodate writers as different as Nashe and Smollett, yet sufficiently active to encourage a rather implausibly reticent Defoe to 'emerge'. It allows otherwise diverse narratives to be grouped together for critical consideration, centralises the biographical pattern, and further suggests that there is some version of *Zeitgeist* at work behind the scenes, nudging writers to produce works within the dominant or emergent traditions.

This kind of generic approach to the literature of delinquency, which echoes the influentially formative work of F. W. Chandler, looks comprehensive, but is in fact rigorously exclusive. It allows for the most heterogeneous writers to be yoked together by violence, without any of them having to face the most pertinent and challenging questions. For an analysis of criminal writing in the seventeenth and eighteenth centuries to be more genuinely informative, capable of indicating features of the surrounding culture, we have to pose more complex questions about historicity, like those formulated by Lennard J. Davis:

> One of the central questions about the origins of genres is – what causes change? Is there a necessary cause, a force, or an aim to changes in literary genres, or are we consigned to a realm of impenetrable forces, complex and shifting uncertainties and vague speculations on taste, style, and so on? . . . It is possible to talk about the necessity for change on a formal level. One could say that the tale was too short to develop a character or a plot adequately, or that romance was too episodic for psychological realism. But buried in such discussions is the unexpected core of necessity. Why should one particular change and not another occur? Are there only formal solutions to formal problems?[14]

In the context of a stimulating discussion of the origins of the English novel and the establishment of the discrete categories of 'fact' and 'fiction', Davis is arguing against the autonomous development of literature, and he poses questions which are very important for understanding the representations of criminality in Augustan England. Although the more elaborate and individualised versions of criminal biography, like *Moll Flanders* or *Colonel Jack*, are inevitably bound up in that inextricable fankle obscuring the origins of the novel, other changes in narrative style or presentation may be more obviously responsive to identifiable social pressures. Developments in the literary treatments of crime are clearly not motivated exclusively by literary or formal considerations, as Parker seems to suggest, but by more stealthy deep-seated social needs and imperatives.

It would be wrong, of course, to deny that forms of writing and genres may establish their own momentum, or that their very existence may encourage imitation and formal development. Had criminal biographies of the most conventional kind not been popular or successful in the commercialised publishing world of Augustan England, then the form would soon have disappeared. Had individual criminal tales and pamphlets not sold in respectable numbers, then it is unlikely that any publisher would have risked the more expensive compilations like Captain Alexander Smith's collection, mentioned above, or, describing a more specialised group of villains, *A General History of the Robberies and Murders Of the most notorious Pyrates, and also Their Policies, Discipline and Government, From their first Rise and Settlement in the Island of Providence, in 1717, to the present Year 1724* by 'Captain Charles Johnson' (probably Defoe). But even to say this is to introduce a material and social dimension in the account of literary causation, through the recognition of the economic importance of popularity and the availability of efficient systems of production and distribution. So in one way, even if the extraordinary range of criminal writing visible throughout the Augustan period may not be an accurate or reliable source of information about the development of crime, it could still be highly informative about the parallel development of what is regarded by some as a slightly more salubrious activity, that of publishing.

However, this is not an avenue I wish to explore for the moment. An account of the bizarre exploits of John Applebee, say, would no doubt be very interesting and welcome, but it would only be a distraction from the present enquiry. For what is being sought here is a clearer perception of the possible meanings of the criminal for Augustan readers, a more articulate way of considering just what myths the malefactor was asked to maintain or represent, and what social and ideological forces brought about any changes in the apprehension of criminality. One of the most interesting attempts so far to tackle this difficult subject has been offered by John J. Richetti.[15] This literary critic rightly believes that Augustan crime writing is not a disinterested body of factual information, but 'an exotic place where mythological simplicities prevail' (p. 24). Even if we might wish to suggest that the mythological elements of these texts are complex rather than simple, the statement seems broadly incontestable, and leads into a very interesting discussion of ways in which these texts disseminate eschatology and apologetics.

Basing his analysis mainly, indeed it seems almost exclusively, on the figures included in Captain Alexander Smith's rather expensive compilation, Richetti concentrates on the representations of two male categories of criminal, the 'Heroic highwayman' (p. 59) and the 'revolted apprentice' (p. 56). His conclusion is a general and definite one about the meaning offered to readers by 'the criminal':

> Given the moral and social context of the age, the popularity of criminal narrative thus processed justifies us in interpreting the criminal (especially the heroic highwayman, relatively innocent of cruel and bloody acts) as a mythical figure of great significance: an embodiment of the secular energies of the age which chafe under the traditional system of social and moral limitations and their religious foundations. The criminal, generally speaking, obtains his compelling stature because he violates the specific taboos of the age, and it will not do simply to resort to psychological truisms, to say only that violent crime has always been fascinating to many.
>
> (p. 59)

It will be obvious that I am greatly in sympathy with the outline of Richetti's argument, and what he says here about the violation of *specific* taboos is extremely important. However, at the risk of sounding pusillanimous, I fear he is trying to engineer a much more uniform and single-mindedly tidy conclusion than his material really offers. As we have already seen, the representation of criminals in Augustan writing is astonishingly diverse, and any attempt to round them up into two discrete groups is inevitably over-prescriptive and becomes too schematic. As Lincoln Faller has shown, even the more limited category of criminal biography is remarkably volatile and inconsistent, and we must remember that the writing about crime goes far beyond the individualised biographical model.

At the end of his argument, Richetti finds himself having to pay tribute to the obvious diversity of crime writing, while simultaneously searching for a meaningful pattern persisting throughout its various forms. What he comes up with is the recurrent motif of religious interpretation:

> This survey of criminal narrative of the early eighteenth century has shown that it is a miscellaneous type, capable of a whole range of entertaining postures, but that these attractions and mythical implications are superimposed upon the biographical pattern created by the religious rubrics of fall, sin, and repentance or damnation.
>
> (p. 59)

Of course, this basic pattern is regularly detectable in that group of texts chosen for close examination, but perhaps Richetti's insistence upon its identification obscures more differences than it reveals similarities, and criminal writing of all kinds may have been able to convey a greater range of meanings than this narrowly typological reading of some possibly unrepresentative narratives suggests.

The point can be made more forcefully if we think beyond even the ill-. defined and rather elastic limits of criminal biographies, and recall the other styles of Augustan writing where criminals were prominent. The title of a 1735 collection indicates some of the paradoxes surrounding the biographies:

> *Lives of the Most Remarkable Criminals Who Have Been Condemned and Executed for Murder, the Highway, Housebreaking, Street Robberies, Coining or Other Offences.*

The emphasis here is on 'Most Remarkable', as commercially it must be. Those criminals offered to the public in this way were by definition treated as exceptional and unrepresentative. But there were also other forms of writing about criminals which did not individuate in this way, and which disseminated instead the notion of gangs or classes of the underworld. Johnson's poem and the various discussions of the 'Mohocks' have already been mentioned, and it is appropriate to remember one other fascinating form: the canting dictionary. These glossaries of criminal argot claimed to give readers access to a world which was both distinct from their own, yet furtively integrated within it. The best known of these odd works is Captain Francis Groses's *Classical Dictionary of the Vulgar Tongue* (1785), which compiles its definitions from a number of Augustan sources, but there are earlier ones which are just as interesting. The best known to contemporaries, as well as the most comprehensive, were *The Canting Crew* (1698) and *A New Canting Dictionary* (1725), but there are less developed versions appended to various biographical pamphlets, including *The Memoirs of the Right Villainous John Hall* (1708), *The Regulator: Or a Discovery of Thieves etc.* (1718) by 'A Prisoner in Newgate' (actually Charles Hitchen), and the 'Key to the Canting Language' contained in *A Genuine Narrative of all the Street Robberies of James Dalton etc.* (1728).[16]

These lexicographical works are particularly interesting in the way they purport to deal with the dialect spoken by a discrete group within society. At a time when London was thronging with inward migrants, all speaking their own very different dialect versions of English, the constitution of a criminal language is a fascinating exercise. Not only does it provide the reticulated taxonomy of a constituent group within society, with its own subtly discriminated attitudes and labels for its own practices, but it does so without the creation of particularly heroic or particularly odious individuals. Rather, this exercise presents indications of the professional criminal, of criminality being the occupation of a distinct group, and of the possibility of criminals being members of a secret society. The myth created by the canting dictionaries is thus one shrouded in mystery, which the investigative efforts of the lexicographers do little to dispel. Just like the anonymous threatening hordes in Johnson's poem, these criminals are not individuated, and their pervasiveness is the most challenging and disquieting feature of their representation.

What we have seen so far is that the Augustan press was infatuated with the representation of criminals. It gave prominence to accounts of remarkable individuals, but also provided an extensive underworld context in which criminal activities made a kind of sense. Although it is extremely difficult to identify the exact meanings of these representations, with their radically differing inflections and interpretations, it is clear that crime was being established as a central feature of urban life, encouraging a sense of danger and threat. The 'myth' of crime was used to explain away the intractable internal problems of contemporary culture, but that only deferred more subtle aetiological questions. If it was crime which caused social disorder, what caused crime? What made people behave criminally?

As usual, the Augustan press offered contending answers to these questions, ranging from the social and economic to the theological and psychological. Although there is a body of writing addressed to the philosophical implications of this question, there was greater concern with the practicalities of crime. How should apprehended criminals be treated? How, if at all, was crime to be prevented? The forum in which these questions were first addressed was the forensic tribunal, and the elaborate rituals of the courtroom and of execution were of the utmost social importance. The press not only offered the most extensive commentary on those criminals still at large, it concentrated, as we have already seen, on the behaviour of the convicted. As we shall now see, its treatment of these matters was as intense and confused and ironically perplexing as its treatment of all legal issues.

TRIALS AND TYBURN

> Ye Gallants of *Newgate*, whose Fingers are nice,
> In diving in Pockets, or cogging of Dice,
> Ye Sharpers so rich, who can buy off the Noose,
> Ye honester poor Rogues, who die in your Shoes,
>   Attend and draw near,
>   Good News ye shall hear,
>   How *Jonathan's* Throat was cut from Ear to Ear;
> How *Blueskin's* sharp Penknife hath set you at Ease,
> And every Man round me may rob, if he please.[17]

In Augustan literature, as we have seen, rumours of the existence of unidentified and elusive groups of contemporary criminals were regularly published, taking their place alongside more detailed and corroborated expositions of the lives of selected remarkable individuals. This persistently popular body of writing has been shown to be extraordinarily diverse and variously nuanced. Exploiting many possibilities of expression both in tone and in content, Augustan writers repeated and disseminated hearsay alongside allegedly factual accounts, rarely distinguishing carefully between them. By the range and inventiveness of its coverage of crime, and its confusing mixture of fact and fantasy, the eighteenth-century press resists a uniform interpretation and refuses to be controlled by a neatly restricted typology. Although sharing many attitudes and perceptions about the current growth of law-breaking and the increasing virulence and violence of felons, the extensive body of criminal texts is clearly capable of supporting and conveying many contending and contradictory meanings.

The prime function of this discourse is to generate a myth of crime, to confront the Augustan public with a barrage of images of lawlessness. But if crime sometimes represented the savagery of nature, the official courts and tribunals of justice might represent the epitome of civilisation. Inevitably associated with the complex myths of visible crime and criminals in Augustan literature were the equally intricate and elaborate authorised ritual performances of the courtrooms and the public sites of execution in Augustan society. These rituals in their turn were also widely discussed in print and their ideological aims and functions were disseminated and occasionally disputed by the contemporary press. Alongside the extensive writing exclusively concerned with criminals, there exists an equally large body of varying commentary on the conventionalised and ritualised activities of judges, juries, gaolers, lawyers and all other participants in these socially important rites.

As contentious and as variously described as the relationship between literature and society, the relationship between myth and ritual is of course another area of great anthropological uncertainty and controversy. Although I wish to employ these terms to describe the workings of the Augustan courts and the supportive or critical commentaries of the contemporary press, I will make no claims here about which of the two should take precedence or priority. What I have to say about criminality as myth and the courtroom and execution as ritual and processional form is primarily suggestive, and should be seen as free of commitment to any particular anthropological theory.[18]

As we shall see, the workings of the Augustan legal system through its authorised courts were attended by great theatrical pomp and ceremony, and reliant on elaborate ritual. The ideological function of these practices, as Douglas Hay has shown, was to offer legitimisation of the law as a solemn and disinterested arbiter, above specific class loyalties, with a view to reinforcing its appearance of gravity and authority.[19] The treatment of the captured felon before the law was ritualised, with the trial conducted through recognised ceremonial processes. However, it is possible to think of a slightly different, complementary sense of 'ritual' observable in the literary representations of those particular criminals apprehended by the law and brought to trial. From the extensive bibliographical evidence, it is possible to see that a great deal of the criminal literature of the Augustan period was concerned primarily with the processional drama of the captured and tried criminal. The biographical narrative of the criminal's life was regularly conducted between sentence and execution, and it was described through a visible system of conventional and recurrent forms, however variously inflected in individual cases.

In obvious contrast to the structure of most traditional twentieth-century crime fiction, which typically starts with a murder and hermeneutically works backwards to identify its perpetrator, the Augustan criminal biography deliberately avoided and dispelled such mystery. The individualised criminal biography conventionally starts with the spectacle of the captured offender and avoids hermeneutics in favour of a more formal pageant-like presentation. As its narrative proceeds, the biography may work back to an aetiological exploration of its subject's crimes and move inexorably forward to the grim and ceremonial moment of execution. The central concern of such texts is to publicise the guilt of the identified criminal, which is presented as incontestable and firmly established from the beginning of the narrative. As the tale progresses, some attention is inevitably paid to what we might consider as questions of motive – why did this particular character behave in this wicked way? And why does anyone behave thus? – but much closer scrutiny is given to a conventionalised step-by-step narrative of the ritual behaviour of incarcerated felons after capture and sentence.

The significance of this recurrent narrative procedure is obvious. By studying the apprehended, tried and imprisoned offender, writers could claim to have authoritative access to the state of mind of one exemplary individual. At the same time, and perhaps more importantly, that singular villain could be taken as a reliable informant for the much more nebulous and undefinable realm of active, uncaught desperadoes still thought to be prowling the streets. By a suggestive process of analogy and extension, based on authenticated exemplary histories, criminal biographers and court reporters could imaginatively invigorate a peculiarly dramatic and powerful individualised narrative of corruption, crime, judgement and death. The functions of these narratives could be different: readers could be reassured by the way these discovered criminals were displayed to be so different from themselves, or horrified by the way they were revealed as fundamentally so similar. Various and inconsistent versions of motive and causation could be offered, emphasising innate wickedness or the force of circumstances, within conventional limits, and the literary effect of the narrative could thus be amended and nuanced.

Common to the presentation of all the criminal biographies was the great emphasis conventionally put on endorsing their genuineness, truth and accuracy. For the exemplary and forensic concerns of the texts to be effectively communicated, readers had to be convincingly assured of the authenticity and recognisability of their contents. Yet at the same time, prospective readers also had to be encouraged to purchase particular pamphlets by the assurance that their narratives were sufficiently out of the ordinary and were capable of incorporating the marvellous. In Defoe's *History of the Remarkable Life of John Sheppard etc.* (1724), the narrative's uncompromising mixture of the accurate and the extraordinary is confronted early on:

> His History will astonish! and is not compos'd of Fiction, Fable, or Stories plac'd at York, Rome, or Jamaica, but Facts done at your Doors, Facts unheard of, altogether new, Incredible, and yet Uncontestable.[20]

Sheppard's story, as it was represented to the Augustan public, was indeed remarkable, and this pamphlet (the first of two written about him by Defoe) is a startling compendium of his various escapes from captivity. In an unusual variant of the established marketing practices, this piece was first published while the central figure was still at large, then extensively revised after his execution one month later. According to Defoe, the citizens of London were being introduced to an authentic account of a figure who, at the moment of publication of the pamphlet, actually walked among them, the subject of intense rumour and speculation.

A more representative example of the desire to authenticate a narrative by first-hand experience of the subject comes in Defoe's *True and Genuine Account of the Life and Actions of the Late Jonathan Wild, Not made up of Fiction and Fable, but taken from his Own Mouth and collected from Papers of his own Writing* (1725). In presenting this rather lugubrious pamphlet, the author gives his work authority over the many rival and competing texts by avowing its unquestionable truth:

> We have the advantage in this account to come at the particular of his story from unquestioned authority, for he was sensible wrong accounts would be published of him, he was not backward to give materials from his own mouth which no body can contradict, and others fully conversant with him, having given the same stories or accounts of the same facts, we have the satisfaction to see them agree fully together, and thereby be assured of the truth of both.[21]

Defoe here claims to have interviewed Wild in Newgate to gain first-hand knowledge of his subject, a claim which we are at liberty to believe if we so desire. However, since the pamphlet includes a graphic account of Wild's execution, the subject is unlikely to be able to substantiate or deny his biographer's claims. The marketing strategy is interesting enough in itself, but, rather than squander our finite reserves of scepticism by looking at Defoe's sneakiness yet again, the important point to make is to emphasise the illusion of authenticity, to see how the apprehended criminal is said to be recorded in the text, following the accepted descriptive conventions, rather than invented. The condemned and eventually executed man is subsequently exhibited to the reader as a genuine part of contemporary culture. Such pamphlets thus exemplify, seem to corroborate, and make concrete the less specific fears about the proliferation of criminals which we have already seen in Johnson's poem and the canting dictionaries.

The most famous of all Augustan crime books, the one known to us through its many revised versions as *The Newgate Calendar*, is based on just these conventionalised exemplary premises. With a lot more gravity and solemnity than wit, it provides personal details of the lives of its catalogue of convicted criminals and describes their differing conduct while awaiting eventual execution, sometimes penitently, sometimes more defiantly. The narratives of their lives are full of corroborative circumstantial detail, and are interspersed with the rather ponderous sermons addressed to them by the prison chaplain, known as the Ordinary of Newgate, and his comments on their careers. Although reliant on a very crude and stylised notion of motivation, the tales do attempt to provide a social context for their participants' activities. The interaction of the religious narrator and the specific historical facts of the narration provides both a material and a spiritual perspective for understanding the exploits of the convicted, and reinforces the possibilities both of divine forgiveness for the penitent and inevitable damnation for the defiant.

The best-known compendium of such accounts was not in fact published under that title until 1773, when a compendious five-volume retrospective version was issued, also known by the more dramatic title of *The Malefactor's Bloody Register*. However, during the Augustan period itself, there were a great many individual pamphlets about specific offenders, purporting to be written by the Ordinary of Newgate (usually Paul Lorrain or John Guthrie). These short pieces were widely available and seem to have been popular, often first sold on the very day of execution. Known as *The Ordinary of Newgate, His Account of the Behaviour, Confession, and Dying Words of the Malefactors who were Executed at Tyburn*, such pamphlets followed a highly conventional narrative pattern throughout this period. The legal historian Peter Linebaugh describes the five discrete sections to be found in the typical account:

> The first described the basic facts of the trial – its date, the magistrates present, the members of the two juries and a summary of the proceedings. The second part cited the Biblical texts from which the Ordinary preached to the condemned and provided a synopsis of the sermons. The third and most valuable part of the *Account* contained

descriptions of the life and crimes of each of the malefactors condemned to death. The fourth part of the *Account*, a miscellaneous but rich section, contained various items – sometimes a narrative purporting to come from the hand of the condemned, sometimes a brief essay on some topic (smuggling or the robbing of country merchants) that the Ordinary (or his printer) thought appropriate. Finally, the *Account* contained a section entitled 'At the Place of Execution' in which was recounted the events of the hanging itself – the condition of the malefactors, the psalms sung or attempts to escape.[22]

Perhaps this presentation is inevitably a bit over-schematic, but in broad terms the suggested pattern is observable across a wide range of texts. For comparative purposes, it is most interesting to notice the relative priority given in particular cases to the various components of the condemned individual's history, as represented through the rather pedestrian imagination of the Ordinary. Compared with the very brief notices of the sentences handed out at particular court sittings (usually without naming those involved or giving details of the charges) which appeared in *The Post Boy* and the *London Chronicle* and other papers at this time, the Ordinary's accounts are much more interpretive and judgemental. Only after the offender had gone through the ritual process of being identified, arraigned, tried, imprisoned and prepared for execution, it seems, could his or her life begin to yield up its full range of meanings for contemporary readers. And although these pamphlets were often ridiculed for their penny-pinching and their morality by more sophisticated (or rival) authors, they helped establish conventions of narration which were widely imitated.

One rather lengthy title from an anonymous pamphlet published by the notoriously unscrupulous crime specialist John Applebee in 1723 shows the kind of narrative pattern that had been established relatively early in the century for the literary representation of particularly interesting criminals and their histories:

> *A Full, True and Particular Account of the Behaviour, Confession and last Words of Thomas Athoe, late Mayor of Tenby in Pembrokeshire, and Thomas Athoe his Son, who were executed on Fryday July 5th, 1723, at St. Thomas's Watering in the County of Surrey, for a barbarous murther by them committed, upon the Body of Mr. George Marchant their Kinsman, in Pembrokeshire, Anno. 1722. The whole Faithfully Publish'd by Thomas Dyche Chaplain to the King's Bench Prison. To which is added The case of the Two Athoes concerning this barbarous Murther.*

This is a representative, albeit spectacular, example of the familiar and domestic murder, a particularly horrifying and persistently fascinating offence for Augustan readers. In the titling (and subsequent marketing) of the pamphlet, it is the authentic full confession and the final words of the convicted felons which are first offered to the prospective reader, attested to and verified by a chaplain, with the explanatory details of the ritual procedures of the trial itself were subject to closer scrutiny, and, on many occasions, the prime focus of attention was the penitent behaviour of the criminal held under legal restraint after receiving the death sentence. And while murders (particularly within the family) were clearly the most attention-grabbing crimes to report, there are many other pamphlets which just as seriously or sensationally discussed individuals convicted of treason, counterfeiting, theft, highway robbery and a great many other capital offences.

Although the offences and offenders were various, and the proposed explanations of their behaviour diverse and inconsistent, one important recurrent function of the descriptive pamphlets was to publicise the consistent workings of the legal system, offering opportunities for authors to validate or criticise its forensic procedures. In the Ordinary's accounts, the legal system is treated uncritically, the procedures of the courts and the pronouncements of judges being described with great respect and awe, and this attitude is representative of most of the official literature. At this time, at least, there were very few attempts to explore possible miscarriages of justice (with the thought of such a horrific possibility never making the short journey across the mind of the Ordinary), and the literature of the trial was for the most part supportive of legal procedures rather than hostile, laying great emphasis on freely-offered confessions and admissions of guilt. There was a controversial case in 1695, which is described in a pamphlet called *Mistaken Justice: Or, Innocence Condemn'd*, but the vast majority of surviving accounts seek to demonstrate that when dealing with individual cases the law got things right a lot more often than it got them wrong, and that those sentenced to death were indeed villains. Of course, this confidence in the ability of courts to identify the guilt of those who appeared before them still left plenty of room for the Jonsonian suspicion that a great many more nameless guilty parties never actually faced trial.

In 1718, for instance, an important collection was published with an elaborate title showing how serious legalist interest and popular sensationalism could be happily combined:

A Compleat Collection of Remarkable Tryals of the Most Notorious Malefactors, at the Sessions-House in the Old Baily, for near Fifty Years Past . . . Together with a Particular Account of Their Behaviour under Sentence of Death, and Dying Speeches. Faithfully Collected from the Books of Tryals, and Papers of Mr. Smith, Mr. Allen, Mr. Wikes, and Mr. Lorrain, Ordinaries of Newgate, from the first Printing of Them, down to This Present Time: and from Other Authentic Narratives.

No attempt is made by the publishers to disguise the sources of this redaction or compilation, or to pass it off as original, and, as it grew to four volumes in 1721, there is every reason to think that such a competent, allegedly authentic collection proved popular with those readers who could afford such a relatively lavish production.

The most interesting general feature of the accounts contained in these and similar volumes is that, in a much more purposeful way than in the extended fictional biographies of Defoe, say, they deliberately shape their narratives around the great ritual moments of the trial, the confinement and the elaborate execution, all conducted with the due ceremonies. The impression conveyed by these repetitive and conventionalised narratives is that the life of the criminal already displays a kind of ritual pattern, before the intervention of the author or compiler. Also, as these volumes came out with great regularity, getting progressively longer and more numerous with each printing, readers were almost inevitably left with the impression that crime was not only widespread, but always growing, even despite the best efforts of the authorities to identify, curtail or eradicate it. Like their hapless confederates the poor, the wicked, it seems, are always with us.

A slightly later title shows the persisting interest in such a narrative pattern, giving greater than usual prominence to the criminal incarcerated and awaiting death, the story thus occupying a period of time which would vary greatly depending on the interval between the trial and the first available 'hanging day'. Once again, the pre-history of the offence is relegated to relatively secondary status:

> *A short Narrative of the Behaviour, &c. of John Barry, while under Sentence of Death, who was executed May 16th, 1746 at St. Michael's Hill Gallows, for causing and procuring to be falsely made, forged and counterfeited, the last Will and Testament of James Barry, who died at his House, in order to secure unto himself his Prize-Money, amounting to at least 1500 l.*

Such a concern with the criminal's final days in prison prior to the trip to the gallows allowed writers suitable opportunities to point conventional warnings about the awful sorry fate of convicted malefactors, to explore the felon's remorsefulness or defiance in the face of imminent death, to propose reforms in the current system of imprisonment (as in the Barry pamphlet) or simply to give as comprehensive an account as possible of the whole circumstances leading up to a particular crime and its terrible consequences (as with the Athoes).

More fundamentally, however, the literary discussion of the captured and executed criminal offered an opportunity for ostentatious display. Through the mechanism of the individualised biographical pamphlet, the named malefactor was put before the public in a more lasting way than at the gallows itself. And of course, as far as Augustan readers were concerned, documentary accounts of those criminals who had been brought to justice and legally despatched, while still capable of causing concern, might be less frightening and more reassuring than the widespread contemporary newspaper reports and rumours of those greater numbers who were successfully evading the law – provided, of course, that readers could be persuaded that the law successfully apprehended as many criminals as possible.

In the absence of any formally organised police force, or any effective alternative method of rounding up suspects, contemporary readers could have little reason for confidence in the ability of the courts to make much impression on the criminal underworld. The captured and executed felon might have been representatively criminal, but he or she could still seem disquietingly unrepresentative in having been apprehended. There remains great uncertainty within these narratives about just how many villains might still be at large, conducting themselves unhindered. The Ordinary's conventional efforts to get condemned villains to inform on their fellows were rarely successful, except when a pardon was offered in return for such information, on which occasions the condemned could wax particularly garrulous. In any case, if the declared aim of these books was to give access primarily to those few unfortunate criminals who were fortuitously brought to justice, who might then describe the customs and language of their teeming unidentified confederates still at liberty, then the effect of such pamphlets must have been much more disconcerting.

The 'cant' dictionaries and the profuse biographical reports helped construct the notion of a large and successful criminal class, and were instrumental in both paying attention to the pattern of the individual malefactor's life and creating and disseminating the ideology of the organised criminal gang. The clearest and in some odd ways the least judgemental representation of the constituents of that class could be found in the records of trials available in the numerous published court reports. There were some impressive records of the most solemn and influential cases, like T. Salmon's *A Compleat Collection of State-tryals, and Proceedings Upon Impeachments for High Treason, and Other Crimes and Misdemeanours*, published in four volumes in 1719. Although these volumes were widely cited by contemporaries, and are of great importance to historians, they are of only limited use in the search for versions of Augustan criminality, being deliberately restricted to the trials of major crimes against the state. Alongside such august reports, and of equal interest to legal historians, there are also various useful manuscript sources available, like the fragmentary notebooks of Dudley Ryder which describe Old Bailey cases from 1754 to 1756 or the various surviving Gaol Delivery Rolls and sundry courtroom ephemera.

However, of greater importance for the present purposes are the many contemporary published records of more mundane court proceedings, covering all the offences brought before normal court sittings.[23] The general title for these was *The Complete Proceedings on the King's Commission of the Sessions of the Peace, of Oyer and Terminer, and of Gaol Delivery*, followed by the name of the particular place in question, and they seem to have been published after every Sessions, though not all now survive. As well as acting as a semi-official record of all cases tried and judgements passed, the session papers were offered for sale to the public in the form of relatively cheap pamphlets. From the evidence of their regular appearance and persistence, their avoidance of over-elaborate legal details or technicalities, and their unembarrassed incorporation of advertisements for popular products like patent medicines, they seem to have been understood by both their producers and consumers as a commercial proposition rather than as a more austere exercise in documentary.

Whatever their contemporary purpose, these surviving papers are clearly of the utmost importance as documentary records of the conduct of trials, and have informed the growing recent investigative work of legal historians. Of particular importance are John H. Langbein's analysis of the Old Bailey Session Papers (OBSP), and J. M. Beattie's discussions of the Surrey and Sussex Assize Papers. However, by the way the reports are shaped, by selection, inclusion, exclusion and emphasis, the session papers not only record the proceedings, but also compose a particular version of the trial, and direct public attitudes towards these ritual practices. This vital point is often under-emphasised by the legal archivists. Langbein, for instance, is particularly enthusiastic about the veridical accuracy and reliability of these documents. While he acknowledges that the earliest surviving Old Bailey Session Papers (from around the 1670s) are highly selective and editorial in their presentation, he is confident that by the 1730s they are more disinterested – 'we have no reason to expect invention in the OBSP . . . The pressures of the market place made for reasonable accuracy in what was reported.'[24] Langbein's belief in the benignity of market forces has a certain charm, but seems to me to be inconsistent with the experience of reading eighteenth-century texts. Of course, the court reports were not total fabrications or hoaxes, as far as we can tell, but the virtually uncritical version of courtroom procedure they offer, full of silences and omissions, is hard to see as wholly accurate, and does not fully represent the versions of the trial available in Augustan writing. While not designed to deceive, the session papers can inevitably only offer a partial and broadly supportive view of how the Augustan courts operated. Whether or not this amounts to 'reasonable accuracy' depends on the nature of the information sought, and the investigator's criteria for acceptability.

I have no wish to quarrel with Langbein's argument about the increasing prominence of lawyers and advocates in trials from the 1730s onwards, which he scrupulously substantiates from the OBSP records. Of course, as he acknowledges, this change was greeted with sustained contempt by most Augustan writers, and lawyers are treated with the utmost scorn in a whole range of different texts. The best-known indictments may be those which recur throughout *Gulliver's Travels*, but the charges that lawyers were men without principle, agents of the devil, wholly unscrupulous and entirely avaricious can be found in an enormous number of diverse books and pamphlets.[25] The point is made with extreme ironic force in *The Beggar's Opera* (1728), where one of Peachum's songs identifies the lawyer as the most dangerous crook to be found anywhere in the contemporary world:

> A Fox may steal your Hens, Sir,
> A Whore your Health and Pence, Sir,
> Your Daughter rob your Chest, Sir,
> Your Wife may steal your Rest, Sir,
>   A Thief your Goods and Plate.
> But this is all but picking,
> With Rest, Pence, Chest, and Chicken;
> It ever was decreed, Sir,
> If Lawyer's Hand is fee'd, Sir,
>   He steals your whole Estate.[26]

For many more sceptical Augustan authors, writing in opposition to the schematised pieties of the Ordinary, it was obvious that the developing rituals of the courtroom and the trial were to be abhorred, and ridiculed as pompous and over-elaborate ceremonies, barely connected with the proper discovery of guilt and dispensation of justice. Any attempt to create an awe-inspiring majestic performance in court was treated with the utmost suspicion by the satirists, who regularly articulated their view that the elevated forms of the legal ritual were only an unsuccessful and unconvincing attempt to disguise a lack of integrity and substance. The lawyer came in for the most searching criticism, but there were equally scathing remarks about judges, juries and the other participants in these formal proceedings. The famous descriptive passage from *The Rape of the Lock*:

> Mean while declining from the Noon of Day,
> The Sun obliquely shoots his burning Ray;
> The hungry Judges soon the Sentence sign,
> And wretches hang, that jurymen may dine

was only one of the most amusingly concise and sly of a great many contemporary criticisms of the length and orotundity of the official court sessions.[27]

The publicising of the courtroom took many forms, then, from the broadly documentary and covertly supportive in the session papers, to the more overtly hostile in the form of satire. Further literary attention was given to the convicted criminal's conduct after the trial, and one of the most interesting bodies of commentary on crime comes in the regularly published collections of 'dying speeches'.[28] One fascinating component in the full ritual of execution, which included a lengthy procession, attended with all manner of bizarre quasi-matrimonial ceremonies, was the opportunity granted to the condemned to address the crowd, who might number thousands, just before being 'turned off'. If the felon felt unable to deliver a personal address, through terror or intoxication, he or she might hand a written speech over to the Ordinary, who would then read it out. In many cases, these valedictory words were rehearsed, and subsequently published. Collections of all the speeches from particularly successful 'hanging matches' exist, like *The Confessions, Behaviour, and Dying Speeches of the Criminals that were Executed at Tyburn, on Saturday the 20th of July, 1700*. Other criminals, like Hogarth's poor Thomas Idle, might have their words printed just before execution, with or (more probably) without their knowledge or consent, and these could be distributed on the day of execution and immediately afterwards. As Sir Leon Radzinowicz illustrates, most Augustan publishers were extremely enthusiastic about this kind of pamphlet. After all, the attractive combination of ease and cheapness of publication and distribution and consistent popularity with readers, not to mention the absence of tiresomely interfering authors, seems to have made the recorded 'last speech' a highly remunerative form for publishers and printers alike.[29]

As the emphasis on true confessions indicates, these stylised speeches were conventionally full of self-recrimination and lingered over the condemned's acceptance of the justice of the capital sentence. The felon facing death might also provide a brief autobiographical sketch, more details of the offence with some attempts at explanation, or might simply bid a hearty farewell to his or her fellows. Of most interest to certain Augustan writers, however, were those hardened figures who approached execution with defiance or irreverence. For some commentators, the theatricality of the final moments at the gallows failed to impress the onlookers with the gravity of the occasion, and in fact encouraged a kind of drunken courage and boastfulness in the criminals, which had potentially bad effects on the audience. Bernard Mandeville puts this case extensively and polemically in his *Enquiry into the Causes of the Frequent Executions at Tyburn* (1725):

> At the very Place of Execution, the most remarkable Scene is a vast Multitude on Foot, intermixed with many Horsemen and hackney-Coaches, all very dirty, or else cover'd with Dust, that are either abusing one another, or else staring at the Prisoners, among whom there is commonly very little Devotion; and in that, which is practis'd and dispatch'd there, of Course, there is as little good Sense as there is Melody. It is possible that a Man of extraordinary Holiness, by

anticipating the Joys of Heaven, might embrace a violent Death in such Raptures, as would dispose him to the singing of Psalms: But to require this Exercise, or expect it promiscuously of every Wretch that comes to be hang'd, is as wild and extravagant as the Performance of it is commonly frightful and impertinent: Besides this, there is always at that Place, such a mixture of Oddnesses and Hurry, that from what passes, the best dispos'd Spectator seldom can pick out any thing that is edifying or moving.[30]

The turbulent and frantic performances at Tyburn attract Mandeville's distaste here for their failure to enact and communicate any worthwhile moral message. At the same time, they seem to excite his covert delight in the paradoxical frustration of purposes, in the 'mixture of Oddnesses and Hurry'. The scene at the gallows is so stubbornly earthly and squalid ('very dirty . . . Dust') that it encourages festivity rather than solemnity, and according to Mandeville the condemned felon regularly went off to tumultuous applause rather than due execration.

Similarly contradicting and problematising the austere and solemn presentations of many of the 'dying speeches' and confessions in print is Swift's poem 'Clever Tom Clinch Going to be Hanged' (?1726). In a lively enactment of the procession and execution, Swift ironically delights in his hero's useless but nonetheless flamboyant defiance, and in the drama of his valedictory courage:

> As clever Tom Clinch, while the rabble was bawling,
> Rode stately through Holborn, to die in his calling;
> He stopped at the George for a bottle of sack,
> And promised to pay for it when he came back.
> His waistcoat and stockings, and breeches were white,
> His cap had a new cherry ribbon to tie't.
> The maids to the doors and the balconies ran,
> And said, lackaday, he's a proper young man.
> But, as from the windows the ladies he spied,
> Like a beau in the box, he bowed low on each side;
> And when his last speech the hawkers did cry,
> He swore from his cart, it was all a damned lie.
> The hangman for pardon fell down on his knee;
> Tom gave him a kick in the guts for his fee.
> Then said, 'I must speak to the people a little,
> But I'll see you all damned before I will whittle.
> My honest friend Wild, may he long hold his place,
> He lengthened my life with a long year of grace.
> Take courage, dear comrades, and be not afraid,
> Nor slip this occasion to follow your trade.
> My conscience is clear, my spirits are calm,
> And thus I go off without prayer-book or psalm.'

Then follow the practice of clever Tom Clinch,
Who hung like a hero, and never would flinch.[31]

It is clear from these pieces by Swift and Mandeville, as from the Hogarth
prints analysed earlier, that the diverse oppositional literature of the time
was eager to exploit failings in the operations of the legal system, and
prepared to draw unexpected and conflicting meanings from its
authorised rituals. In this particular poem, Swift enjoys the mock-heroic
spectacle of the drunken roaring Clinch, making his 'stately' procession to
the gallows, with his 'calling' and his defiant gallantry. The picture given
of this 'proper young man' is in direct contradiction to the conventional
moralising of the Ordinary, or the tacitly supportive accounts of the trial
found in the session papers. As usual, Swift was eager to exploit the
disparity between what this ritual was designed to convey and what it
actually did, and he offers a reading of Tyburn which is in opposition to
the official line. Clinch himself encourages his listeners to exploit the
opportunities created by the 'rabble' to engage in some remunerative
pilfering. Instead of offering the grim spectacle of the due processes of
the law at their most terrible, the scene at Tyburn enacts a kind of theatre
of courage and spirit, turning Clinch into a celebrity, famous for fifteen
minutes, but finally ending in bathos.

Although many Augustan writers offered their own inflections of such
ironic commentary, Swift in particular was drawn to the tragi-comic
ceremony of the public execution, and the conflicting meanings offered by
the spectacle of the criminal. He satirically dramatised the rituals of the
published confession in his 1722 Dublin pamphlet, *The Last Speech and
Dying Words of Ebenezor Elliston, who was Executed the Second Day of
May, 1722*. The piece is another hoax, fraudulently declared to be written
by the condemned man himself, 'Published at his Desire, for the
Common Good', and it acted as a parodic rival to the genuine broadsheet
offered by Elliston, a well-known Dublin criminal executed for horse-
stealing. The absurdity of the whole business is emphasised by
extravagantly over-playing the efficacy of such confessional pieces, in an
intrusive editorial footnote added in 1735:

N. B. About the Time that this Speech was written, the Town was
much pestered with *Street-Robbers*; who, in a barbarous Manner would
seize on Gentlemen, and take them into remote Corners, and after
they had robbed them, would leave them bound and gagged. It is
remarkable, that this Speech had so good an Effect, that there have
been very few Robberies of that kind committed since.[32]

Remarkable indeed, since Ebenezor Elliston's recitation lays the entire
blame for such crimes upon the cowardice of the victims rather than the
rapacity of the perpetrators. Despite Elliston's statements of high intent,
his whole demeanour gives no grounds for confidence in his desire to
amend the world, and he seems more concerned to set the record straight

than to put the world to rights. In fact, the whole speech is smoothly confused and riven with baldly-stated internal contradictions, vexing rather than diverting us, making a clear interpretation of its alleged author very elusive and perplexing.

Prominent in this welter of confusions and inconsistencies is the moment when Elliston adopts the recognised forms of penitence without truly feeling any trace of it:

> AND First, I cannot say from the Bottom of my Heart, that I am truly sorry for the Offence I have given to God and the World; but I am very much so, for the bad Success of my Villainy in bringing me to this untimely End . . . And therefore although in Compliance with my Friends, I resolve to go to the Gallows after the usual Manner, Kneeling, with a Book in my Hand, and my Eyes lift up; yet I shall feel no more Devotion in my Heart than I have observed in some of my Comrades, who have been drunk amomg common Whores the very Night before their Execution.
>
> (IX, 38)

Elliston's account complicates every issue it touches upon. He looks penitent, but is not; he is sorry for his failures, but would repeat them given the chance; and he accepts the justice of his sentence, while emphasising that he cannot help but be a rogue. In fact, on closer inspection it becomes clear that this apparently conventional pamphlet is one of Swift's complex exercises in disorientation. Elliston gives a portrait of the criminal's life which is painful and disturbing, but yet Swift does not allow us to pity him, or indeed to adopt any single attitude towards him. Extenuating circumstances of a kind are offered (whores and drunkenness), but these do not extenuate. Proposals to eradicate crime are put forward, but they are so unlikely and doubtful that they do not persuade. The overwhelming impression of this brief piece is to bring together the abject horrors of the criminal life and the hopelessness of official measures to combat crime, without the balancing provision of any more positive perspective.

In many ways, *Ebenezor Elliston* epitomises much of the Augustan literary commentary on apprehended criminals, in an intense and dramatised form. What Swift's piece does is compress the contending images of heroism and villainy, making his malefactor almost impossible to read or clearly identify. The language used to describe criminals, which Elliston claims to be clarifying, is becoming fraught and unable to carry single meanings. And the fact that Swift's hoax was only one of a number of pamphlets claiming to be the authentic final words of the condemned man only adds to the multi-vocality and confusion. The combination of glamour and squalor prominent in 'Tom Clinch' and Mandeville's *Enquiry* is reiterated in Elliston's account, but his final words are more disconcerting: 'GOOD People fare ye well; bad as I am, I leave many worse behind me.' It is this discomforting recognition of the virulence and unmanageability of crime which the Augustan press could intermittently disseminate. Alongside the supportive session papers and trial reports, the literature of the apprehended criminal could carry many contending and contradictory images. In Swift's version, Elliston seems to take on the multiple significances in an alarming and destabilising way, and is being asked to carry the suggestion that the greatest rogues never appear before the courts. To see how the relation between criminals and 'great men' was developed, and to recognise what other significances the criminal could be asked to convey, we need to leave the literature of the trial aside, and move to more imaginative constructions.

NEWGATE PASTORAL

Our selves, like the Great, to secure a Retreat,
When Matters require it, must give up our Gang:
   And good reason why,
   Or, instead of the Fry,   /
   Ev'n *Peachum* and I,
Like poor petty Rascals, might hang, hang;
Like poor petty Rascals, might hang.[33]

The extensive body of writing about criminals so far discussed in this chapter has made prominent its claim to deal with real events and with living (or recently executed) individuals, in however fantastic or caricatured a form they may seem to us to have been represented. Although the diverse products of the Augustan press examined in the preceding discussions were all inevitably selective and interpretive in their presentation of crime, making them all to some extent distorting and judgemental, the events thereby portrayed and the characters who participated in them were almost invariably alleged to be genuine. Although we must always remain sceptical about the precise accuracy of the various crime reports, we must remember that their authors and publishers sought to claim veridical authority by upholding at least the vestiges of verisimilitude.

In the session papers and the orthodox criminal biographies, as well as in so many periodicals and canting dictionaries, the illusion of circumstantial authenticity and impartiality was maintained very strenuously, if not always entirely persuasively. Despite this quasi-factual presentation, there were certainly clear internal tensions within specific texts, and perplexing disparities of tone when more obvious editorialising broke out, as we have seen in Mandeville and in Blackstone, and elsewhere. However, although ideological confusions unsettled and disturbed the progress of many texts, most of the Augustan writing concerned with crime seen so far explicitly sought to stigmatise criminality severely, and to validate or criticise the legal system's ability to cope with the situation thus revealed. That is to say, the literature examined so far may have purported to describe or report criminality, but in fact it invariably and stealthily packaged and interpreted events for the reader. Only in more complex and deliberately ironic efforts, like Hogarth's prints or Johnson's *London* or Swift's impersonation of Ebenezor Elliston, were the creative possibilities of distortion or misrepresentation deliberately given any attention and seriously confronted. These stylisations and exaggerations, though, were employed purposefully by their authors, surrounded by uncertainties and hesitations about the possibilities of accuracy, and the discomforting intensity of the ironic texts was generated by their potential applicability to the real world.

However, perhaps the most exciting and persistently popular literary representation of early eighteenth-century crime, criminals and justice is a deliberate and unembarrassed work of fiction: John Gay's extraordinarily successful musical play, *The Beggar's Opera*. First published and performed in London in 1728, it enjoyed great success in its first theatrical season and was revived frequently throughout England during the Augustan period to widespread popular acclaim.[34] There can be no doubt that it is Gay's exuberant wit and his inventiveness which have kept his ballad opera in the standard theatrical repertoire, rather than its accurate or caricatured documentary portrayal of an identifiable Augustan underworld. Indeed, by being performed so frequently, the play has gradually acquired a reassuring covering of patina, lending it an enjoyable sense of timelessness and giving its characters the appearance of entertaining pantomime figures. Like that other great Augustan popular success, *Robinson Crusoe*, this work seems to be with us always, no longer enveloped in the aura of its historical situation, and inevitably taking on the power of fantasy. As a result, it may well now be the case, as Michael Denning argues, that Gay's work has become 'too familiar a play'.[35]

It is also possible, of course, that the ubiquity and power of the famous 1928 Bertolt Brecht/Kurt Weill adaptation, *Die Dreigroschenoper* (*The Threepenny Opera*), have overshadowed and obscured the original text, making it difficult for late twentieth-century readers or audiences to retrieve the contemporary cultural significance of Gay's piece, or appreciate its immediate historicity. For some critics, this removal of the play from the tangles of its local surroundings is only to be welcomed. As Peter Elfed Lewis approvingly puts it, 'one of the effects of the comic stylization is to lift the play out of its immediate 1720s context and so universalize it'.[36] Yet this search for the universal rather than the specific in Augustan literature seems to me to be misguided and unhelpful, both theoretically and practically. Lewis seems to see the local context of the play merely as a convenient vehicle for presenting the author's real, deeper concerns: 'Gay, too, is dealing with human nature and society in general rather than with the England of George I, Walpole, Handel, and Wild' (p. 59).

The notion of 'society in general' seems far too broad and abstract a philosophical construction for Gay's piece, however much of a fable it may appear to be. At the same time, the undefined and imprecise idea of universal 'human nature' seems a poor substitute for the much more interesting immediate and local concerns of a play as densely allusive as *The Beggar's Opera*. Instead of parading before us these abstract phantoms, the play seems to me to be intricately embedded in its historical surroundings, even if most modern readers (and theatrical producers) find the act of reconstruction required to see this a difficult one to perform. I would not wish to argue, of course, that this play is a disinterested work of historical record, with the author at last providing the source for an accurate picture of its times, free from distortion or disfiguring partiality. My emphasis on the fictional elements in factual discourse is not to be paralleled by equally confident statements about the accuracy of fiction. Nonetheless, by exploring the immediate social contexts in which the play intervened and with which it interacted, we may discover much about contemporary Augustan perceptions of crime, and about the possible roles of the press in its more imaginative forms in disseminating or transforming the received ideas through powerful and suggestive metaphors. The criminal underworld is elaborated and exploited in this play, not to represent or reinforce timeless truths about the nature of humanity or society, but to represent in a metaphoric way the very connections that Gay and other oppositional writers could see between figures like George I, Walpole, Handel and Wild. Readers in search of profound insight into 'society in general' and 'human nature' may thus skip the rest of this chapter, and probably the rest of this book.

The original suggestion for the composition of *The Beggar's Opera* seems to have come in one of Swift's letters to Pope in 1716, where he considered the possibility that Gay might produce a 'Newgate pastoral, among the whores and thieves there'.[37] Swift's suggestion may simply have been offered to encourage Gay to write another straightforward burlesque incorporating topical references to crime and some mock-pastoral elements, like his earlier work *The What D'Ye Call It* (1715), to which the later play bears some incidental similarities of plot, or like his unperformed tragi-comical piece, *The Mohocks* (1712). This may also have been an attempt by Swift to initiate another jaunty collaborative Scriblerian project, like *Three Hours after Marriage* (1717), without necessarily involving any more complex political resonances, and there are brief hints of such a topic embedded in *The Memoirs of Martinus Scriblerus*.

Gay's response to this hint is not known, but does not seem to have been initially very positive. Apart from the song called 'Newgate's Garland' or 'Blueskin's Ballad', probably written in collaboration with Swift and first published in 1724 after its incorporation in John Thurmond's rarely performed miscellaneous afterpiece *Harlequin Sheppard; A Night Scene in Grotesque Characters*, there is no evidence that Gay was immediately inspired by the possibility of writing such a piece, or even that he thought seriously about Swift's suggestion. However, in his characteristically casual and dilettante way, Gay seems to have held on to the idea of the 'Newgate pastoral' and eventually got round to developing it into *The Beggar's Opera* eleven years later.

After Gay had completed work on this play in 1727, he circulated the text to friends for comments, his literary advisers probably including Pope, Voltaire and William Congreve. Given his unfortunate financial plight after his losses during the South Sea Bubble, Gay certainly needed some revenue, and he clearly hoped his new play would prove more remunerative than his earlier theatrical work, and more successful than his pursuit of patronage. But however much they wished to be supportive, his readers' responses were not particularly encouraging, with most of them seeming rather baffled by the play's mixture of styles and forms, its mingling of the romantic and the cynical, its 'low' Newgate setting, and its relaxed exculpatory ending. And when he subsequently approached theatres, there was initially considerable reluctance to put the play on to the stage in the form presented. Amongst others, Colley Cibber rejected it as unsuitable for the Theatre Royal in Drury Lane, possibly on political grounds, possibly out of personal antipathy, and it was eventually produced, with some straightforward commercial trepidation, by John Rich at Lincoln's Inn Fields in January of 1728.

Despite these initial uncertainties, and some substantial confusions during rehearsal about the music and presentation of the songs, the performed play seems instantly to have caught the public's imagination. For Augustan theatre-goers, if not always for contemporary commentators and critics, *The Beggar's Opera* was a remarkable financial and artistic triumph, 'making Rich gay and Gay rich', as a contributor to *The Craftsman* put it within a week of the first night. Full of popular songs and airs, eventually attracting the attention of the most fashionable audiences and the participation of the established theatrical 'stars' of the day, the raffish and surprisingly genial atmosphere of this play gave Augustan criminals their most sympathetic and well-received publicity.

But as well as being a successful popular entertainment in its own right, and a boisterous burlesque treatment of the current taste for Italian opera, the play was also a buoyant and potentially subversive political intervention, greatly informative in helping us understand the ways more ironical oppositional Augustan writers could apprehend, transfigure and metaphorically exploit the significance of contemporary crime, criminals and the existing system of justice. For although its underworld characters are deliberately stylised and caricatured in their presentation, and stand on their own as imaginative creations, they are also capable of being closely associated with known figures in eighteenth-century London life, many of whom are still identifiable. The play's central ironic meaning is summed up by the eponymous beggar at the end:

> Through the whole Piece you may observe such a similitude of Manners in high and low Life, that it is difficult to determine whether (in the fashionable Vices) the fine Gentlemen imitate the Gentlemen of the Road, or the Gentlemen of the Road the fine Gentlemen.

> (II, 64)

Such a witty invigoration of the almost conventional comic comparison of gentlemen and rascals is most obvious in the play in Gay's jocose presentation of the romantic highwayman figure in Captain Macheath, whose speeches combine criminal cant and heroic gallantry in a much more 'gentlemanly' and occasionally pathetic way than in Swift's presentation of Tom Clinch. However, the various and suggestive connections between high and low life, and the concerns with the paradoxes of real and poetic justice, are also dispersed throughout the entire action to interesting and complex effect.

Gay's main point about the pervasiveness and political significance of crime in contemporary life had already been animated, as we have seen, in his occasional poem/song 'Newgate's Garland', which was inspired by the near-fatal assault on Jonathan Wild by Joseph Blake, known as 'Blueskin', at the Old Bailey in 1724. Although badly slashed across the throat, Wild survived the attack, only to be hanged the following year. In this hearty ballad, Blueskin is unaware of his failure and prematurely celebrates Wild's death as a great moment of liberation for all the other less audacious criminals lurking in society:

> Some say there are Courtiers of highest Renown,
> Who steal the King's Gold, and leave him but a Crown,
> Some say there are Peers, and some Parliament Men,
> Who meet once a Year to rob Courtiers again.
> > Let them all take their Swing,
> > To pillage the King,
> Now *Blueskin's* sharp Penknife hath set you at Ease,
> And every man round me may rob, if he please.[38]

Through his character's words, the author is here making both a specific and a generalised point about the ubiquity of corruption, and about the low standards of behaviour pervading the highest realms of the land, a view already familiar from much contemporary and recent writing, and perhaps in this context not expected to be taken very seriously. In its light-hearted way, the poem can be seen as one of the first recognisably anti-Walpole satires to appear on the English stage, part of the growing

but sporadic oppositional campaign of the mid-1720s designed to disparage
the man himself and the 'Robinocracy' he had created, also visible at this
time in *Gulliver's Travels* and *The Dunciad*, and in papers like *Mist's
Weekly Journal*, where the representation of Walpole as arch-criminal
was first elaborated in 1725.[39] But without over-strenuously drawing the
specific parallel between Wild and Walpole, the ballad simply exploits a
suitable topical opportunity to give an incongruous and droll re-working
of a conventional idea, appropriating the metaphor of crime to describe
the workings of government and courtiers, witty and ironic in its
expression, but unimpassioned in its attitudes.

Although it includes many similar songs, *The Beggar's Opera* goes
much further than this occasional poem, and makes some much more
subversive and explicit connections between the play and the political
world in which it participates, using the world of organised crime as a
suggestive mediating trope. The author claimed to have carried out first-
hand research for the play at Newgate (involving yet another alleged
interview with Jonathan Wild, who seems to have spent his final days
besieged by men with notebooks), and to have based most of his
characters on genuine underworld figures of the day. Wild himself is
represented again through the figure of Peachum, as we shall see, and
Macheath resembles the conventional contemporary stage presentation of
the popular escapologist Jack Sheppard. However, in more complex
allusive ways, the whole play is imbued with further sly and oblique
references to recognisable contemporary figures, and hints broadly at the
similarities in values and practices between the underworld and the
corridors of power.

The immediate informing social context is tantalisingly and brilliantly
transfigured in Hogarth's painting of a scene from the drama in
performance, first sketched in 1728.[40] The picture exploits the play's
fashionable success, seeing it in many different ways as a nexus through
which respectable and criminal figures could be brought into stimulating
juxtaposition. It is a depiction of a tableau from Act III, Scene xi; the
dramatic moment when the chained Macheath is flanked by his two main
lovers, Polly and Lucy, who in turn are beseeching their respective
fathers, Peachum and Lockit, on his behalf. It shows the part the Beggar
refers to as 'a Prison Scene, which the Ladies always reckon charmingly
pathetick' (II, 3). All the main participants in the drama are gathered
together on stage simultaneously, giving the artist amongst other things
the opportunity for an interesting formal experiment in group portraiture,
replicating and parodying the more respectable figures in his contemporary paintings of noble families. As often happened, Hogarth produced
several versions of the picture, and the developments from one to the
next give a fascinating insight into his interpretation of the central
meanings and significances of the play.

In the earliest versions of the picture, the artist was content to place his central figures in a conventional stance in the centre of the canvas, and to surround them with a thinly-sketched generalised context of theatre and audience. Our attention is thus concentrated exclusively on the formal relationship between the figures on the stage. However, by the fourth version, painted for John Rich to hang in his theatre in 1729, Hogarth was prepared to offer a much more complex statement within the painting, retaining the basic design and shape of the first, but creating a much more detailed and suggestive context for it. The eventual result not only provides an interpretation of the play, it makes suitably suggestive connections between the drama, the stage and the audience, and identifies many of the furtive relations between them. The picture thus offers a 'story' which is as provocative and as excitingly structured in a single and static form as the more dynamic narrative presentation of *Industry and Idleness*.

The material feature of contemporary theatrical practice which Hogarth exploits in his final version is the provision of seats on the stage itself, where the wealthiest spectators could both watch the play and be simultaneously admired by less privileged members of the audience. The transformation of spectators into vicarious participants created by the layout of the Augustan playhouse is reproduced in Hogarth's painting by the physical proximity of recognisable aristocratic figures sitting very close to the actors impersonating criminals and prostitutes. By this simple juxtaposition, Hogarth then provides a spatial realisation of that 'similitude of Manners in high and low Life' which is the central generating idea of the play. Furthermore, he makes the point clearer by the way the actress playing the most popular character in the play, Polly Peachum (Lavinia Fenton), seems to be looking past her illicit lover on stage, Macheath, towards her even more illicit lover off-stage, a figure identifiable as the Duke of Bolton, with whom she subsequently ran off. The Duke seems to be staring back at his mistress, and the innuendo is confirmed by the representation of a satyr which is lowering over his head, pointing at him. Fact and fantasy are thus brought startlingly close together, with subterfuge and imposture permeating both the play and the world surrounding it, giving the painting and the drama it depicts a slyly interventionist role, disrupting clear social demarcations.

Hogarth's painting hints at rather subtle and entertainingly scandalous connections between the play and its social context, associating the theatre with one kind of licentious behaviour, as many hostile Puritan writers did, and offering a comment on the appropriateness of the unorthodox romantic theme of the play. Alongside these gossipy interactions, however, there were other more obvious parallels between the figures performing on stage and those watching them remarked upon by a great many contemporary commentators. Gay himself had already indicated his sensitivity to a 'similitude of Manners' between those in power and those out of it in a letter of 1723:

I cannot indeed wonder that the Talents requisite for a great Statesman are so scarce in the world since so many of those who possess them are every month cut off in the prime of their Age at the Old-Baily.[41]

The 'similitude' was thus not confined to the erotic behaviour of highwaymen and dukes, whores and actresses, it also suggested resonant resemblances between those under legal suspicion and those above it. In keeping with this increasingly commonplace Augustan perception, *The Beggar's Opera* draws together a great many references to crime, particularly to organised crime, all designed to enact and replicate the satiric analogy between the successful criminal and the powerful statesman. Specific parallels can be identified between Gay's work and the existing body of contemporary criminal literature, showing how he incorporated and used material from the extensive literature about Jack Sheppard and Jonathan Wild in particular in the construction of his characters, but it is less important to itemise these borrowings than to demonstrate the ways Gay transformed his sources into a composite picture of social corruption starting from the top, and to indicate how he playfully exploited the widely-disseminated notion of the criminal gang.[42]

The general taint of money and corruption is initiated right at the beginning of the play, when its presiding deity, the master bourgeois manipulator Peachum, poring over his accounts, makes the conventional comparison between his career and that of the lawyer:

A Lawyer is an honest Employment, so is mine. Like me too he acts in a double Capacity, both against Rogues and for 'em; for 'tis but fitting that we should protect and encourage Cheats, since we live by them.

(II, 4)

The perfidious and unprincipled lawyer is here represented as being no better than the double-dealing thief-taker and processor of stolen goods we see Peachum revealed to be. The paradoxical analogy between lawyer and criminal was sufficiently well known and established to set the frame of satiric reference for the rest of the play. Right at the beginning, then, audiences would be familiarised with the burlesque treatment of crime which was being initiated, but the point of comparison in this play is not restricted to lawyers, as Peachum's first song shows:

Through all the Employments of Life
    Each Neighbour abuses his Brother;
Whore and Rogue they call Husband and Wife:
    All Professions be-rogue one another.
The Priest calls the Lawyer a Cheat,
    The Lawyer be-knaves the Divine;
And the Statesman because he's so great,
    Thinks his Trade as honest as mine.

(II, 4)

Associated with the unromantic, self-preserving insights of Peachum are the equally money-based arguments of Lockit, who sees the contemporary world as a fully combative arena – 'Every one of us preys upon his Neighbour, yet we herd together' (II, 46) – and who likens his contemporaries to pikes, who eat each other when necessary. Yet although these stark visions are given much space in the drama, the main thrust of the play is paradoxically not to explore the inherent competitiveness of the world nor to legitimise the clear-sighted criminal after the fashion of the picaresque novel. Instead, Gay sets out deliberately to 'be-rogue' and 'be-knave' the statesman. These cynical statements are not incorporated so that we may see them demonstrated to be true, but so that we may see them pervading the beliefs and practices of more socially elevated figures than a thief-taker and a gaoler. Peachum clearly represents the master criminal Jonathan Wild, but, just as Fielding was later to do, Gay equates that great bourgeois figure of the underworld with equally great men in the so-called respectable world. And the target of this satiric attack is not just a general one, on the pretensions of all 'Great Men'. Its real aim is a specific and elaborate, albeit teasing, unveiling of the quasi-criminal and cynical procedures of the then Prime Minister, Robert Walpole.

When Peachum anatomises his gang, with a view to turning in its less profitable members, he singles out for special consideration one 'Robin of Bagshot, alias Gorgon, alias Bluff Bob, alias Carbuncle, alias Bob Booty' (II, 6). This rather unappealing multi-faceted figure is clearly a version of Walpole, who is thereafter dispersed throughout the play, appearing at times as Peachum, at others as Lockit, at others even as Macheath. Like Peachum, he is extremely powerful in his world, but wholly unscrupulous and treacherous in the maintenance of that power. Like Lockit, he is the acknowledged master of his realm, notoriously concerned with the 'garnish' it will bring him, an equation made easier by the gaoler being first played at Lincoln's Inn Fields by a suitably corpulent actor. And like Macheath, who normally represents a different code of conduct, he has embarrassing problems with his various lovers. Where the romantic highwayman has to negotiate between his two whores, Polly and Lucy, not to mention the others, Walpole famously had to arbitrate between the competing and exhausting claims of his wife, Lady Walpole, and his mistress, Molly Skerrett.

All these different perspectives on the one figure are confusing, and they are interspersed with overlapping incidental caricatures of other contemporary figures, most of whom were identified for contemporary readers in *A Compleat Key to the Beggar's Opera*, first published in *The Craftsman* in February 1728, and reprinted in Christopher Bullock's *A Woman's Revenge; or, A Match in Newgate* later in the year.[43] The cumulative effect of this dispersal of reference and disruption of clear allegorical significance is one of constant flickering, of potentially savage satire being held in check by light-heartedness and geniality, and of accumulating surprise at the reversals of roles, the mingling of the ironic, the pathetic and the potentially tragic, culminating in the casual reprieve and festive comic dance at the end. The criminality of the participants is never in doubt, but that does not restrict them to the conventional postures of the biographies, nor limit their capacity for representing more elevated social classes. And by dispersing his representation of Walpole through various figures, Gay partly ensures his own safety by making the identification deniable, while brilliantly insinuating the idea that Walpole is the consummate, composite master-criminal.

Although Gay seems deliberately to have confused the play and softened its capacity for producing outrage, no-one seems to have doubted that Walpole was the real target of his wit. As Swift put it in a letter to Gay in February 1728, 'Does Walpole think you intended an affront to him in your opera? Pray God he may.'[44] Swift returned to the play in a paper in *The Intelligencer* later in the same year, where, in a densely ironic passage, he denies the connection between criminals and statesmen in terms which make the identification remarkably clear:

> My Reason for mentioning *Courts*, and *Ministers*, *(whom I never think on, but with the most profound Veneration)* is, because an Opinion obtains, that in the *Beggar's Opera*, there appears to be some Reflection upon *Courtiers* and *Statesmen*, whereof I am by no Means a Judge.
>
> It is true, indeed, that Mr. Gay, the Author of this Piece, hath been somewhat singular in the Course of his Fortunes; for it hath happened, that after Fourteen Years attending the *Court*, with a large Stock of real Merit, a modest and agreeable Conversation, a *Hundred Promises*, and *five Hundred Friends*, he hath failed of Preferment; and upon a very weighty Reason. He lay under the Suspicion of having written a Libel, or Lampoon against a great Minister. It is true, that great Minister was demonstratively convinced, and publickly owned his Conviction, that Mr. Gay was not the Author; but having lain under his Suspicion, it seemed very just, that he should suffer the punishment; because in this most reformed Age, the Virtues of a Prime Minister are no more to be suspected, than the Chastity of *Caesar's* Wife.[45]

It was true that Gay had been humiliated in his search for preferment – in 1727 he had been offered, and had refused, the minor post of Gentleman Usher to Princess Louisa – and he blamed Walpole for this slight, probably with good cause. Swift's essay mixes a caustic attack on Walpole's interference and ability to harbour grudges with a sly stab at the rumours of his wife's infidelities. The effect is to heighten Gay's identification of the Prime Minister and the ever-suspicious Peachum, under the guise of pretending not to understand why anyone would detect any such similarities. That the identification was often made, and that it hit home, can be seen in the way Walpole arranged the suppression of

Gay's much less pointed sequel, *Polly* (1729), and in the way he encouraged rival, more supportive plays at the same time.[46]

As the play progresses, then, it adroitly mixes cynicism about the virtual universality of criminal motives, with a worldly acceptance that really nothing much better can be expected. The awfulness of Peachum is made quite clear from the outset, and is unremitting until his final cry of 'There's Comfort for you, you Slut' (II, 59) to his daughter. At the end, he is not brought to justice, and Macheath's request that two of the 'Fry', Ben Budge and Matt of the Mint, try to have Peachum arraigned and sentenced to death is seen to come to nothing. Nonetheless, although he is a consummate villain, in the hearty circumstances of the ballad opera Peachum's villainy is still containable and could remain largely unintimidating for the audience, until they make the specific connection with Walpole. So although the tenor of the play (the shabbiness and corruption of contemporary politicians) is elaborate and disquieting, the vehicle (the shabbiness and corruption of contemporary criminals) is familiar and relatively comfortable.

As a result of this failure of emotional equivalence between tenor and vehicle, the romantic roguery of Macheath, with his two lovers and his 'four Wives more' (II, 63), takes over the centre of the play from the bourgeois account-book mentality expressed by Peachum and Lockit.[47] Immediately after Lockit has preached self-preservation at all costs and the overpowering value of money, Macheath offers a glimpse of a much more gentlemanly code – 'When my Friends are in Difficulties, I am always glad that my Fortune can be serviceable to them. You see, I am not a meer Court Friend, who professes everything and will do nothing' (II, 48). Macheath represents a much more expansive version of criminality than the tawdry style of his rivals, and can be used intermittently to provide a critique of Court standards. However, unlike his counterpart in the non-fictional criminal literature of the time, Jack Sheppard, Macheath is reprieved from the gallows at the last moment. The Beggar apologises for this acquiescence in providing a happy ending at the behest of the Player, seeing it as a cosy triumph of poetic justice over the justice of the courts:

> Had the Play remain'd, as I at first intended, it would have carried a most excellent Moral. 'Twould have shown that the lower Sort of People have their Vices in a degree as well as the Rich: And that they are punish'd for them.
>
> (II, 64)

In an intriguing gesture, Gay thus incorporates his sharp satiric moral, but does not enact it. With the pastoral taking over Newgate, albeit momentarily, the fantasy of a happy ending is performed, even though it has already been stripped of significance by the Beggar's interjection, and, in Swift's terms, Gay's humour takes the place of his wit. But the effect of this festive ending is complex, particularly in terms of its presentation of contemporary justice, and it reveals interesting indications of the limits which were set on possible literary presentations of criminality.

The sudden reprieve for Macheath predictably displeased many severe commentators, like Sir John Fielding, who saw it as a pernicious influence on the impressionable. But in one sense, it could be made to fit the demands of the drama, and still maintain in a striking but indirect way the social critique developed earlier. As we saw in the previous chapter, one of the ways the Augustan legal system sought to demonstrate its impartiality and capacity for clemency was by the regular use of discretion and reprieves through the Royal prerogative of mercy. Such a strategy at the same time increased the fearsomeness of the courts and heightened the drama of the hanging day, by introducing capricious reversals and sudden transformations.[48] Gay was able to exploit this suddenness in order to maintain the lightheartedness of his production, but he does not present it as a plausible act of institutional clemency, rather as a necessary gesture of respect for perceived generic decorum.

The Beggar's proposed ending was to be demonstrative of his view that the 'lower Sort of People' are punished for their vices:

> To make the Piece perfect, I was for doing strict poetical Justice. — *Macheath* is to be hang'd; and for the other Personages of the Drama, the Audience must have suppos'd they were all either hang'd or transported.
>
> (II, 63)

The poetical justice is clearly offered as superior to actual justice, which would have found it difficult to round up and punish all the personages. Lockit, after all, is a well set up establishment figure. So the proposed ending is envisaged as a poetic fantasy, fitting the deeds, but not to be taken seriously as a piece of verisimilitude. However, it is to be replaced by an even more ridiculous fantasy. As the Player puts it: 'The Catastrophe is manifestly wrong, for an Opera must end happily.' So the fantasy of effective justice is replaced by the more absurd, if more soothing, fantasy of merciful and lenient courts, 'to comply with the Taste of the Town'. By this device, Gay can provide a suitably festive ending, while making it clear that any such satisfactory conclusion is purely arbitrary and whimsical. 'Justice' in real terms is neither done nor seen to be done, and the play comes to climax by deliberately and skilfully skirting all the issues it has raised. But, by announcing this act of avoidance, Gay simply makes all the problems prominent and still intractable.

This discussion of the play has concentrated on its satirical presentation of the idea of justice and its indirect but powerful representation of Walpole. But for contemporary audiences Gay's play was distinguished by its two strong female parts, Polly and Lucy, and the interaction of women, criminality and the law was one of the most agitated and contested areas of commentary in Augustan literature. As we shall now see, the legal position of women provided many Augustan writers with a subject they could neither ignore nor articulate with full clarity.

3   The harlot's progress

DOUBLE STANDARDS

> What are your laws, of which you make your boast, but the fool's wisdom and the coward's valor, the instrument and screen of all your villainies, by which you punish in others what you act yourselves, or would have acted, had you been in their circumstances? The judge who condemns the poor man for being a thief had been a thief himself, had he been poor. Thus, you go on deceiving and being deceived, harassing, plaguing, and destroying one another, but women are your universal prey.[1]

These powerful words are spoken by Millwood, the notorious 'lady of pleasure' in George Lillo's play *The London Merchant* (1731). Defiantly, as she is about to be carried off to trial and subsequent execution, she denounces the law which judges her as an instrument of male power. As she has come to see it, the law is bereft of the principles of justice, expressing and articulating instead only the hypocritical male desire to subjugate and suppress women. Within the play, Millwood is certainly presented as an evil figure, a dangerous temptress representing to contemporary audiences a female Machiavelli, but yet her final outburst remains impressive and cannot be instantly dismissed.

The London Merchant was a very popular eighteenth-century play, traditionally performed for audiences of apprentices on the Boxing Day holiday, its success arguably deriving from the way it brought together so many points of ideological contention in a melodramatic and accessible way. However, despite its contemporary popularity, the play has subsequently drifted out of prominence, with Millwood being seen by some modern critics as a feebly melodramatic villainess – 'a risible immoral vamp of the flimsiest shocker' – but by others more sympathetically as a forerunner of Ibsen's tragic heroines.[2] Leaving the intrusive and diverting questions of literary merit aside, it remains obvious that Millwood's fiery denunciation of the law is the real climax of the piece, offering a tragic perception that darkens the otherwise clear moral sentiments, historically important in reaching beyond the confines of the theatre to address eighteenth-century culture at large. Although her statements in their dramatic context may be seen as extravagant and malevolent, once they have intruded they cannot simply be dismissed, and they hang ominously over the final act. As the allegorically named Thorowgood says, 'Truth is truth, though from an enemy and spoke in malice. You bloody, blind, and superstitious bigots, how will you answer this?' Within the play, no answer or rebuttal is even attempted.

With the benefits of hindsight, it seems obvious that there is something chillingly accurate about Millwood's perception. Furthermore, Lillo's inability to dispel this dark view from his play and reconcile the conflicts it creates indicates the extent of contemporary ideological confusions surrounding men, women and the law. Eighteenth-century English gentlemen, perhaps by inheriting some of the free-and-easy attitudes conventionally associated with the licentious court of Charles II, seem to have lived by a very obvious double standard in their dealings with women, and their law, rather than arbitrating in a wholly disinterested manner, seems to have expressed and legitimised their will to power. Calling these men 'bloody, blind, and superstitious bigots' may have been an unusually outspoken accusation, but it is one which, on the evidence available, is extremely difficult to dismiss.

As we have seen, the statute, and in particular the laws concerned with property, made sure that many people in eighteenth-century England were disenfranchised and deprived of the right to full participation in their society. However, even in this illiberal context, the treatment of women seems particularly severe and oppressive. Something of the climate of confusion surrounding notions of a woman's proper place in society and the relative legal status of the sexes can be seen in the astonishing series of private journals kept throughout the 1760s by James Boswell. With a jaw-dropping combination of candour and insensitivity, Boswell recorded his sexual adventures as a young Scotsman on the make in London at the very end of the Augustan period:

> I should have mentioned last night that I met with a monstrous big whore in the Strand, whom I had a great curiosity to lubricate, as the saying is. I went into a tavern with her, where she displayed to me all the parts of her enormous carcass; but I found that her avarice was as large as her a---, for she would by no means take what I offered her. I therefore with all coolness pulled the bell and discharged the reckoning, to her no small surprise and mortification, who would fain have provoked me to talk harshly to her and so make a disturbance. But I walked off with the gravity of a Barcelonian bishop. I had an opportunity tonight of observing the rascality of the waiters in these infamous sort of taverns. They connive with the whores, and do what they can to fleece the gentlemen. I was on my guard, and got off pretty

well. I was so much in the lewd humour that I felt myself restless, and took a little girl into a court; but wanted vigour. So I went home, resolved against low street debauchery.[3]

There are many remarkable features about this passage, like the dramatic collision of vocabularies, where the lexicon of carnal pleasure jostles the language of moral self-assurance, where complacency and misogyny and sexual desire contend for supremacy, as they do in so much Augustan writing by men about women. But for me the most significant element is the way Boswell overcomes the internal tensions in his rhetoric and emerges so startlingly unabashed by his conduct.

Boswell may be momentarily embarrassed by his lack of 'vigour', but he seems singularly proud of his ability to drive a hard bargain, and what we might now call his street wisdom. In his narrative, the roles of victim and predator are blithely and silently switched, without the narrator noticing that anything odd is going on. The exploiter (Boswell) becomes the potential sufferer, and the humiliated victims ('monstrous big whore' and 'little girl' – their names are not thought important enough to include) become in his perception the real culprits. Through this perspective, if any party has sinned, it is the 'monstrous big whore' and her avarice, rather than Boswell. For gentlemen playing in the buyer's market of eighteenth-century metropolitan street prostitution, the customer was always right. Engaging in 'low street debauchery' was presented as though it held potential dangers only for the innocent strolling consumer, who envisages himself as the possible victim of the wiles of others. In this straightforward commercial transaction, Boswell has the right to bargain: the others only have the capacity to cheat.

Such casualness may now seem extraordinary, but in one very important way Boswell's smug perception of himself was perfectly accurate, incorporating as it did a faithful reflection of the position of men and women before the law throughout the preceding period. All through this adventure, and the host of others like it, Boswell was not breaking any enforceable laws, or doing anything that was likely to bring him up before any court in London. He may have been behaving shabbily, as he occasionally admits, but he would have been astonishingly unlucky to have been arraigned for 'lewdness', as the laws were very imperfect and, at this time, unenforced. For the Augustan gentleman, provided he could resist the temptations of his own sex or common farmyard animals, the laws governing sexual behaviour were of negligible effect. Even in those areas of the country where church courts were still effective in dealing with sexual crimes like adultery or fornication, whoremongering was not seriously punished: Blackstone talks of 'the feeble coercion of the spiritual courts' which treated such behaviour with 'tenderness and lenity' (IV, 64).

Practically, therefore, Boswell is quite within his rights to insist on his innocence. Dealing with these raffish women required a sensible gentleman to keep his wits about him, but whoring was much less dangerous and potentially embarrassing than mingling with *real* criminals, like pick-pockets or footpads. There were no such easy circumstances in which gentlemen would so imperturbably patronise these characters. If there was a danger for males given to whoring, it lay in the risk of contracting disease or in the long-term spiritual impoverishment such behaviour initiated or in the possibility of falling for a swindle like 'buttock and twang'. For the women involved, however, things were much grimmer. They held a different status and did not enjoy immunity from prosecution. For them, as we shall see, the whole business contained material dangers and was highly illegal. According to the laws in force throughout the Augustan period, it was all their fault. Blackstone again, commenting on the punishment for brothel-keeping, unveils the misogynistic ideological basis for such an attitude – 'such an offence as the law presumes to be genuinely conducted by the intrigues of the female sex' (IV, 79). The law then was prepared to intervene in whoring, but only to punish the whores and their (female) supervisors. Despite his general air of frankness, Boswell does not seem to find it necessary to mention that the protective 'armour' he carried with him included the full tolerance of the law.

Of course, it has to be remembered that the manic-depressive, sexually incorrigible Boswell was by no means a fully representative figure from whose behaviour general conclusions may easily be drawn. Even Lawrence Stone admits as much. Also, the examples chosen from his *Journals* come rather late in the century, and might not be wholly representative of earlier behaviour. However, Boswell's total inability to treat his sexual partners as fellow human beings and his failure to recognise that he was exploiting them (albeit with legal immunity) are very telling and may accurately be seen as representing in a heightened and stylised form a structure of feeling symptomatic of his class and his time. After all, even those who advised Boswell and other young rakes to desist from whoring argued usually that it was bad for *them* to give in to their urges and mix with unclean women, rather than that it perpetuated a system of sexual exploitation and might be more obviously harmful for the women involved.

In his intermittent moral fits, even Boswell himself seemed to accept the immorality and shabbiness of his behaviour. After meeting and befriending the censorious figure of Dr Johnson, he tried to get his exuberant carnal urges under some sort of control:

Since my being honoured with the friendship of Mr. Johnson, I have more seriously considered the duties of morality and religion and the dignity of human nature. I have considered that promiscuous concubinage is certainly wrong. It is contributing one's share towards bringing confusion and misery into society; and it is a transgression of the laws of the Almighty Creator, who has ordained marriage for the mutual comfort of the sexes and the procreation and right educating of children. Sure it is that if all the men and women in Britain were merely to consult animal gratification, society would be a most shocking scene. Nay, it would soon cease altogether. Notwithstanding of these reflections, I have stooped to mean profligacy even yesterday. However, I am now resolved to guard against it.

Despite these high-flown words, and his recognition of the powerful moral arguments involved, Boswell's attempts to bring his yearnings for 'animal gratification' under control were never conspicuously successful. The wonderful bathos of the penultimate sentence represents his egregious failure yet again to match deeds and words. Indeed, the memorandums for the passage quoted above are even less pious and humble than the finished version. They include, in a mixture of cipher and plain English, the exhortation '[Swear to have no more rogering before you leave England] except Mrs.------- in chambers.'[4] The flagrant hypocrisy of his attitude is made even more comically graphic in Holland the following year when he discusses these matters with the cosmopolitan Belle de Zuylen (Zélide). She casually entertains the possibility of an amicable husband who might turn a blind eye to her occasional dalliances with other men. Boswell, clearly shocked by her desire to enjoy a taste of those very freedoms he has lingeringly described in his own career, comments: 'In short, she seemed a frantic libertine.'[5]

The problem of 'animal gratification' or 'lewd humour' is seen by Boswell in his more lucid moments as one which might affect the constitution of society. His behaviour may well have been eccentric or idiosyncratic or more virulent than that of many gentlemen, but the way he articulates the problem, and his unexamined assumption that different standards should apply to men and to women, are perfectly consistent with the descriptions of sexual conduct and gender relations inscribed in the statute up to this point. In its categorisation of sexual morality, the law was virtually unambiguous: a chaste woman's place was in the home; an unchaste woman's place was in the wrong. Although the statute had not radically altered, the post-Restoration climate of tolerance associated with memories of the Merry Monarch and his ample courtesans had begun to lose force, even assuming it had existed earlier in any significant way at all. By the early eighteenth century, pressure groups like the societies for the reformation of manners were seeking to orchestrate an enforcement wave to clean up the streets, without, it must be said, any very obvious success. Their efforts, of course, went more vigorously into punishing loose women rather than their clients. Boswell's remorseful voice articulates this more repressive structure of feeling just as surely as his boastful voice reverberates with its hedonistic opposite. The fact that he could contain this flagrant contradiction within the confines of single diary entries says much about the ideological tensions and fissures he inhabited and exploited.

The social and legal status of women in the Augustan period was thus consistently fraught and radically compromised. They could achieve respectability and a degree of self-government, but only on terms very strictly drawn up by men through the law, and they could never legitimately enjoy the same personal freedoms as men. Women, be they honest or dissolute, played no part in framing or drawing up legislation, nor in implementing it. They could, as we shall see, write polemics about their lowly status, or agitate for change, but with no confidence of being taken seriously, and every chance of being slandered and derided. There were no female judges, or lawyers, or legislators. Although a woman might sit on the throne, no other important public offices in church or state were available to females. Women could not vote, and only on rare occasions could they sign contracts independently. In an unscholarly but fervent historical analysis of the subject in 1779, William Alexander saw that British women had traditionally occupied an entirely unenviable role:

> for the most part, but improperly, or slightly educated; and at all times kept in a state of dependence, by the restrictions of a severe legislation, which, in the management and disposal of what property is allowed them, commonly cramps the freedom of their will. Dishonoured and disgraced beyond all possibility of redemption by the commission of faults, which in the men are hardly considered as anything but acts of gallantry.[6]

Alexander puts the case polemically, but what he says can be corroborated by looking at the legalists of the earlier eighteenth century. Blackstone, for example, has some startling things to say about married women:

> By marriage, the husband and wife are one person in law: that is, the very being or legal existence of the woman is suspended during the marriage, or at least is incorporated and consolidated into that of her husband.
>
> (I, 430)

As far as the law was concerned, the married woman became little more than a valuable chattel, part of her husband's retinue, a way of preserving property and ensuring that a man's wealth would be properly transmitted by lineage to his genuine male offspring. The key ideological component in this process had to be the unimpeachable and inviolable chastity of the wife, which ensured a male's confidence in the legitimacy of his offspring

– 'upon that all the property in the world depends' as Dr Johnson famously remarked.[7]

This extraordinary reification of the female identity often disguised itself as a necessary and protective paternalism. Women, it was often argued (almost invariably by men), were just not constituted stoutly enough to undergo the full rigours of education and responsible citizenship. The regularly-voiced opposition to female scholarship and learning served just as well to deny women their full rights to participation in legal society. As a correspondent in *The British Apollo* in 1708 put it 'they are cast in too soft a mould, are made of too fine, too delicate a composure to endure the severity of study, the drudgery of contemplation, the fatigue of profound speculation'.[8] This apparent care for the tenderness and vulnerability of women was a way of legitimising their disenfranchisement, and providing for them a very limited repertoire of acceptable behaviour. Also, it offered a way of negotiating between the avowed commitment to the impartiality of the law and the intense attachment to a patriarchal model of family and society. While men must guard themselves against those crafty monstrous big whores and their accomplices, enjoy them though they may, they must simultaneously protect that most valuable and fragile creature, the good wife or *femme couverte*. The two categories must remain distinct, at all costs, creating a climate of continual suspicion of women. If some women were crafty and licentious, who was to say that all women might not be so? The intersection of 'animal gratification' and the security of lineage is not easily managed, and the tensions produced by the uncertainty about the nature of women leave their legitimate activities deeply compromised and circumscribed.

The body of statute thus contained few images of women, and in as much as it offered a commentary on women's actions it was a commentary on their incipient criminality. In one sense, the law did genuinely espouse and articulate the doctrine of equal rights: men and women were equally liable to be tried for most criminal offences. Bridget Hill, in discussing eighteenth-century women, claims that 'their legal existence, in so far as they had one at all, was that of under-age children'.[9] There is much truth in this, but even if the law conferred few rights on women, it encumbered them with many more duties than it did under-age children. Although women might not be granted many of the liberties that men enjoyed, and might be partly protected by their husband's status, they were under many of the same constraints to avoid what men were legally restrained from doing. As a result, women who stepped out of line and were apprehended might be hanged, transported, burnt in the hand, flogged, pilloried and treated with the full severity of the penal code when circumstances dictated, just like men. In that sense at least, they enjoyed the dubious privilege of full citizenship.

However, that is not the whole story, and the gender of the accused seems to have been taken into account more often in the practices of the courtroom than in the statute itself. As J. M. Beattie has persuasively argued, women may have been arraigned as often as men, but they seem to have been convicted proportionately less often:

> Taking all property crimes together, the treatment of women was substantially different from that of men, for women were more likely to be acquitted and, if convicted, to be found guilty of a lesser charge than that stated in the indictment.[10]

As well as being eligible for these apparent acts of clemency, women might be reprieved of capital offences if they could prove they were pregnant – 'pleading the belly' as it was known – and they often had their sentences lessened by the 'pious perjury' of courts deliberately understating the gravity of offences. This tempering of severity towards women has been rather implausibly explained by one eminent historian as the result of an 'instinctive chivalry'.[11] No such chivalry seemed to operate once women had been convicted, or in other areas of eighteenth-century life. It seems more likely that the reason for such restraint lay in a broadly utilitarian view of punishment – by having so little power, women were thought to pose less threat to the community and so could confidently be treated with less severity.

Against this minute amount of positive discrimination in favour of women, we must place those more numerous and important features of the law which were significantly harsher for them, where the double standard became more oppressively apparent. There were a few particularly heinous crimes which only women could commit, which were punished in the most startlingly barbaric of ways. A wife who murdered her husband (like a servant who killed his or her master, or a clergyman who murdered his ecclesiastical superior) could be found guilty of the crime of 'petty treason'. For this, she could be burned alive. The same atavistic punishment applied to female counterfeiters. Blackstone, in a very odd passage, argued that this was an essentially merciful dispensation in favour of women. The proper punishment for such a breach of fealty would really be hanging, drawing and quartering (the traditional punishment for males convicted of high treason), and women were excused such rough handling 'as the natural modesty of the sex forbids the exposing and publicly mangling their bodies' (IV, 93). Although the public floggings of half-naked women at Bridewell might be thought sufficient to disprove this, Blackstone retreats apologetically into the Celtic twilight by seeing the practice descending from 'the laws of the antient Druids' (IV, 204).

In keeping with his desire to point out the superiority of the British legal system, and in particular its noble avoidance of continental practices of torture, Blackstone worries away at this point, trying to turn an act of great ceremonial savagery into one of commendable restraint and courtesy:

> The humanity of the English nation has authorized, by tacit consent, an almost general mitigation of such part of these judgements as savour of torture or cruelty . . . and there are very few instances (and those accidental or by negligence) of any persons being embowelled or burned, till previously deprived of sensation by strangling.
>
> (IV, 370)

The monstrous big problem of legalised barbarity in the treatment of women just refuses to go away, despite Blackstone's most strenuous efforts to excuse it as a kindness ('almost general', 'very few') or blame it on some old Druids. As with the earlier passages from Boswell, but in a more deliberate and self-conscious way, the language here is trying to carry the pressures of an internally-riven ideology, and the tone of apologetic urbanity fails to disperse effectively the stresses it has to confront.

The other pressure point in the ideological construction of women through the law was sexual assault. When Blackstone discusses the crime of rape, he reveals his hesitancy by calling on precedent and higher authority. He refers back to the earlier writings of Sir Matthew Hale, the seventeenth-century legalist, whom he directly quotes: 'rape is a most detestable crime, and therefore ought severely and impartially to be punished with death' (IV, 215). This is a bald, unequivocal statement, and seems to offer women reliable security against physical abuse. However, the real message follows when the necessary reservations become apparent: 'but it must be remembered, that it is an accusation easy to be made, hard to be proved, but harder to be defended by the party accused, though innocent' (IV, 215). Blackstone and Hale, true to their deepest allegiances, seem united in their concern for the possibilities of slanderous accusation of a male, which takes precedence over their duty to preserve women from attack and offer them reliable redress for suffering. William Eden, the later reformer, confirmed the gravity of the crime of rape, but mitigated it by adding that it was 'peculiarly open to the divine prerogative of pardon'.[12] In an astonishing yet entirely predictable transformation, it seems to be the women who become the dangerous party yet again, and helpless men who become the victims.

Women seeking redress through the courts for alleged rape were thus put to inordinately great lengths to prove the offence, and they had to withstand a grim test of character in the process. From the most recent studies of the evidence available, it seems that juries were much more likely to convict a man on a charge of attempted rape than on a charge of rape itself.[13] Indeed, the statistics indicate that the death penalty was very rarely carried out on rapists at this time. Radzinowicz demonstrates that from the total of 678 executions in London and Middlesex between 1749 and 1771, only two were of convicted rapists. Such a small number can be put in perspective by noting that the same number of villains were put to death for the much less grim-sounding offence of 'personating others to obtain prize money'.[14] This reluctance to carry out executions is most uncharacteristic of the period, not matched in other fields. It may be partly explained (if not excused) by the law's persistent refusal to interfere in sexual matters other than to condemn 'unnatural acts' – two sodomites also suffered capital punishment in this group – but it can also be seen to draw on uncertainties about the status of the injured party. That a woman had successfully fought off an attacker meant that she had remained chaste, and so retained her value as a respectable figure. The violated woman seems to have been a much less credible witness to her own character, subject to gruelling and potentially humiliating examination in public. As a result, there is every reason to believe that such officially-sanctioned hostile treatment of injured women led to rape being seriously under-reported to the courts, and that such cases as did come to trial were terrible ordeals for the aggrieved party.

The law thus seems to have created and authorised a very restricted typology of female possibility, reinforcing suspicions of female duplicity and making explicit the double standard that was implicit in much male behaviour. It seemed to recognise only two types of women. It valorised and encouraged the obedient, silent, chaste wife as a fit spouse for a male who could be as headstrong, noisy and lewd as he thought fit. In polar opposition to this image, the law stigmatised women who behaved as independent, sexual creatures, capable of self-government – such women were whores, and were not legally protected. Men should be on their guard constantly against their deceptiveness and cunning. Virtually no interim possibilities were offered, with even widows and spinsters attracting little legal protection. Although the law espoused the cause of equal rights and protectivism, its actual operations were much more patriarchal. The resulting tensions between the avowed independence of the law and its assertive use as an arm of male power are clearly visible in very diverse writing. As we have seen, these tensions are close to the surface of a text like *The London Merchant*, and it is obvious that similar quasi-legal problems are part of the ostensible fabric of a whole range of other eighteenth-century works, from *Moll Flanders* to *Clarissa* to *Amelia*. These problems are certainly prominent in Blackstone's writing, part of his overt project being to make them disappear or seem unimportant. Most interestingly, they are equally visible in Boswell's journals, without the author being very aware of them. Internalised and unconscious as they are there, we may see them retrospectively in a way that he himself would have failed to recognise, and Boswell's silence says more about his unspoken assumptions than any degree of self-consciousness could provide.

As we might expect, the press produced a body of writing to disseminate these official images of women, suppressing the ideological fissures they contained. There were a number of overtly polemical pieces justifying the legal subordination of women, like Richard Allestree's *The Lady's Calling* (1673) and Hannah Woolley's *The Gentlewoman's Companion: or, A Guide to the Female Sex* (1675). These pious and apologetic seventeenth-century texts survived through many editions, and were joined by a great many conduct books and guides to etiquette, raising in this specific context the whole debate about subordination and rights and equality that is central to the social and political philosophy of the post-Restoration period. The question was discussed in Locke's essays on government, and in the diverse replies to them. And as we shall see, the literary periodical as it developed in the early eighteenth century was a key site for the elaboration of a more comprehensive female typology. More important, however, were the less overt manipulations of this message, and the various subversive attempts to create radical alternatives and to undermine the authorised practices by creating more complex images of women.

That the law was not always or universally thought to be an authoritative or incontestable guide to human conduct, articulated by infallibly wise judges, can be seen later in the century with the case of Justice Buller. In 1782, in the course of a judgement, Buller ruled that it was acceptable marital practice for husbands to beat their wives, as long as the stick used was no thicker than the man's thumb.[15] No sooner had he made this preposterous statement than the print shops were flooded with dozens of cartoons and caricatures of the learned magistrate measuring thumbs, selling sticks, and so on. The lampooning of Buller shows that the press had taken on a more actively oppositional role later in the century, with the freedom to comment on contemporary events and the technology to do so quickly. It also shows that the judiciary was no more thought to articulate popular feeling in the later eighteenth century than it is today. Earlier in the century, there is less evidence of such a close linking of event and commentary, such a direct or unmediated confrontation of ideologies. The prevailing ideology of the law was hegemonically more powerful in the Augustan period, and less blatantly contested, but there are still a number of interesting alternative voices available, offering oblique commentaries on legal concerns and providing different perspectives on female possibility.

When Mary Wollstonecraft published *A Vindication of the Rights of Women* in 1792 she produced the most articulate and considered defence of the integrity of women that eighteenth-century readers had encountered. Although it is possible to see that great book as a radical break from the past, as a moment of discontinuity, it actually consolidates a great deal of less well-known earlier work. The ideas Wollstonecraft articulated so forcefully had been part of the fabric of discussion for a much longer period, even if they had traditionally been stigmatised and marginalised – a process which subsequent commentators have done little to reverse.

In the later seventeenth century, a number of women, influenced by the egalitarian element in Puritan thinking, argued in favour of a more active social role for females. As early as 1673, Bathsua Makin had produced *An Essay to Revive the Antient Education of Gentlewomen*. In 1696, the better-known Mary Astell wrote *A Serious Proposal to the Ladies for the Advancement of Their True and Greatest Interest*, and in 1696, Judith Cook published *An Essay in Defence of the Female Sex*. In these pamphlets, and in a number of others like them, the manifold advantages of having women as active participants in society were thoughtfully discussed and advocated. Although based on the value of education to women, rather than on the value of educated women to the economy, these proto-feminist arguments are similar to some of those put forward by Defoe, also writing in Puritan traditions, in his *Essay Upon Projects* (1697). These provocative ideas were further rehearsed, in that author's characteristic down-market recycling way, in his *Conjugal Lewdness* (1727) and *Augusta Triumphans* (1728). Many further examples of female advocacy can be found, from less well-known writers, like Lady Mary Chudleigh's *The Ladies Defence* (1701) and the splendidly titled *Women Not Inferior to Men or A Short and Modest Vindication of the Natural Right of the Fair Sex to a Perfect Equality of Power, Dignity, and Esteem with the Men* (1739) by 'Sophia'.

As well as recovering these polemical and controversialist pieces, we can see that much print was expended on the occasional prominent females in public life, and on what was seen as a slightly scandalous development in female participation in society. Although women were isolated from most areas of the public sphere, quite properly and naturally, according to Pope in his 'Epistle to a Lady', they could legitimately participate in a more active way in a few. Even these, however, were held to have an exciting or intimidating *demi-mondaine* air about them. In the immediate post-Restoration period, the most celebrated women had been notorious courtesans, but in the early part of the eighteenth century, other avenues of opportunity were opening up, carrying still the *frisson* of dubious morality. As actresses, women were becoming celebrities in the theatre and, as authors, they were increasingly prominent in the emerging form of the novel. These were without doubt culturally important activities, but they occupied a curious, twilight status, and the women who participated in them were often caricatured as freaks or prodigies, rather like the intriguing female prize-fighters advertised in the London press in the 1720s. Both the stage and the page were widely represented as unwholesome venues for disreputable activities, populated by loose and unscrupulous characters.[16] It is as though forcefulness and wit were stigmatised as being in themselves unfitting for respectable women, suitable though they might be for whores, and, although no legal sanctions could be brought to bear on such flagrant females, the whole cast of eighteenth-century misogyny and male suspicion was turned against them.

There were certain exceptions to this general climate of hostility, but they are not powerful. John Duncombe's poem, *The Feminiad* (1754), was an attempt to enumerate a pantheon of successful public women. However, he struggles to find many who fit his bill, possibly because his criteria for inclusion are stiflingly timid:

> The modest Muse a veil with pity throws
> O'er Vice's friends and Virtue's female foes;
> Abash'd she views the bold unblushing mien
> Of modern Manley, Centlivre, and Behn;
> And grieves to see One nobly born disgrace
> Her modest sex, and her illustrious race.[17]

Duncombe thus excludes the most interesting female writers on deeply conservative moral grounds, and seems only to permit women to write if they can do so without stepping out of domestic rectitude. His poem eventually becomes a patronising and unsatisfactory attempt to reconcile the ideological tensions in the understanding of women by relying wholly on the paradigm of the chaste wife, in a way which reproduces the conflict between the constant heroine and the scholarly Mrs Bennet in Fielding's *Amelia*. It recognises the legalised repression, but does not offer to protest about it, concentrating instead on the small number of women who succeeded against the odds.

Later, in 1774, his poem was expanded and partly contested by Mary Scott's *The Female Advocate*, which more fruitfully created a catalogue of impressive women, ranging throughout recorded European history. Although still not particularly radical or outspoken, Scott's poem has a confidence based on the more assertive understanding of female possibility which had developed throughout Europe by the later part of the century. In the Augustan period, however, it is much harder to find many utterances which can maintain this buoyant tone unapologetically or which display any real confidence in the audience's desire to hear of such controversial possibilities.

Since the legally-reinforced typology of the time created an apparently exhaustive scheme of docile wives or active whores, publicly prominent women carried the taint of disreputability with them. As a result, they were all ideologically coerced into the second category. The connection between female wit and sluttishness was a commonplace of seventeenth-century and Augustan writing, used to stigmatise and belittle a host of female writers from Aphra Behn to Lady Mary Wortley Montagu and beyond, all casually diagnosed as suffering from 'the scribbling itch'.[18]

Readers will be familiar with Pope's terrible caricatures of Eliza

Haywood and Susanna Centlivre in *The Dunciad*, deeply offensive misrepresentations which still seem to dominate critical thinking about those writers, and with the whole elaborate tradition of misogynist Juvenalian satire which disfigures Augustan male writing. So pervasive was this hostility to the female pen and to the kind of woman who might be interested in putting herself on display in print, that even some intelligent women seem to have internalised it, as readers and as writers. The 'scandalous memoir', for instance, in which fallen women recounted their fate, turned female writing into a form of confessional, as though the only thing women might find to write about was their shame. And even these pieces attracted gendered hostility – Elizabeth Montagu, on reading the enjoyably scandalous *Memoirs* of Laetitia Pilkington, felt that they demonstrated the regrettable but apparently inevitable connection between wit and licentiousness:

> It is often said that Wit is a dangerous quality; it is there meant that it is an offensive weapon, and is a perilous thing in society; but Wit in women is apt to have other bad consequences; like a sword without a scabbard it wounds the wearer and provokes assailants. I am sorry to say the generality of women who have excelled in wit have failed in chastity.[19]

It might be unwise to make too much of the subliminal associations in this passage between 'wit' and the manly, penile sword without a scabbard. However, the fact that this is an intelligent female writer repeating as an acceptable commonplace the view that witty women can be no better than self-destructive whores shows us how effective the contemporary campaign of misogynistic ideological propaganda had been.

The press thus seems to have acted alongside the law in surreptitiously-constraining but highly effective ways to disseminate and legitimise the double standards by which many eighteenth-century men lived. The double standard could allow men to behave sexually more or less as they wished, free of guilt, by drawing on the notion that women really deserved no better treatment. Economically, the creation of a large group of women with no visible means of support encouraged the growth of cheap prostitution, which remained illegal but in which only the women were punished. In this elaborate, sustained and collective act of self-deception and transference of blame, the law and the press were mutually supportive. The statute did not always overtly criminalise female behaviour. Rather it achieved its ideological purpose by encouraging the climate of opinion in which only two authorised images of women prevailed. On the one hand, there was the legally-sanctioned wife, the *femme couverte*, a wholly domestic creature, virtually invisible before the law, possessing few rights. On the other hand, there were the rest, all squeezed together into the remaining capacious category of 'whores'. The legal encoding of women was binary (may the reader forgive the antique terminology) and thereby exhaustive. The contemporary press could not help but assimilate these ideas, and disseminated them through conduct books, periodical essays and other didactic forms.

However, as we have already seen, the press and the stage also carried on a more dynamic function, by providing a forum in which these categories could be contested and usurped, where ideological conflict could be carried on in relative safety, and where a kind of resistance movement could be built up. Bearing in mind the evidence of such ideological tension and conflict, not only between texts but within them, it is now appropriate to go on to look at these hostilities through examining the monstrous big body of eighteenth-century writing concerned with 'whores', a grouping, if eighteenth-century authorities may be believed, at once loose and all-embracing.

THE WHORE'S RHETORICK

The boundaries of respectable female behaviour were drawn so carefully in eighteenth-century England that a host of women were inevitably stranded outside them. The legal and social status of those excluded was profoundly unhappy. They enjoyed few rights, and only on very rare occasions were they able to seek legal redress by suing successfully for assault or breach of promise. In literature, however, fallen women could be treated more expansively than in the courts. Later in the century, they could be represented as proper objects for the sensitive reader's sympathy and pity, like Emily Atkins in the brothel in *The Man of Feeling* (1771) or Olivia Primrose in *The Vicar of Wakefield* (1766), or Lady Vane in *Peregrine Pickle* (1751).[20] Even later, in Victorian fiction, they emerge as poor unfortunates to be rehabilitated by intelligent philanthropy. But although these later structures of feeling had their basis in the Augustan period, and can be seen in undeveloped form in works by Steele, Richardson, Johnson and Hogarth, they are not given prominence in the writing of the time. In the literature of Augustan England, the most characteristic response to miscreant women was a prurient mixture of overt disapproval and covert fascination, articulated with various degrees of self-awareness and disguised by various layers of irony.

The stealthy glamorisation of the criminal woman, incompletely hidden by a veneer of disapproval or outrage, can be detected in a number of places. In language itself, an elaborate fantasy of the criminal underworld was sustained by the entropic generation of terms to describe the inhabitants of that world, male and female. Captain Francis Grose, in 1796, recorded a catalogue of early eighteenth-century titles which he claimed were used by the 'canting crew' to describe their women: 'Bawdy Baskets, Autem Morts, Walking Morts, Doxies, Delles, Kinching Morts, and Kinching Coes.' Elsewhere, he offered definitions of female forms like Abbess, Arch Dell, Ballum Rancum, Barber's Chair, Brimstone, Blower, Bunter, Buttock, Cat, Covey, Crack, Demi-Rep, Dimber Mort, Dodsey, Drab, Drury Lane Vestal and many others.[21] The replication of these terms, with so many subtle shades of difference between them, is designed to convey a sense of a reticulated criminal world just outside the reader's reach – foreign, frightening and fascinating.

Like the literature of exotic travel, or indeed like *The Beggar's Opera*, Grose's dictionary gives a sense of a culture that is very extraordinary, yet in some ways recognisable and overlapping with the world of the bourgeois reader. The women in this elaborate fabrication represent a challenge to the authorised version of docile and domesticated woman-hood, but a challenge which is at once rendered exciting and manageable by its clear and convenient categorisation as deviant. It may be part of the reader's world, but it is a part which is for most of the time invisible or subterranean. To enter this fabulous place, you have to be prepared to pass through the door marked 'criminal'. As we shall see, artists willing to offer sustained narrative treatments of criminal women (Defoe, Haywood, Hogarth, Cleland) were able thereby to explore the nature of a woman's lot, and to offer innovative and contesting definitions of gender. But such definitions were always to some extent compromised by the 'otherness' of the examined women's illegality, which gave them an aura of the underworld, but stripped them of power.

Grose's pseudo-documentary technique is clearly designed to entertain and perhaps to titillate. Like the Elizabethan 'cony-catching' pamphlets, his lexicon imbues its reader with the spurious glow of sophistication, offering vicarious dalliance in the reassuring and acceptable guise of admonitory caution. It is an enjoyable phrase-book, but, like all the other 'canting' dictionaries, it cannot be taken very seriously as a description of a genuine linguistic practice. A more austere, more accurate and much more genuinely disturbing piece of lexicography is given in this 1755 *Dictionary* definition by Dr Johnson:

> WHORE: 1. A woman who converses unlawfully with men; a fornicatress; an adultress; a strumpet.
> 2. A prostitute; a woman who receives men for money.

Whereas Grose invigorates and dramatises female criminality by creating an imaginative inventory of its different terms, Johnson cuts through the façade and shows how the one harsh word could cover nearly everything, as in fact it did under the law. Grose creates enjoyable ambiguities about the appropriate classification of his women, about which particular inflection of criminality they might display, and about which sub-category they might belong to. The law, though, was insufficiently interested in these varieties to recognise them, discriminate between them, or dignify them as separate criminal offences. Working within this generalising tradition, Johnson dispels any over-fastidious uncertainties with an emphatic act of incorporation and assertion. The meaning of sense (1) is so stark and unambiguous, given the bounds of lawful 'conversation', that the term must encompass an awful lot of women. And the proximity of sense (2) shows terrible mistrust and intolerance entrenched in the language, to be reproduced by the statute. Having the same word to describe a prostitute and an adultress, a loose woman and a professional strumpet, indicates that the possibility of drawing official moral or legal distinctions between them was not thought important, and the nuances we can subsequently recognise may even have been invisible to many upright citizens of the time.

Such restricted vision is surely indicative of a profoundly narrow view of legitimate female possibility, and it betrays a disconcerting willingness to resort to unsubtle laws to regulate and constrain women's sexual behaviour. The law here seems to be coincident with an official morality, at least as far as women are concerned, and it seems very unambiguous in its categories. Johnson's definition does not of itself rule out the possibility of a more meticulous or discerning classification, like Grose's, but it forces any such scholarship into a subsidiary role, making it merely a numbering of the streaks of a particularly gaudy tulip, to cite an appropriate reference. The important point here is the decisiveness and dismissiveness of Johnson's terms, and their apparent interchangeability. As far as the authorised version of the English language was concerned, women who did not cleanly fit the recognised categories of virgin, spinster, wife or widow were simply whores, and no greater subtlety of description was required. As we shall see, Johnson's own attitude to deviant women could be much more compassionate and sympathetic in practice than in theory, certainly much less exploitative than Boswell's, but the language available to him does not seem to have encouraged or facilitated such charitable impulses.

Although canonical eighteenth-century literature is liberally festooned with genteel fallen maidens, the most problematic and persistently destabilising literary representation of women as whores can be seen in contemporary pornography (the word literally means 'description of the life, manners, etc. of prostitutes'). Pornography, of course, existed long before the Augustan period. If the prostitute belonged to the oldest profession, the pornographer was almost as antique. Learned citizens during and before the eighteenth century had their traditional access to erotica through the respectably ancient work of Catullus, Ovid, Petronius and others. Also, from the number of contemporary references made, they seem to have maintained a quasi-scholarly and pseudo-legitimate interest in the subject through their apparent familiarity with Aretino's *Postures*. Although it is hard to tell how many people had actually read this book, it is clear that a great many had heard of it. Less schooled readers, of course, would not have had access to this expensive and Latinate material, but they certainly had their own versions of pornography in the popular jest-books and through the strong oral traditions of bawdy jokes. During the late seventeenth century, however, the newly activated Grub Street press produced a great outpouring of affordable native English pornography, incorporating bawdy tales, directories of whores, sexual instruction manuals, catalogues, lewd dialogues and all sorts of smutty stuff, which seems to have sold sufficiently well to maintain a number of specialist publishers.[22]

By its very nature, not much of this material was publicly discussed or has survived. There is no reliable evidence about circulation or readership, but the wide currency of pornography is obvious from the court actions against various publishers, particularly the well-documented trial of Edward Curll in 1727 for his part in offering a new edition of a particularly filthy book called *Venus in the Cloister*. However, the availability of pornography to potential consumers can also be seen in the references to the easiness of buying smutty pamphlets in Pepys's diary – Pepys was an avid collector of these things – and in the casual allusion in *The Country-Wife* (1675) when Horner tells Lady Fidget that although he has just come back from France, he has nothing for her: 'I have brought over not so much as a bawdy picture, new postures, nor the second part of the *École des Filles*.'[23] That such a reference can be so casually thrown off in a play, without contextual explanation, suggests that these titles enjoyed much topical celebrity.

The snide suggestion in Wycherley's play is that pornography appealed to women's secret salacious appetites – a characteristically misogynist line. However, the available early texts rather suggest that they were written with male readers in mind, offering to confirm the sense of lasciviousness and rapacity thought by some to be disguised by the demure façade of women's polite behaviour. In one respect, this attitude is simply the official line expressed differently, dramatising the desire to repress women's sexual awareness. But in another way, pornography had the paradoxical capacity to enhance the role of women by giving more animated accounts of their sexuality and diminishing the authority of males, although at some cost.

One such book is *The Whore's Rhetorick Calculated to the Meridian of London and Conformed to the Rules of Art in Two Dialogues* (1683). Like a number of these works, including *L'École des Filles*, it purports to be an instructional dialogue, where the naïve young girl Dorothea is taught the arts of successful metropolitan whoring by the worldly old Mother Creswel – a notorious bawd whose place in the fabric of popular culture can be seen again by the casual references to her in Otway's *Venice Preserv'd* (1682) and elsewhere, and who can be compared in notoriety to the Mother Haywood Fielding mentions in *Joseph Andrews*.[24] This book is clearly not pornography in the sense of attempting to create sexual arousal in its readers. Instead, it offers an entertainingly satirical and frank account of contemporary sexual behaviour, in which male hypocrisy is the real target. Despite appearances, it is clearly not addressed to women – 'I hope the Reader will supply her other parts with *his* imagination'[25] – and it gives a droll and worldly account of the stupidity of men led by their carnal appetites. In so doing, it works within the perspective of the double standard, recognising the exploitation of women by male institutions, but offering compensation by investing self-aware women with secret powers:

> It were impossible so many Whores should daily become such spectacles of misery, such objects of pity and compassion, if they would make the right use of half that wit, nature and their own experience has furnished them withal: they needed not fear the Constables Staff, or the justices Warrant, a public whipping or a private one at *Bridewel*, where Sir *William* knocks, and keeps time with the Lash; they might scape the Halter, starving in a corner, rotting of the Canker, or the *French*-Pox, if they were not filthy idle, ridiculous, negligent, absurd asses, sots, extravagant, lewd, the Devil and worse . . . If then notwithstanding, these ignorant bawling, scurrilous, drunken, stripping Sweep-Kennels do sometimes work wonders, and govern the World: If privy Councellours, Judges, Aldermen, Doctors, Dukes, Lords, Colonels, Knights and Squires maybe made beasts on by these stupid Jades; how thinkest thou might the Cullies be handled by Women of sense and understanding?
>
> (p. 45)

The pathetic fate of shabby whores is acknowledged here, but Mother Creswel wastes no sympathy on these useless creatures. As far as she is concerned, they have none but themselves to blame. If only, suggests Creswel, these women were astute enough to realise the extraordinary power they could easily possess. Were they willing and able to exploit their native abilities to the full, men of the highest ranks would soon fall helplessly under their control. The lamentable experiences of the unsuccessful whores are elaborated, not as an argument against whoring, but as a warning about what happens if you are not very good at it, or very intelligent. The material rewards open to the astute whore are made obvious by the detailed portrait of the stupidity of so many men only too ready to be led by the horns. The unambiguous message for Dorothea is that by becoming an accomplished 'posture-mistress' she can control her own life, exercise sway over men, and thereby achieve security and status.

The laws against whoring are thus presented by the old bawd as feeble and hypocritical attempts to protect men from themselves, by protecting them from common whores. However, these laws are no more than partly effective in that they only deter stupid women, and are rarely enforced.

Even when they are enforced, they only apply to cheap street-walkers, and not to the more protected women ensconced in well-maintained brothels. As things stand, according to Creswel, men are so remarkably and predictably unintelligent about sex that they will happily and energetically consort with the lowest sort of whores in search of satisfaction. Whatever else this might lead to, it certainly creates marketing and business opportunities which shrewder women may exploit. The profoundly Hobbesian cynicism of the book emerges when the instructress describes the overwhelming power of money:

> You must look on it as the great business of your life, to please others, and enrich your self. Fancy your self subjugated by an inevitable decree to satisfie any with the most lascivious appetite, provided he comes with Gold in his Purse, and is willing to purchase at your rates. You must forget the distinction of Gentleman, and Mechanick; but let men be divided in your books under the names of Poor, Rich, Liberal, and Niggardly.
>
> (p. 53)

Creswel's argument is an amusing, tongue-in-cheek variant on the belief in market forces which sustained the growth of early eighteenth-century commerce, anticipating Mandeville in its frankness and panache. It reverses the perspective seen in Boswell's *Journals* and gives the real power to the dependable or innovative supplier of a commodity always much in demand. However, in an ironic and deliberately unsympathetic way, Creswel reproduces Boswell's perception that men might be the real victims of this project. The disquieting notion that powerful men may harbour secret depraved desires which they will pay anything to satisfy is juxtaposed with the even more disquieting idea that the women they use may set the terms of the transaction and may drive unusually hard bargains. The male belief in masculinity and potency, it seems, may also be an illusion fabricated by shrewd women for their own purposes. The entire arena of sexuality is thus presided over by women, whatever the law may say to the contrary. In the absence of male pimps, or even the procuring 'waiters' mentioned by Boswell, the whole enterprise seems to be run and regulated by women, who share the secret rules of the game with each other and thereby achieve extensive power by stealth.

The Whore's Rhetorick does not contest the law concerning prostitution by protest or confrontation, but it does surreptitiously infiltrate a defiant reworking of the terms of reference. After all, it suggests, by making prostitution illegal, men have merely succeeded in raising the prices, and in taking the operation of the transactions out of their immediate control. Instead of stripping women of power, all that the repressive legislation has achieved, according to Creswel, is the transfer of power to those women sufficiently astute to exploit the enfeebling weaknesses of men. In the second part of the book, Creswel describes the remarkably simple sexual techniques which ensure success, and make the customer feel that he is getting his money's worth, and the transparently easy means of flattering male vanity. Any chance of being legally apprehended is made to seem like a minor inconvenience, only occasionally interfering with trade. Strict enforcement of the existing legislation, as demanded by the societies for the reformation of manners, could certainly make the supply difficult, but it could do nothing to limit the demand. According to this book, only incompetent or unfortunate whores need suffer and, ironically, the waves of enforcement only served to make the position of established discreet madams and their employees rather more secure.

Legally, the transaction between whore and client was a prohibited commerce in which only the woman might be punished. Already, from a brief discussion of the meanings of pornography, it is possible to see literature surrounding this simple model with ironic complications and reformulations. In contrast to the legal fiction of evil women preying on hapless male victims, some printed versions suggested that it was the men who were lecherous and the whores innocent; others, that the men were witless gulls of crafty females, who deserved everything they got; and yet others, that both parties were equally wanton, engaged in a purely carnal activity, beyond moral or legal censure. The various uncertainties about how best to describe the commerce of prostitution are very obvious in a lot of diverse writing. Part of this hesitancy arises from the ambivalence of the authors, when the avowed aim of documenting and castigating vice is often only the flimsiest of pretexts for a much more prurient exploitation of low-life. Such moralistic protestations, barely disguising the author's enjoyment of vicarious dalliance, can be clearly seen in John Dunton's intermittent and slightly ridiculous periodical *The Night Walker, Or, Evening Rambles in Search after Lewd Women* where the pleasures of rambling are made tastier by the sprinkling of a little self-righteous disapproval over them. In his bizarre self-analysis in *The Life and Errors of John Dunton, Late Citizen of London* (1705), the author rather unconvincingly reproved himself for this escapade:

> As for my own part, I am sorry for the frolic, and would not act it over again; but if any of the discoveries we made, do but give others an abhorrence of that wicked generation of Night-Walkers, I shall willingly bear the little censures I may meet with.[26]

Dunton's reservations are scarcely persuasive, since it seems most unlikely that a periodical with so splendid and enticing a title was really designed to generate 'abhorrence' for its contents. It is much more probable that Dunton was simply cashing in on the popular vogue for scandalous revelations, anticipating the subsequent techniques of tabloid journalism, enjoying the role of worldly, seen-it-all-before guide and the stance of cosmopolitanism it offered him.

A less apologetic approach to the same sort of material was used by

Ned Ward in his contemporary documentary journey, *The London-Spy*, first published in monthly instalments between 1698 and 1702, which gave him many opportunities to describe the operation of the law in sexual affairs. Amongst a whole range of entertaining and rather seamy adventures, he persistently evoked images of legal practice. Visiting Bridewell, he witnessed the treatment of convicted prostitutes, and it is fascinating to see how he insinuated a judgemental and sceptical version of events into what starts as an orthodox descriptive account:

> my Friend . . . led me up a pair of Stairs into a spacious Chamber, where the Court was sitting in great *Grandure* and *Order*. A Grave Gentleman, whose Awful Looks bespoke him some Honourable Citizen, was mounted in the *Judgement-Seat*, Arm'd with a Hammer . . . and a Woman under the Lash in the next Room; where Folding Doors were open'd, that the whole Court might see the Punishment Inflicted; at last down went the Hammer, and the Scourging ceas'd . . . Another accusation being then deliver'd by a *Flat-Cap* against a poor Wench, who having no Friend to speak on her behalf, Proclamation was made, *viz. All you who are willing* E---th T----ll, *should have present Punishment, pray hold up your hands*: Which was done accordingly: And then she was order'd the Civility of the House, and was forc'd to shew her tender Back, and tempting Bubbies, to the *Grave Sages* of the *August Assembly*, who were mov'd by her *Modest Mein*, together with the whiteness of her Skin, to give her but a gentle Correction.
>
> Finding little *Knowledge* to be gain'd from their proceedings, and less *Pleasure* and *Satisfaction* from their Punishments; my Friend and I thought it better to retire, and leave them to Flog on till the Accusers had satisfied their *Revenge*, and the Spectators their *Curiosity*.[27]

Ward forces us to entertain doubts about the probity of this tribunal by a series of sly interventionist nudges. The proximity of the 'tempting Bubbies' to the 'Grave Sages' makes clear the voyeurism and prurience implicit in this legal proceeding, and gives Ward the opportunity to imply the conventional anti-Puritan attitude, common in late seventeenth-century pornography. Wilhelm Reich's perception that the authoritarian personality expressed unrecognised sadistic yearnings was anticipated by a host of post-Restoration pieces describing the alleged Puritan enjoyment of flagellation, encouraged by the well-known story of Zachary Crofton, who flogged his maid to death. Ward's talk of 'Revenge' and 'Curiosity', and the construction of the public arena encourage us to consider these clear intimations of legalised sadism. In an earlier part of his jaunt, Ward had quizzically described the curious masochistic practices of 'Flogging-Cullies', and in Bridewell he shows grave magistrates who seem to believe it better (and even more enjoyable) to give than to receive.

Another writer who made this connection between the solemn judiciary and hidden sexual desire was Defoe, in his jaunty poem 'Reformation of Manners' (1702). Here he describes the pleasure taken by Judge Jeffries, an ironmonger turned sheriff, in the humiliation of convicted females:

> Old venerable *Jeph*, with trembling Air,
> Ancient in Sin, and Father of the Chair,
> Forsook by Vices he had lov'd so long,
> Can now be vicious only with his Tongue;
> Yet talks of ancient Lewdness with delight,
> And loves to be the Justice of the Night:
> On Baudy Tales with pleasure he reflects,
> And leudly smiles at Vices he corrects.
> The feeble tottering Magistrate appears
> Willing to Wickedness, in spite of Years;
> Struggles his Age and Weakness to resist,
> And fain wou'd sin, but Nature won't assist.[28]

By making this connection, alongside his other accusations against the judiciary, Defoe says little about the status of prostitutes, but he does force us to entertain great scepticism about the purity and disinterest of their judges.

These Grub Street writers give frank accounts of the lives of whores, in which a climate of scepticism is created around the workings of the legal system, discrediting any male claims to purity of heart or rectitude. In the overtly ironic or cynical writing we have seen so far, including the pornography, little sympathy may be offered for the apprehended women, but, at the same time, little real authority or integrity is granted to their judges. Similar scandalous revelations about proclivities of the clients of these 'posture-mistresses' sustain the knock-about imaginary biographies of celebrated individuals, in pamphlets like the *Authentick Memoirs of the Life Intrigues and Adventures of the Celebrated Sally Salisbury* (1723), or any of the other accounts of this particularly notorious woman.[29] The overall import of the whore-stories is that, despite all the legally-reinforced protestations to the contrary, high-life and low-life are in some respects very close together, equally dominated by the acquisition of money and the expression of sexual desire. Pornography then offers a critique of class and gender, analogous to the implicit connections made in much criminal writing, demonstrating the concealed similarities between men and women, between the law-abiding and the criminal, using the demarcations of the law to dramatise its revelations. It is not difficult to imagine the mixture of shock and satisfaction a bourgeois audience might find in the revelation that the upper classes were pox-ridden whore-mongers, being systematically fleeced by the calculating women they hired to satisfy their perverted, wanton lusts.

In most of the writing discussed so far, there are manifest uncertainties and hesitations, but no real sense of profound disturbance or inability to get things into some kind of organising perspective. The overriding tone is world-weary lassitude, laconically or wryly expressing the ways of the world. Although Blackstone's confidence and Boswell's self-assurance may be exceptional, they share the overall feeling of acceptance of gendered differences, sometimes reproduced in the pornographic or ironic writing. Yet just as Blackstone has to smooth over the difficulties raised by the 'Bloody Code' and Boswell gets into psychological tangles in his imagining of women, there are attempts to describe whores which more forcefully exploit the contradictions and bring to light much more disturbingly the turbulence expressed through the whole business of prostitution.

The most dramatic and unsettling of these is Swift's poem 'A Beautiful Young Nymph Going to Bed'. Written around 1731, published in 1734, this poem tortuously negotiates between the misogynistic tradition of Juvenalian satire and the growth of humanitarian or philanthropic attitudes, articulating a number of different perceptions of women, and gaining its power from the unresolved tensions between them. As far as literary critics are concerned, it is conventionally grouped with other Swift poems – specifically 'The Lady's Dressing Room', 'The Progress of Beauty' and 'Cassinus and Peter' – amongst his most virulently scatalogical works, and there is no doubt that its concern with the seamier aspects of carnality is deeply disquieting. It also has many points of reference to a number of late seventeenth-century poems belittling women's claims to beauty, all maintaining the misogynist line of Juvenal's Sixth Satire. Unlike those other poems, however, which seem to articulate and indirectly express the complex psychology of their authors, the 'Beautiful Young Nymph' is attached to a genuine social concern, and its battery of obnoxious language is used partly as an offensive against its subject and yet partly also as a challenge to its readers.

Just as *The Beggar's Opera* is described as a Newgate pastoral, this poem can be thought of as a Drury Lane idyll. That is to say, Swift brings the pastoral language of Arcadia to bear on an inappropriate and incongruous subject, an old whore undressing and falling asleep. The consequent disparities between tenor and vehicle are adroitly used to explore the true significances of his description. The author gives the poem the sub-title 'Written for the Honour of the Fair Sex', and so initiates his highly intricate game of obliquity and indirection by making a startling and almost wholly misleading statement of chivalric intent.[30] Immediately, the poem adopts a mock-panegyric style and situates its subject amid elaborate, predominantly negative language:

Corinna, pride of Drury Lane,
For whom no shepherd sighs in vain;
Never did Covent Garden boast
So bright a battered, strolling toast;
No drunken rake to pick her up,
No cellar where on tick to sup.

(ll. 1–6)

The effect of this catalogue of denials is to strip the subject of dignity under the guise of investing her with tribute. The anti-pastoral references in the 'shepherd' at once display her availability (no one sighs for her *in vain*) and her failure to attract (no one sighs for her *at all*). The 'No' in 'No drunken rake' and 'No cellar' has the syntactical force of a reassurance (she is safe from drunken rakes) but the meaning of a jeer (not even drunken rakes want her). By the end of this brief introduction, Swift has created a pitiable figure whom he does not allow us the luxury of pitying, and he has given the reader the reassuring confidence of privileged insight.

Once we are firmly on course to taunt this woman, to participate vicariously in her elaborate humiliation, she begins systematically to dismantle herself and come apart before us:

Then, seated on a three-legged chair,
Takes off her artificial hair:
Now, picking out a crystal eye,
She wipes it clean, and lays it by.

(ll. 9–12)

The catalogue continues until she has removed eyebrows, 'plumpers', teeth, a steel corset, bolsters and garish make-up, leaving only a sorry and abused carcass, in very bad repair:

With gentlest touch, she next explores
Her shankers, issues, running sores;
Effects of many a sad disaster,
And then to each applies a plaster.

(ll. 29–32)

This all seems like conventionally coarse misogynist banter, the kind of thing we get from Rochester, employing gruesome shock tactics which could be quite enjoyable for thick-skinned readers as long as everything rushed along and did not leave room for serious consideration. The woman has no more substance than the personalities invented in a joke, and as long as she remains an illusion, there is no need to entertain any deeper concern. But there is a disturbing undertone in the presentation which cannot be dispelled, which Swift maintains by the continuous disrupting of perspective. The woman who is taken to pieces before us is grotesque and nauseating enough, but she is disconcertingly silent and apparently automated. We remember that all these efforts at surface renovation have been unsuccessful – she is returning alone, at the relatively early time of midnight – and yet the bathos of her performance is too quietly mechanical and routine to be simply amusing. By this technique, readers are forced into embarrassment, made to feel uncomfortably voyeuristic. The ritualistic nature of her disintegration is not simply entertaining, as Henri Bergson's notions of comedy might lead us to expect. Instead, the woman's self-destruction seems at once sombre and riotous, methodical and madcap, solemn and deranged.

Once she has returned to her native self, she seeks rest. Tormented by 'pains of love' – venereal rather than emotional, we are invited to think – she takes a sleeping pill. But no rest comes, and Swift conducts us through the chamber of horrors that constitutes her imagination:

> Of Bridewell and the compter dreams,
> And feels the lash, and faintly screams.
> Or, by a faithless bully drawn,
> At some hedge-tavern lies in pawn.
> Or to Jamaica seems transported,
> Alone, and by no planter courted;
> Or, near Fleet Ditch's oozy brinks,
> Surrounded with a hundred stinks,
> Belated, seems on watch to lie,
> And snap some cully passing by;
> Or, struck with fear, her fancy runs
> On watchmen, constables and duns.
>
> (ll. 40–52)

The mood has changed, and Swift is making us suffer with his subject. The possibilities build up, but no comforting solution is envisaged. The series of unappealing fates is made to seem exhaustive, and makes our earlier amusement at the absurd spectacle of Corinna seem distasteful and exploitative. The feeling of threat, the anxieties and the hopelessness of this passage make it bleak and shocking reading. And yet, it still refuses to allow us the simple escape of pity.

After this frightening glimpse of Corinna's disturbance, the poem never really settles on a consistent tone, and it becomes increasingly fraught and internally riven. Looking for a way out of the ideological and poetical impasse, Swift first of all takes refuge in the farcical:

> Corinna wakes. A dreadful sight!
> Behold the ruins of the night!

A wicked rat her plaster stole,
Half ate, and dragged it to his hole.
The crystal eye, alas, was missed;
And Puss had on her plumpers pissed.

(ll. 57–62)

The mocking tone here tries for a consistently superior attitude to the
distressed woman, but it does not come off. For this farcical collapse to
work, Corinna would have to have previously been invested with
pomposity or an inappropriate sense of her own grandeur. But this
episode just heaps misery upon misery, and the attempt to stand aloof
and laugh cannot be adroitly managed. The images are just too grotesque
and distasteful – remember she has to put these 'plumpers' back in her
mouth – and the poem becomes cruelly and rhetorically taunting.

Yet Swift cannot leave the problem alone. His next voice is an earnest
attempt at a compassionate consideration of suffering:

The nymph, though in this mangled plight,
Must every morn her limbs unite.
But how shall I describe her arts
To recollect her scattered parts?
Or show the anguish, toil, and pain,
Of gathering up herself again?

(ll. 65–70)

This is the most forthright acknowledgement in the poem of Corinna's
humanity. She is no longer presented as an absurd comic automaton, but
as someone who lives a life of persistent pain, which the poet cannot
seem to find a consistent attitude towards. Like Corinna, it might be said,
the poem has gone to pieces. It has fragmented itself and its even, urbane
tone has been scattered around. The semblance of civility and superiority
has been stripped away, and no adequate voice has been discovered to
articulate the awfulness of the revelation. In looking for a way of
handling this profoundly unsettling and volatile complex of attitudes,
Swift's questions are not rhetorical. The only method he has for
describing this woman to begin with is the sneering tone of the anti-
pastoral, which initially looked like an unemotional piece of verbal
dexterity. Corinna, in other words, was just used as an opportunity
for Swift to show off. But in describing her at all, the poet has been
forced to confront his own complicity in her exploitation, and his
rhetoric does not allow him to evade this problem with a casual or glib
summing-up.

Having expressed his inability to conclude or continue, Swift gets out of
the poem by simply retreating into a cheap sneer:

The bashful muse will never bear
In such a scene to interfere.

Corinna in the morning dizened,
Who sees, will spew, who smells, be poisoned.

(ll. 71–4)

Like one of her clients, Swift feels himself debased by this encounter, and leaves a motto at the end which is humiliatingly inhumane for both parties. As readers, we are implicated in the whole business, as we too have spent the night with this woman in our experience of the poem. Swift's willingness to exploit his subject, in which we are incriminated, shows how disturbing and unsettling such an encounter must be. And it shows how a liberal concern for the well-being of one individual cannot co-exist with the hopelessness of the situation and cannot express itself in any beneficial way, becoming wholly inarticulate and ineffectual.

At the end, the poem seems to confront its own nihilism, only to run away from its implications, and the failure to provide a consistent perspective makes it a very disconcertingly unstable poem to read. Whereas some critics feel able to describe this final passage as 'very brief, a spasm of irritation', I feel the climactic rancour at the end displays a much more radical failure of perspective, an inability to decide which party in this transaction is the more loathsome. The voice of the poem becomes as uncontrolled as the mad voice of the narrator of the final book of *Gulliver's Travels*. Despite the fact that this woman is right in front of him, in pain and suffering, Swift is unable to cope by falling into either easy sentimentalism or wholehearted mockery and he humiliatingly resorts to a blustering guilty outburst which fails hopelessly to bring the whole poem together.[31]

Swift clearly attempts to strip the glamour away from whoring, but it is very interesting to see him doing it partly from the whore's point of view. Much of the poem's capacity to disturb comes from the way we sometimes peek clandestinely at Corinna, while at other moments we are forced to participate in her imaginings. The combination of impersonal scrutiny and intimate knowledge, analogous to the act of prostitution itself, gives the poem an insecurity of approach which makes it seem internally unstable and very disquieting to encounter. Although the whole piece singularly fails to reconcile the tensions it generates between curiosity and exploitation, its ability to infiltrate even an intermittent trace of sympathy for Corinna and her plight makes it very different from other similar contemporary pieces of male writing, like the passage on Drury Lane in John Gay's long poem *Trivia: Or, The Art of Walking the Streets of London* (1716).[32]

Swift's Corinna was a sorry and bedraggled sight, incapable, it seems, of attracting any but the most credulous or desperate. Gay's street-walking whores, however, are much more seductive, and are presented as a much more alluring threat to males:

'Tis she who nightly strowls with saunt'ring Pace,

No stubborn Stays her yielding Shape embrace;
Beneath the Lamp her tawdry Ribbons glare,
The new-scower'd Manteau, and the slattern Air;
High-draggled Petticoats her Travels show,
And hollow Cheeks with artful Blushes glow;
With flatt'ring Sounds she sooths the cred'lous Ear,
My noble Captain! Charmer! Love! my Dear!
In Riding-hood, near Tavern-Doors she plies,
Or muffled Pinners hide her livid Eyes.
With empty Bandbox she delights to range,
And feigns a distant Errand from the *Change*;
Nay, she will oft' the Quaker's Hood prophane,
And trudge demure the Rounds of *Drury-Lane*.
She darts from Sarsnet Ambush wily Leers,
Twitches thy Sleeve, or with familiar Airs,
Her Fan will pat thy Cheek; these Snares disdain,
Nor gaze behind thee, when she turns again.

(III, 267–84)

Gay's coquettish whores are very different from Corinna. They are artful, enticing and confident, like the women in *The Beggar's Opera*. The impression Gay creates here is of women of a distinctly gendered high passion ('livid Eyes', 'wily Leers') who remain fully in command of themselves and the situation. Although the description incorporates references to the real shabbiness of the women ('tawdry', 'slattern'), its general direction is to enhance their availability and blowsy attractiveness. Once again, as in Boswell, the women are seductive sirens, impelled by desire, and the men are the victims. The vocabulary for describing males in this passage is consistently unflattering – 'the cred'lous Ear' – and the women are presented, almost literally, as 'Snares'. The description may be much more positive than many contemporary images of women, in that it at least gives these women charm and power, but it is inevitably compromised by its suggestions of predatoriness and criminality. The whores are presented as vibrant women, active and sexy and self-assured in gender-specific ways, but these talents only serve to make them more dangerous to males.

As in Dunton's periodical, the admonitory voice is used here to legitimise lingering descriptions of the alluring temptresses. As the passage continues, Gay spells out the gravity of the female threat with an admonitory tale for his implied male audience:

I knew a Yeoman, who for thirst of Gain,
To the great City drove from *Devon's* plain
His num'rous lowing Herd; his Herds he sold,
And his deep leathren Pocket bagg'd with Gold;
Drawn by a fraudful Nymph, he gaz'd, he sigh'd;

Unmindful of his Home, and distant Bride,
She leads the willing Victim to his Doom,
Through winding Alleys to her Cobweb Room.

(III, 285–92)

No graphic details of their congress are given, and the focus remains exclusively on the 'Yeoman'. As a result of his recklessness and naïvety, he loses all his gold, gets into a brawl, and eventually discovers something even more awful:

Ah hapless Swain, unus'd to Pains and Ills!
Canst thou forgo Roast-Beef for nauseous Pills?
How wilt thou lift to Heav'n thy Eyes and Hands,
When the long Scroll the Surgeon's Fees demands!
Or else (ye Gods avert that worst Disgrace)
Thy ruin'd Nose falls level with thy Face,
Then shall thy Wife thy loathsome Kiss disdain,
And wholesome Neighbours from thy Mug refrain.

(III, 299–306)

There is no doubt that Gay is exploiting (and enjoying) the Virgilian contrast between the wholesome country and the diseased town, confronting rustic naïvety with urban lasciviousness. The tone of the passage is much more playful and teasing than fully admonitory, as can be seen by comparing this little story with the sombre procession of a similar encounter in Wordsworth's 'Michael'. Yet the poem is still attached to a serious issue, and, however sceptical or playful it may seek to be, it still surreptitiously disseminates the prevailing ideology of female sexuality as a threat.

Gay's poem thus includes a much simpler apprehension of whores than Swift's. The only complication it seems to introduce is the comic deflation of the gullible male. Otherwise, it shows the whore as the attractive, dangerous creature, whose passions or whose abilities to feign passion make her a persistent threat to otherwise upright citizens. Once again, the whore is the bearer of the stigma. As in *The Whore's Rhetorick*, she is cynical and fraudulent. She is not presented as a hapless fallen woman whom we could or should pity, but as a seasoned coquette whom only the sophisticated urbanite can cope with. In this part of *Trivia*, the forces of law and order are conspicuously absent, as they are in Boswell's journals. In Swift's poem, however, the interaction of the whore and the law is much more problematic, and the intrusion of Bridewell into the episode makes the whole business harder to assess rather than easier. In broad terms, then, Gay's piece briskly avoids the complexities of the issue, by seeing it more or less through the official perspective. He accepts the existence of whores as part of the day-to-day fabric of London life, worth seeing, with due caution. Swift complicates matters, and reveals many of the ideological tensions and difficulties which were also less disturbingly brought out in Ned Ward and in some of the pornography. Swift's tone is moving some way towards the anger and intensity of Blake's 'youthful harlot' in his poem 'London', whereas Gay's is a more tolerant and sanguine acceptance of the status quo.

It would certainly be wrong to see Gay's poem as an unambiguous attempt to disseminate the authoritarian ideology of the evils of whores – his women seem too luscious and playful for that – but he still does little to contest the authorised version. What these two very different poems share, however, is the sense that whoring was a visible part of the city, and that it represented some kind of social problem, which the law seemed to be addressing rather clumsily. The pragmatic approach, looking for what might be done to improve matters, is not adopted by Boswell, Ward, Swift or Gay. Nor does it figure in this formulation in pornography, where it is the law, not the whores, which is the problem. But many commentators did recognise the existence of a problem in prostitution, and many solutions were offered in the press, involving either an amendment of the law or a more radical change of attitude. It is these we will go on to look at now.

MODEST PROPOSALS

The writing we have seen so far has expressed a diverse range of attitudes to prostitution and to the law, ranging from exasperation to resigned tolerance. However, it was obvious to Augustan writers and readers of all shades of opinion that, if the punitive law was meant to deter prostitutes, it had most definitely failed, and all the extensive commentary on whoredom had to take account of the flagrancy of this legislative failure. Although some pieces did overtly contest the assumptions about gender and conduct embedded in the statute, most worked within its parameters, insinuating degrees of scepticism, stealthily undermining the legally reinforced idea that women were essentially different from men in terms of sexual conduct. In the pseudo-instructional dialogue, for instance, some of the cynical arguments put forward by bawds amusingly reformulated sexual politics to show that, in a variety of surprising ways, men might not always be on top. In the conducted tours of London, on the other hand, the law might be seen to encourage practices which seemed a bit doubtful, but it was still a fundamentally necessary instrument in the regulation of sexual desire, which happened in this case to be locally incompetent.

The substance of most of this writing, however, was not any particular deficiencies in the legislation, but a series of complex negotiations between the whore's attractiveness and her loathsomeness, an irreconcilable and frightening contradiction, or an amusing irony, depending on the point of view adopted. For some writers, this tension could be seen as a question of individual conduct, while for others it was a matter of social organisation, perhaps representing specific national as well as gender characteristics. Prostitution was the point of contact between 'animal gratification' and illegality, and as such it was associated with questions of social morality and the best constitution of society, as formulated and reformulated by contemporary writers.

The social perspective on prostitution is best represented by travel writers and polemicists, all of whom shape narratives to present the case they want to make in its most convincing light. The most common argument presented throughout the period is that the extraordinary number of whores visible on the London streets represented a national scandal, and that the crude reliance on corporal punishments to discourage this led to a failure in the efficacy of the law, which in turn brought the whole project of legislation into disrepute. That there were said to be 107 brothels operating unhindered in the vicinity of Drury Lane alone in 1725, as one scandalised commentator claimed, was not evidence of a peculiar lustiness in Londoners, but rather an indication of the ineptness of existing English social policy.[33] What many commentators seem to have been struck by was the great quantity of prostitutes, and the reluctance of the law to provide a workable structure to regulate their practice. Although the comfortable and hospitable brothel had been long established in Paris and Amsterdam, for instance, the exclusive and expensive *bagnio* only gradually began to be part of London's facilities, even then of necessity catering exclusively for better-off clients. To provide for the lower classes, the lusty rustics like Gay's yeoman, and the transients, a great many women were to be seen plying their trade at large in the public highways.

It was this feature which arrested the attention of the traveller J. W. von Archenholz, whose retrospective account of metropolitan street life was published in 1789:

> London is said to contain fifty thousand prostitutes, without reckoning kept mistresses. The most wretched of these live with *matrons*, who lodge, board, and clothe them. The dress worn by the very lowest of them is silk, according to the custom which luxury has generally introduced into England. Sometimes they escape from their prison, with their little wardrobes under their arms, and trade on their *own bottoms*, when, if they are unfortunate, or happen not to be economical, they are soon dragged to the gaol by their creditors.[34]

There is some indication here that the English love of 'luxury' is to blame, an argument which finds differing echoes in Defoe, Mandeville, Henry Fielding and many more orthodox Puritan writers, but von Archenholz puts more emphasis on the wretchedness and plain inefficiency of the proceedings, and points to the flagrant incompetence of the legal practices involved.

Later in the century, Patrick Colquhoun's systematic enumeration of metropolitan criminals included 2,000 bawds and the extraordinary figure of 50,000 'Unfortunate Females of all descriptions, who support themselves chiefly or wholly by prostitution'. Colquhoun used this obviously inflated and undiscerning (and unsupported) figure to boost his overall numbers of miscreants up to the inflammatory total of 115,000, and there is certainly no reason to see it as an accurate description of the real state of affairs in the 1790s or before.[35] What is important, however, is to see that the problem was being formulated by many commentators as a collective one, with the attendant suggestion that there was some widespread social responsibility to rectify things. Otherwise, it was often argued, everyone was tainted with the disgrace. The simple diagnosis of the phenomenon as the public manifestation of the evil desires of women was being replaced by the view that some more subtle explanation had to be found, and that the introduction of more and more severe legal sanctions against individual prostitutes might not be the whole answer. The press, once again, can be seen surrounding the official legal line on punishment with various contending reformulations and alternatives.

In fact, there is one literary feature of the Augustan period which can be identified as helping to initiate the first moves towards a less punitive approach. Paradoxical though it may sound, the move away from the emphasis on 'sin' as an explanation of the vast numbers of whores on the London streets towards an attempt to deal with the problem socially can be seen in the development of a literature of individual philanthropy in the periodical essay and the early novel. The periodical essay is a particularly interesting form here, initially identifying 'bawds' as the real culprits, then moving away to see the blame lying in the conjunction of male predatoriness and the economically disadvantaged condition of women. In the *Tatler* and the *Spectator*, and in the many imitations of these successful works, the curious reader was given a commentary on the affairs of the day, conducted for the most part through a gentlemanly ethos, with particular attention to the etiquette of urban life. In one of Steele's papers for the *Spectator* in 1712, he offers a 'Consideration of poor and publick Whores'.[36] Sensitive to the dangers of self-righteousness (as well he might be) he is reluctant to adopt a strictly moralistic perspective, and avoids falling into easy, hypocritical censure. Indeed, the young whore he encounters is presented as an appropriate object for enlightened pity rather than pious vilification:

> we stood under one of the Arches by Twilight; and there I could observe as exact Features as I had ever seen, the most agreeable Shape, the finest Neck and Bosom, in a Word, the whole Person of a Woman exquisitely beautiful. She affected to allure me with a forced Wantonness in her Look and Air; but I saw it checked with Hunger and Cold: Her Eyes were wan and eager, her Dress thin and tawdry,

her Mein genteel and childish. This strange Figure gave me much Anguish of Heart, and to avoid being seen with her I went away, but could not forbear giving her a Crown. The poor thing sighed, curtsied, and with a Blessing, expressed with the utmost Vehemence, turned from me.

Once again, this passage is struggling to maintain its composure or evenness of tone. The tension between desire and charity is openly acknowledged, but the further tensions between sympathy and patronage, and between desire and distrust, are less consciously confronted. Steele is presenting himself as sufficiently adept to see through the affected charms that might take in Gay's rustic, but too charitable to give the kind of lingering and fastidious analysis that Swift undertook. Steele suffers from 'Anguish of Heart', but is unable to conceive of a solution to the obvious problem. He slips her a coin (albeit a valuable one), and slinks off 'to avoid being seen with her', and her parting 'Vehemence' is a brief reminder of the whore's basic hard-heartedness. Although, then, he recognises some philanthropic responsibility, he retains the notion that contact with whores is undignified and demeaning for males, and potentially distressing.

Such concern with the status of the worldly gentleman means that Steele's analysis can only move a short distance from the gendered moralism of the official legal account. He is more sympathetic to this girl than the law would normally be, and he reserves his full condemnation for 'those Hags of Hell whom we call Bawds'. Steele sees the whores as innocent victims of evil procuresses, probably simple country girls entrapped by artful metropolitan crones. The tender-hearted gentleman is thus absolved of all responsibility for the institution of whoring, and his occasional charitable gestures are as much as he need do. In a later paper, #274, Steele recognises that the 'Arts and Gallantries of crafty Men' are undoubtedly involved, and that 'most Part of what we in our Youth think gay and polite, is nothing else but an Habit of indulging a Pruriency that way' (II, 567). So males are at least partly incriminated by their native lustfulness, but once again the real responsibility lies with 'the impotent Wenchers and industrious Haggs who are supplied with, and are constantly supplying new Sacrifices to the Devil of Lust' (II, 567). Although Steele introduces further comple﹍ities into the discussion with a letter from 'Pucella', the kept mistress of an impotent old rascal, in #276, the fundamental point of his analysis remains the same: men may be naturally over-boisterous, but the moral responsibility for whoring lies not primarily with them but with a specific exploitative group elsewhere, in this case 'evil procuresses'.

'Mr. Spectator' thus offers some sympathy for whores but does not thereby antagonise his readership. Women, after all, are still to blame. It is interesting to compare the scapegoating of procuresses, as it appears here and in many other pieces, including *Clarissa*, *The Harlot's Progress* and Jonas Hanway's *Plan For Establishing a Charity House* (1758), with the more universal accusatory and censorious tone of Samuel Johnson in the *Rambler* in 1751. Johnson gives a sombre account of the miserable life of prostitutes through a first-person narrative tale by 'Misella', in which she describes how she was seduced by her benefactor, thrown on the streets and mistreated by virtually everyone she subsequently encountered. Unlike Steele, Johnson takes the opportunity to identify the guilty parties:

> They neither employ the graces of fancy, nor the force of understanding, in their attempts; they cannot please their vanity with the art of their approaches, the delicacy of their adulations, the elegance of their address, or the efficacy of their eloquence; nor applaud themselves as possessed of any qualities, by which affection is attracted. . .
>
> Many of these despicable wretches does my present acquaintance with infamy and wickedness enable me to number among the heroes of debauchery. Reptiles whom their own servants would have despised, had they not been their servants, and with whom beggary would have disdained intercourse, had she not been lured by hopes of relief. Many of those now rioting in taverns, or shivering in the streets, have been corrupted not by arts of gallantry which stole gradually upon the affections and laid prudence asleep, but by the fear of losing benefits which were never intended, or of incurring resentment which they could not escape; some have been frighted by masters, and some awed by guardians into ruin.[37]

It is interesting that this powerful denunciation contains no gender-specific terms until the final clause, but it is still clear that Johnson/Misella is accusing gentlemen of being the corrupters of helpless women. No longer is there any easy recourse to blaming witch-like bawds or procuresses for the miserable state of affairs, rather the strength of the accusation lies in its breadth and its inclusiveness. By not specifying the villain, Misella hurls her accusations at the male readership in general, challenging them by refusing to produce the luxury of a scapegoat.

As Misella's descent from kept mistress to common street-walker accelerates, she encounters a number of strolling gentlemen like 'Mr. Spectator'. The first responds to her distress with contempt:

> he seized me by the hand, and drew me into a neighbouring house, where when he saw my face pale with hunger, and my eyes swelling with tears, he spurned me from him, and bad me cant and whine in some other place; he for his part would take care of his pockets.

The second importuner takes more notice of Misella's distress, but only sees it as an opportunity for his personal gain:

another soon addressed me in the same manner. When he saw the same tokens of calamity, he considered that I might be obtained at a cheap rate, and therefore quickly made overtures, which I had no longer firmness to reject.

The narrative ends with a very disturbing account of the whore's wretched existence, and with an uncompromising call for philanthropy and humanitarian concern:

> If those who pass their days in plenty and security, could visit for an hour the dismal receptacles to which the prostitute retires from her nocturnal excursions, and see the wretches that lie crowded together, mad with intemperance, ghastly with famine, nauseous with filth, and noisome with disease; it would not be easy for any degree of abhorrence to harden them against compassion, or to repress the desire which they must immediately feel to rescue such numbers of human beings from a state so dreadful.

The final verb 'rescue' is most interesting, in the way it calls for help and aid, rather than for greater punishment or discouragements. Johnson seems to have been both more severe in his understanding of male depravity, and more lenient in his assessment of female frailty, than most of the writers we have seen so far. Elsewhere in his work, this grave sympathy towards women reappears. In reporting a conversation with Johnson in 1763 (the year of the 'monstrous big whore' episode) Boswell records that 'we talked of the wretched life of such women; and agreed, that much more misery than happiness, on the whole, is produced by illicit commerce between the sexes'.[38] Although Boswell fails to draw parallels between this austere view of sexual 'commerce' – the financial pun is no doubt accidental, but it is resonant – and his own private behaviour, he recognises the power of Johnson's remarks, and does not attempt a counter-argument.

These periodical essays thus show a drift from a mixture of charity and embarrassment, awkwardly contained in a single piece, to a powerfully expressed righteous indignation. The severity of Johnson's dictionary definition is retained as a piece of classification, but increasingly tempered by a more sympathetic understanding of what it means for a woman to be a whore. Those women who have fallen into prostitution are beginning to be seen as victims, in need of care and attention, rather than as criminals, in need of punishment or deterrence. At this transitional stage, there remain a number of contending theories about exactly who they are victims of, about whether blame should be transferred from the whores themselves to their procuresses or to their clients. As the magistrate Sir John Fielding put it:

> Who can say that one of these poor children had been prostitutes

through viciousness? No. They are young, unprotected, and of the female sex; therefore become the prey of the bawd and the debauchee.[39]

The developing emphasis on the whore as legally unprotected victim can be found in a lot of mid-century writing. By looking at this shift in emphasis, and at the support it lent to the philanthropic plans of such reformers as Jonas Hanway and Saunders Welch, it is possible to argue, as W. A. Speck does, that the Augustan period saw a gradual but persistent change in attitude towards prostitutes, starting with the public floggings in Bridewell or at the cart's tail, and culminating in the opening of the relatively enlightened Magdalen Hospital for Penitent Prostitutes in 1758. Indeed, it is possible to see the Magdalen Hospital as only one branch of a thriving growth in philanthropic institutions, like the Foundling Hospital, the Marine Society for Educating Poor Destitute Boys to the Sea, the National Truss Society, and even the Society for the Ruptured Poor, all no doubt thought by their instigators and supporters to be noble and high-minded projects, charitably designed to relieve unnecessary suffering.[40] Whether they invariably seemed quite so benign to the recipients of such benevolence is another matter.

Any progressivist argument about the demonstrable growth in charity has to confront the vicissitudes of the contemporary press, and the underlying hypocrisy of the institutions themselves, which sought only to ameliorate suffering, not to address its causes or seek to eradicate it. In discussing the Magdalen Hospital, for instance, some recent writers have argued that, rather than representing a fundamental change in punitive policy, it was simply an agent of the repressive paternalistic regime operating in a different, less obviously coercive guise:

> These refuges, asylums, reformatories and shelters were not necessarily penal, but what they established was a wide, interlocking carceral network, based on the assumption that females needed a firm paternalistic hand to guide their development.[41]

Women could be kept in these refuges for indefinite lengths of time, at the behest of magistrates, and it is not clear just how voluntary their eventual discharge could be. While incarcerated, they lived a spartan life of hard work and rigorous religious training, designed to bring them to full penitence through a long, dull shock. Once again, the focus of attention in the treatment of prostitution was on altering the behaviour of the woman involved, not on rectifying the society which created her, or on admonishing the men who exploited her. Even the stress on 'penitence' in the hospital's title indicates that the problem was still being formulated as a matter of gendered individual wrongdoing, of women's traditional propensity to 'sin'. Although the penal strategy obviously changed during this period, from relying on corporal punishment to favouring incarceration, the thinking behind it remained profoundly paternalistic and conservative, being dependent on a pessimistic view of the possibilities of reform, and on the notion that the vicious, like the poor, might always be with us.

It is clear, then, that the dominant and legally reinforced ideology of Augustan England retained its hostility to women, albeit in mediated form, and understood prostitution as primarily their fault. But that was not the only strand in discussion, and different proposals were just as vociferously voiced. The terms of Johnson's accusation, for instance, were not likely to be dispersed by the setting-up of a few workhouses for apprehended prostitutes. Similarly, there were a number of projectors who argued that only a more radical change in the structure of society would lead to the improvements required. Defoe, for instance, identified the problem in *Some Considerations Upon Streetwalkers* (1726) as a result of the coincidence of too many bachelors and too few economic opportunities for women. His solution was a typically pragmatic and financial one, based on differential taxation incentives for married couples. Not long after, he tried to address these difficulties constructively as part of the plan to make Augustan London the most thriving city in the universe. In *Augusta Triumphans* (1728), writing under his experienced pseudonym 'Andrew Moreton', he said:

> The lewdest people upon earth, ourselves excepted, are not guilty of such open violations of the laws of decency. Go all the world over, and you'll see no such impudence as in the streets of London, which makes many foreigners give our women in general a bad character, from the vile specimens they meet with from one end of the town to the other. . .
>
> How many honest women, those of the inferior sort especially, get loathsome distempers from their husbands' commerce with such creatures, which distempers are often entailed on posterity?[42]

The drift of Defoe's argument, as imbued as ever with economic language ('commerce', 'entailed'), is that the law should more strictly circumscribe male behaviour, to protect women and improve society as a whole. Prostitution is not a symptom of an exclusively female sinfulness, but yet another example of the human capacity to fall from grace. Although Defoe believed it would be impossible to produce a utopian world from which sin would be entirely eradicated, he still maintained confidence in the human capacity to act upon circumstances so as to improve them. In a broad attempt to balance and strengthen relations between the sexes, and so weaken the hold of whores, Defoe suggests the introduction of severe penalties for wife-beaters, and for those who selfishly and, as things stood, quite legally confined their wives to asylums. Compared with most of the other commentators, he seems scrupulous to look after the neglected rights of women – 'Some may think this too low a topic for me to expatiate upon, to which I answer, that it is a charitable and a Christian one, and therefore not in the least beneath the consideration of any man who had a woman for his mother.'

In trying to exert pressure upon social policy on behalf of mistreated women, Defoe/Moreton directly addresses the only powerful female available to him:

> Most gracious and august Queen Caroline! Ornament of your sex, and pride of the British nation! The best of mothers, the best of wives, the best of women! Begin this auspicious reign with an action worthy of your illustrious self, rescue your injured sex from this tyranny.

The notion of marriage as legalised tyranny is outspoken, but can be found in many other Defoe pieces, notably *The Family Instructor* (1715) and *Conjugal Lewdness, or Matrimonial Whoredom* (1727). Similar arguments can be found in Mary Astell and Jonas Hanway, all sharing the notion that reciprocity of rights within marriage, rare enough in any case, was more commonly a feature of the less well-off than of the upper classes, and that prostitution was yet another way in which the rich exploited the weakness of the defenceless poor. Once again, then, the critique of marriage and the treatment of women intersects with what might loosely be called a 'class' dimension, and for those writers who saw women as poorly treated, whoring was regarded as a vice encouraged by the upper classes and of debilitating effect for everybody.

The proposals of Defoe and Sir John Fielding, to take just two rather differently motivated pamphleteers, share a sense that society can be made to work better by a campaign of amendment and reform, conducted within the limits of the existing statute. Their confidence in the possibility of improvement, by intelligent social engineering, is representative of the orthodox line on social policy. There was room for great differences of opinion about the kinds of amendment which should be encouraged, but there was a broad level of agreement, sustaining the activities of the commentating press, that *something* could and should be done. These positivist arguments existed in the space between two types of fatalism. On the one side, there were extreme religious interpretations of the problem, which saw rife prostitution as a symptom of the irretrievable and inevitable collapse of moral integrity. A good example of this style is the 1749 pamphlet *Satan's Harvest Home: Or, The Present State of Whorecraft, Adultery, Fornication, Procuring, Pimping, Sodomy, etc.*, in which the conglomeration of vices in the title represents a catalogue of the leisure interests of the fallen inhabitants of Augustan London, seen as the new Gomorrah. Even more interesting are the arguments on the other extreme, which start from the notion that whoring can never be fully eradicated, and go on to suggest that prostitution should therefore be encouraged, as long as it is adequately supervised. These proposals were put with splendid paradoxical vigour by Bernard Mandeville. He

first advocated the social utility of prostitution – the public benefit of this
private vice – in his *Fable of the Bees*:

> Who would imagine, that Virtuous Women, unknowingly should be
> instrumental in promoting the Advantage of Prostitutes? Or (what still
> seems the greater Paradox) that Incontinence should be made
> serviceable to the Preservation of Chastity? And yet nothing is more
> true. A Vicious young Fellow, after having been an Hour or two at
> Church, a Ball, or any other Assembly, where there is a great parcel of
> handsome Women dress'd to the best Advantage, will have his
> Imagination more fired than if he had the same time been Poling at
> *Guildhall*, or walking in the Country among a Flock of Sheep. The
> consequence of this is, that he'll Strive to satisfy the Appetite that is
> raised in him; and when he finds honest Women obstinate and
> uncomatable, 'tis very natural to think, that he'll hasten to others that
> are more compliable. Who wou'd so much surmise, that this is the fault
> of the Virtuous Women? They have no Thoughts of Men in dressing
> themselves, Poor Souls, and endeavour only to appear clean and
> decent, every one according to her quality.[43]

The ironies here are more clearly stated than is sometimes the case in
Mandeville's work. In this passage, the conflation of churches, balls and
assemblies makes its point openly enough, as does the splendidly
dismissive language used to surround these vain women – 'Flock of
Sheep', 'obstinate and uncomatable', 'Poor Souls'. We are left with the
impression of artful ladies, deliberately stirring up desires they then
refuse to satisfy. And if their chastity provokes incontinence in others, so
too the incontinence of others protects their purity. In a further sardonic
twist to the argument, Mandeville defends the provision of prostitutes as
a necessary bulwark to protect the safety of conventionally decent
women:

> Where Six or Seven Thousand Sailors arrive at once, as it often
> happens at *Amsterdam*, that have seen none but their own Sex for
> many Months together, how is it to be suppos'd that honest Women
> should walk the Streets unmolested, if there were no Harlots to be had
> at reasonable Prices?

Mandeville's presentation gives an ironically inflected and stylised version
of a particularly pragmatic case, in keeping with his overall strategy of
showing the hidden utility of vice in society. Rather than deplore
whoring, or offer genteel pity for the individuals concerned in it, he gives
a swashbuckling account of its commercial value and large civic benefit.

In *The Fable of the Bees*, prostitution is only one of the many
institutions which enable societies to prosper. Mandeville developed his

argument in a more concentrated form in a pamphlet exclusively devoted to the topic, *A Modest Defence of Publick Stews* (1724). Writing as 'Phil-Porney', the author ridicules the claims of the societies for the reformation of manners to have improved matters in any significant way. In fact, he argues, they have simply endangered those very things they claimed to have set out to protect:

> what better could we expect from your Carting of Bawds, than that the Great Leviathan of Leachery, for want of these Tubs to play with, should, with one Whisk of his Tail, overset the *Vessel* of Modesty? Which, in her best Trim, we know to be somewhat *leaky*, and to have a very unsteady *Helm*.[44]

The echo of Swift and Hobbes in the reference to the 'Leviathan' and his tubs gives some indication of the tone of the piece. Like Hobbes, Mandeville is putting forward an economical idea, devoid of casuistry or a too fastidious concern for morality. Like Swift, in his own modest proposals, Mandeville is confronting the hypocrisies of his time by extrapolating them to their conclusion, and surrounding them with elaborate comic embellishments and a battery of puns and quibbles. Something of the precision with which he entertains his basic idea – which is deliberately provocative and yet seriously meant – can be seen in his concern for the standardisation of the franchise arrangements for his retail outlets:

> For the better Entertainment of all Ranks and Degrees of Gentlemen, we shall divide the twenty Women of each House into four Classes, who for their Beauty, or other Qualifications may justly challenge different Prices.
>
> The first Class is to consist of eight, who may legally demand from each Visitant Half a Crown. The second Class to consist of six, whose fix'd price may be a Crown. The third Class of four, at half a Guinea each. The remaining two make up the fourth Class, and are design'd for Persons of the first Rank, who can afford to Pay a Guinea for the Elegancy of their Taste.
>
> (p. 13)

Sound business principles, easily identifiable by the twentieth-century reader, are being applied here, and Mandeville goes on to establish a code of practice for medical inspections, the maintenance of order in the brothels, and the care and attention of the customers. The benefits, he claims, would be obvious: the 'French Pox' could be kept under control, disorderly women would come under official supervision, young men's '*Spermaticks*' (p. 22) would have a legitimate outlet, and the whole fraudulent enterprise of private whoring would fall into disrepute. Men, women and the community at large would reap the benefits of institutionalising what is already going on, and there should be no need for equivocation or prevarication in the implementation of these highly effectual and desirable measures.

Unlike the other writers dealt with here, Mandeville is expatiating upon his theme largely for its own sake. He is dramatising and satirising contemporary sexual and commercial practice through a semi-earnest proposal to legalise whoring. In this, he belongs more with the distanced, ironic commentators like Hogarth than with the interventionist, philanthropic agitators like Hanway. Mandeville's merry frankness and his enjoyment of provocation put him in a category of his own somewhere between the pornographers and the reformers, in that his manner of presentation forms an embellishment which is enjoyable for its inventiveness and its cheek, rather than for its relevance or its accuracy. In that sense, he is nearer to the novelists and artists who dealt with whores than the pamphleteers, and the connections lie in his overall ironic stance and his delight in surrounding an outrageous single point with a distracting fog of detail and pseudo-scientific precision.

Although Mandeville shares the imaginative inventiveness of the creative artists of the time, his scheme is presented in a mock-formal way, and it does not need to dwell on the consequences of the project for those most strongly affected by it. The 'product' he is selling is, after all, not merely a piece of stock, but, just as in Swift's later *Modest Proposal*, a human being. Quite deliberately, Mandeville assumes that the whores who will satisfy his customers need to be maintained with all the care and attention of prime business assets, but of course they are to have no say in matters which concern them. In fact, they are to be treated as slightly privileged and pampered slaves, a pattern of argument which has parallels in Hogarth and Defoe. Although Mandeville sees his whores as valuable commercial commodities, other contemporary writers were keener to explore the issue more from the women's point of view, or from what they assumed was the women's point of view. In so doing, as we shall now go on to see, they provided further reformulations of the legal position, which intensified, complicated, and even subverted it.

WOMEN OF PLEASURE

The most famous and complex representation of a prostitute's career in eighteenth-century English art is undoubtedly William Hogarth's series of engravings known as *The Harlot's Progress* (1731). The title of the sequence is clearly ironic, since Hackabout's career in the prints is presented through a number of selected episodes which are not at all cumulatively triumphant. Like the legendary Solomon Grundy, Hogarth's harlot has a career which is brief, but packed with significant incident. Starting as a country girl arriving in London, she is taken up by a procuress, becomes the mistress of a wealthy Jew, then a common prostitute, spends some time confined in Bridewell, dies, and gets buried.

Just like Tom Idle, then, or the eponymous hero of *The Rake's Progress*, the emblematic prostitute undergoes a life of accelerating depravity, and, after her initial success as a rich man's kept woman, her 'progress' is downhill all the way.

However, the artist composes this pageant for us in a way that does not allow us any comfortable feelings of superiority over the central figure, or indeed any consistency or stability of response at all. Once again, Hogarth presents an apparently simple moral homily, which on closer inspection does not live up to the clarity of its stated scheme, but which reveals instead a corrupt world whose values are almost entirely commercial and where we are allowed no unqualified confidence in the moral authority of the law or of religion. As with the *Industry and Idleness* sequence, and *The Rake's Progress*, the final scene has more bathos about it than gravity, and the covert effect of the entire series is to destabilise the more orthodox legal and moral attitudes which the overall pattern of the narrative seems initially to reinforce. Hogarth's technique, as before, is to offer what looks like a very simple admonitory scheme of sin and punishment, and then to complicate and subvert it internally by the provision of small but significant incongruous details.[45]

The tale of Hackabout is disquieting because her decline and her eventual fate seem so inevitable and yet so beyond her control. Although one recent commentator claims that '*The Harlot's Progress* simply does not make sense unless we assume that Moll has quite cold-bloodedly chosen a route which leads to her death from venereal disease', Hogarth gives no such unambiguous indications that cold-blooded choices are being made or could be made by his heroine.[46] When she arrives in London, the young girl has to leave her rustic past behind her (graphically represented by the left-hand side of the print with its horse and cart and dreamy parson) and she has to cope with the challenges of London unassisted. The city presents itself to the newcomer as welcoming and approachable, but it is obvious to us that it is threatening. Not only is the new arrival being befriended by a figure recognisable as Elizabeth Needham, a well-known bawd who was so roughly treated during an appearance in the pillory in 1730 that she died soon after, but she is also being furtively sized up by the notorious whoremonger Colonel Francis Charteris, whose predatory exploits had already been unveiled in a number of pamphlets and in persistent reports in the *Grub-Street Journal*. Amidst these identifiable accomplished libertines, Moll (if that is her name: Hogarth only calls her 'M. Hackabout') looks no more worldly and experienced than the lolling goose she has brought with her, and it may be that she too is being lined up as a tasty dish for some other rich person's table. The print thus seems to be offering a particularly stark portrait of innocence entering a cruel and unfriendly world in which it may not survive.

However, despite what Speck claims, the engraving offers no real sense of the central figure's frame of mind or ability to understand what is really going on. She does not seem decisively to choose a life of crime and depravity, but she seems to acquiesce in it happily enough, in the absence of any other clear alternative. To begin with, Moll is protected only by a tiny and ineffective pair of scissors, and she does not notice that the country parson has turned his back on her. Indeed, throughout the sequence Moll's eyes are never focused on what is happening around her, and never meet anyone else's. As a result, it is very difficult for us to interpret her behaviour confidently, and we can never be sure of the degree of knowingness in her choices. She remains an object for our contemplation, rather than a figure who fully recognises her surroundings and interacts with others. We watch the tableau, which compiles various images of the harlot, but we are deprived of any access to her interiority. It may be that she is innocently being entrapped, or it may be that she has decided to seek this path quite deliberately – the expression on her face in the first print could carry suggestions of meekness or of innocence or of complicity.

Hogarth thus seems to be using his central figure as a device to introduce a panorama of wicked London types, inviting a very sceptical analysis of the conventional standards of metropolitan behaviour, but he also leaves us uncertain about the true meaning or significance of Hackabout. He avoids presenting her as an unambiguously evil woman, yet does not reproduce Mandeville's contending idea that whores are no more than commodities to be supplied to the ever-eager London markets. Instead, this harlot is intermittently a pathetic, exploited figure (Plates 4 and 5), and a knowing, confident whore (Plates 2 and 3). Both meanings are provided, and the prints simply accumulate the different images of prostitution which expressed the ideological confusions surrounding women's sexuality and the law, without seeking to reconcile them or arbitrate decisively between them.

In the second plate, briskly eliding Hackabout's early career and dramatising her most triumphant moment, Moll is a kept woman, surrounded by opulent materials, taking tea with her wealthy Jewish protector. Her room is richly furnished and well-appointed, showing all the fashionable paraphernalia of the day, including an escaping lover, a mask from a ball, an elaborate tea service, a young black attendant and a monkey. She is dressed in a lavish gown, worn in a fashionable *deshabillé*. If Hackabout has indeed chosen this life, it looks at this point as though she has been wise to do so. If she has not, then she has been singularly fortunate. Her expression is confident and worldly, looking into the middle distance as she nonchalantly upsets a tea-table so that her casual lover may creep out unnoticed by her more regular partner and protector. We are not told what has led to Hackabout achieving this eminence, but the print captures the moment of discovery when the tensions and duplicities are most obvious and her comfortable life begins to collapse, and its inclusion of casual inconsistencies encapsulates the confusion of values which she has come to inhabit. The oblique hint of Old Testament justice in the sombre biblical prints on her wall is not to be seen as a moralistic or sombre intrusion by the artist, but as a reminder of the double standards by which these wealthy people lived.

After her relatively successful period as a kept mistress, Moll falls into much less salubrious company. In the next picture, she is in a distinctly low-life, Drury Lane world, and seems to be working as a common street-walker. Once again, her face has the erotic, confident expression of one of the characters in Gay's *Trivia*. The wealthy Jewish patron has not been replaced, but there is a box by her bed containing the belongings of James Dalton, a well-known highwayman executed in 1730. Her room includes the standard equipment for versatile whoring, and on her wall she has pictures of Gay's MacHeath and the rabble-rousing preacher Dr Sacheverell, controversial contemporary celebrities of the profane and sacred worlds. As she is checking some stolen goods with her raddled maid, she is about to be apprehended by a group of watchmen headed by a figure identifiable as Sir John Gonson, the Westminster magistrate famous for his rather disconcerting zeal in the legal pursuit of whores and for his elaborate sermonising in court. As he enters Hackabout's room, his fervour seems to leave him momentarily, and he looks around with puzzlement. The dramatic moment allows Hogarth to establish the ironies of the entanglement of the criminal world and the self-righteously virtuous. Without making it over-emphatic, Hogarth invites scepticism about Gonson's motives, a pattern of thinking which was also regularly invoked in the more scurrilous press, comparable with Defoe's description of Jeffries or Ned Ward's presentation of the magistrates at Bridewell. As a result, the artist avoids any easy categorisation of his harlot as either pathetic victim or vile temptress. She remains, instead, an enigmatic figure, who is given meaning not by her own motives, which inevitably remain elusive, but by the eclectic company she keeps and the contradictory conventional images she invokes.

The ironies are continued in the Bridewell picture, where Moll retains her wealthy dress, just as the bankrupt gambler beside her retains some vestiges of his previous smart deportment. Her facial expression, however, has turned into one of pathetic suffering, oddly juxtaposed with the leering and shabby figures around her. Hogarth's presentation of Hackabout has ceased to emphasise her confidence, and is beginning to offer her up as a sacrificial victim. But yet he still does not allow us the full luxury of the stable perspective of compassion, as the agents of authority who punish her are not easy to read either. Because her imprisonment has been plausibly provoked by the ambivalent figure of Gonson, we cannot be absolutely confident that it is justice alone that has brought her to this place. And, as Hogarth presents it, Bridewell is only a den of rogues, where the woman overseeing the hemp-beating is proprietorially fingering Moll's dress and the male officer looks dour and unforgiving. The overall impression is that this place of confinement does little to break the spirit of the women it deals with, or bring them to abhor their wicked ways, and that it is wholly ineffective in the suppression of vice. From the lubricious Creswelite figure in Plates 2 and 3, Hackabout has turned into an injured Magdalen who stands with the bruised dignity of the heroine of a 'she-tragedy', like Nicholas Rowe's *The Fair Penitent* (1703), or like the conventionalised persecuted maiden, to be represented most intensely by Richardson's heroines.

Of course, this switching of the presentation of Hackabout is destabilising and disturbing as we try to fit the meaning of the sequence together. The icons of whoring that Moll expresses contradict each other, and make it hard for us to gauge the direction or intended significance of the whole narrative. By making the same figure at different times represent the lascivious, self-seeking whore, and the forlorn persecuted maiden, already familiar to contemporary readers from the writing of Haywood and Manley, Hogarth is interrogating the prevailing ideology of female sexuality most rigorously, and infiltrating scepticism about the adequacy or exhaustiveness of the legal categories. As Moll's 'progress' continues, she becomes less significant in the narrative. After Bridewell, she seems no longer capable of conveying meanings, and her face is wholly blank in Plate 5 and invisible in Plate 6. In her death scene, in Plate 5, she is surrounded by confusions. Her quack doctors are coming to blows about how best to treat this patient, her attendant is shouting at them, another maid is ransacking her clothes-chest, and a child is looking in a puzzled way at some meat cooking. The scene grimly replays the deliberate confusions of Plate 2, also composed around an overturned table, but the blank, expressionless face of Moll is a sardonic reference to her original enigmatic impassivity in Plate 1. The final scene virtually does without her, showing an elaborate lying-in-state. Moll's corpse is enclosed in a coffin out of our sight, and the picture surrounds it with a gallery of conventional female expressive types, ranging from a directly lascivious leer on the far left to the protestation of wretchedness on the extreme right. In between, we see representations of curiosity, genteel weeping, hard-heartedness and vanity. The two adult males seem to represent the exhaustive male typology of imbecility and lustfulness. In the middle of the picture sits an impish child, unconcernedly fiddling with a toy. As usual with Hogarth's sequences, the ending is ironically and disconcertingly bathetic.

In one way, then, I agree with Speck's claim that *The Harlot's Progress* does not make sense unless we see Moll cold-bloodedly choosing her life. Not that I think she does, but I am happy to think the sequence does not strictly make sense. If by 'making sense' we mean producing an unambiguous, clear utterance which communicates a single meaning to its audience, then Hogarth's work does not satisfy the criterion. Instead of embellishing a single idea with corroborative and supportive details, Hogarth provides a battery of significances, compiling a range of female images in the commodious figure of Hackabout, and surrounding her with a gallery of types and possibilities which defy single inclusive interpretation. What we eventually get from a reading of *The Harlot's Progress* is not easy to identify. Hogarth does not compose a parable or moral homily, although, as with *Industry and Idleness*, it looks at first as though one is promised. Instead, through the complications of the narrative, we get an interrogation of the meaning and significances of the illegal woman, showing that the range of existing images is riven with contradictions and ironies.

The constituent images that Hogarth draws together can be isolated in other Augustan writing. We have already seen the tradition of the lascivious whore in pornography and in Boswell's journals, and we can set it beside the tradition of the persecuted female which was prominent in much contemporary women's writing. I have already mentioned the popular 'she-tragedies' of Nicholas Rowe, best exemplified by *The Fair Penitent* (1703), but an even clearer dissemination of the ideology of female suffering can be seen in the extended fiction of Mary de la Rivière Manley and, more problematically, Eliza Haywood. The novels by these women authors enjoyed a great deal of contemporary celebrity, if not always approval. They mingle their social and political themes with close attention to women's issues, and provide another repository of female images which can fruitfully be identified and separated.

To take the best-known first, Manley's *The New Atalantis* (1709) is a complex work, which has an elaborately-coded political meaning, where specific personalities appear in only slightly disguised form. As well as being a political satire, however, the work is full of interpolated tales in which the ideology of female innocence and the double standard are scrutinised. The most interesting of these is the story of Charlot, a version, it seems, of the well-known scandalous seduction of Stuarta Howard by the Earl of Portland.[47] This particular narrative is a conventional one where a Duke seduces the young girl of whom he is guardian, then, tiring of her, leaves her to the sad fate of a fallen woman. Inside this tale, Manley insinuates an intermittently cynical critique of the legally-enforced ideology of gender, ending with a defiant accusation of the iniquity of the double standard. The Duke himself is socially adept:

> The Duke had a seeming Admiration for *Virtue*, wherever he found it, but he was a Statesman, and held it incompatible (in an Age like this) with a Mans making his Fortune, *Ambition*, *desire of Gain*, *Dissimulation*, *Cunning*, all these were serviceable to him: 'Twas enough he always applauded Virtue, and in his Discourse decry'd Vice.

(I, 52–3)

Instead of educating his ward in the requirements of the public world, the

Duke instils in Charlot 'cold Precepts of Education' (I, 58), so that she will be pure enough and innocent enough to marry his son. However, his plan to erect a protective cloister around the girl falters when he falls in love with her himself, and he introduces her to more worldly considerations by letting her read widely and showing her the town. Under this tutelage, Charlot begins to discover the possibilities of desire and eventually she and her guardian become lovers. After some time, however, he yearns for a more sophisticated mistress, and marries a Countess. Charlot is left in desolation and despair.

The most unorthodox and interesting features of Manley's account are the ways it acknowledges the female capacity to entertain desire, and the nonchalant way in which she reveals the ways of the world. It was these features of her writing, along with various rumours about her personal life, which helped create her scandalous reputation. However, her work is not only an exercise in the erotic, it is also an examination of the politics of the constructed female identity. At the end of Charlot's tale, there is a moralistic summary which forcefully exposes the double standard:

> Men may regain their Reputations, tho' after a Complication of Vices, *Cowardice*, *Robbery*, *Adultery*, *Bribery*, and *Murder*, but a Woman once departed from the Road of Virtue, is made incapable of a return; Sorrow and Scorn overtake her, and, as I said before, the World suffers her to perish loath'd, and unlamented.
>
> (I, 83–4)

Although the Duke's behaviour throughout this escapade is entirely legal, he would be immune even to acts of flagrant criminality. The women, however, are presented as the exploited objects of male lust, to be constructed by the men who control them in the ways they desire. It is striking that within this orthodox seduction tale Manley introduces complicating hints of other female possibilities. As Jane Spencer points out, 'the Duke's fatherly relation to Charlot is analogous to the general relation of men to women under patriarchy – figures of authority controlling their lives'.[48] This seduction tale is thus more emphatic than Hogarth's sequence in the way it accuses men, and offers a critique of patriarchy in action. Yet it does not rely for its force on some unexamined idea of intrinsic female purity. In Manley's tale, women are more complex and more variously motivated creatures, capable of exerting influence and holding sway, and the notion of their essential innocence is seen as an elaborately fabricated male fiction.

Manley thus reproduces the legal position of men and women, in order to contest it or introduce a note of strident protest about it. Her contemporary Eliza Haywood produced other reformulations of the suffering maiden, though these are significantly compromised by an unexamined attachment to more orthodox gender distinctions. In her enormous range of popular fictions, Haywood presented a range of female types, which mostly correspond to the legally-reinforced image of passivity, but which gradually infiltrate more assertive possibilities.[49] In the extremely popular novels *Love in Excess* (1719) and *Philidore and Placentia* (1727), Haywood produced heroines who lived stylised lives of subservience, largely unprotesting. In the first of these narratives, there is another possibility presented through the figure of the aggressive Aloisa, who gives the unattractive alternative to the more passive heroines, Amena and Melliora. In other novels, particularly *The British Recluse; or, The Secret History of Cleomira* (1722), the warring impulses of subservience and assertion are internalised in the twin heroines, Cleomira and Belinda. Both these women have been slaves to passion, and have been seduced by the same man. However, their lives are not over as a result, and they can still develop the capacity to live independently. In another novel, pleonastically titled *The Agreeable Caledonian* (1728), the more aggressive, self-determining female is analysed in the fiend-like character of Clementina, whose assumption of independence becomes the excuse for a career of predatory wickedness. By constructing this range of possibilities, and recognising, although in a compromised way, the narrowness of the authorised models, Haywood was partly disseminating and partly contesting the ideology of law. As Mary Anne Schofield puts it, Haywood's novels 'register quite directly the social and moral tensions of her age – tensions generated by the collision of male supremacy and female idolatry with a barely emerging yet subversive sense of women possessing a special kind of selfhood'.[50]

These female writers used the conventional image of the seduced maiden to create a climate of confusion around the carefully-defined legal identity of women. Further confusions, with the strength of dissidence behind them, can be detected in Defoe's two extended narratives with female protagonists, *Moll Flanders* (1722) and *Roxana* (1724). I have already mentioned Defoe's engagement with women's issues in his pamphlets and conduct books, and his occasionally involuntary involvement with the law throughout his career is well known. In much of his fiction, too, the problematic legal status of women is a prominent feature. In *Colonel Jacque* (1722), for instance, there are suggested parallels between the positions of wives and slaves on a plantation in Virginia. Even in *Robinson Crusoe* (1719), a novel not distinguished by its fastidious concern with women's lives, the brief sketch of the narrator's mother at the beginning implies much about the patriarchal system which the whole book is agitated about. In the sequel, *The Farther Adventures of Robinson Crusoe* (1720), there are extensive discussions of marriage and connubiality as the old Crusoe tries to establish a working community on his island. A particular kind of female criminal attracted Defoe's attention in *A History of the Pyrates* (1724), with his discussion of the spectacular careers of Mary Read and Ann Bonney. But it is in *Moll Flanders* and *Roxana* that the legal status of women is most sharply debated. These long narratives are both tales of criminal women: Moll is at different times a thief and a whore; Roxana is also a whore, albeit a high-class one, and (at the least) an accomplice to the murder of her daughter. The thieving and murder have already been discussed at length elsewhere. However, there are very interesting differences of emphasis between these two tales in their discussion of women and sexuality, and in neither case are we given any unmediated version of the legal perspective.

Much has now been written about both books, and I have no wish to reiterate points made elsewhere.[51] However, it is worth comparing the two narratives in this particular context, to see how they interrogate female identity, and offer a critique of the law while so doing. In *Moll*, for instance, Defoe starts from the tale of the seduced maiden, and, like Haywood, he shows the possibilities of resilience. When Moll is seduced by the young man of the family she works for, the potentially catastrophic loss of innocence is made relatively insignificant by Moll's laconic acceptance of change. At the point of seduction, Moll articulates the familiar lament:

> putting the Purse into my Bosom, I made no more Resistance to him, but let him do just what he pleas'd; and as often as he pleas'd; and thus I finish'd my own Destruction at once, for from this Day, being forsaken of my Vertue, and my Modesty, I had nothing of Value left to recommend me, either to God's Blessing, or Man's Assistance.[52]

Although Moll says these powerful words at the appropriate moment, her subsequent behaviour is very different. Acknowledging the 'fallen maiden' style, she goes on to refute it by rebuilding independent identities for herself time and again throughout her narrative. Her virtue, even at this stage, she sees as a 'Trifle' (p. 25), not worth fighting for. Indeed, instead of falling into a decline once she is forsaken, she marries her seducer's brother, and seems to live quite comfortably with him until he dies. She is able to do this because of her awareness of the unappealing alternative, brought home to her by her first lover:

> Thus he wrought me up, in short, to a kind of Hesitation in the matter; having the Dangers on one Side represented in lively Figures, and indeed heighten'd by my Imagination of being turn'd out to the wide World, a meer cast off Whore, *for it was no less*, and perhaps expos'd as such; with little to provide for myself; with no Friend, no Acquaintance in the whole World, *out of that Town*, and there I could not pretend to Stay; all this terrify'd me to the last Degree.
>
> (p. 56)

The stark legal dichotomy between respectable wife and despicable whore is acknowledged here, but Moll always seems to find a way of negotiating the tensions it creates and surviving as comfortably as possible in the grey area between the categories.

Although she lives outside the law most of the time, Moll does not lapse into a life of thorough-going prostitution, celebrating the possibilities of female power, as the figures in *The Whore's Rhetorick* do. For one thing, as has often been noticed, her narrative is disappointingly inexplicit for anyone seeking the pleasures of detailed pornography. When she talks of her sexual encounters, she does so cursorily, with a brisk and unfussy embarrassment, as though the details are not worth the reader's attention: 'as for the Bed, &c. I was not much concern'd about that Part' (p. 225). Moll persistently avoids the cynical and assertive frankness of pornography, just as she avoids the passivity and self-pity of the conventional fallen maiden. As a result, some of her erotic dealings get surrounded by monstrous big equivocations and self-deceptions, but they do offer an account of prostitution which is frank and woman-centred, yet not especially prurient. Indeed, in comparison with her relatively sympathetic treatment of the pressures upon women, Moll's portrait of male whoremongers is scathing and accusatory in the extreme:

> WOULD such Gentlemen but consider the contemptible Thoughts which the very Women they are concern'd with, in such Cases as these, have of them, it wou'd be a surfeit to them: As I said above, they value not the Pleasure, they are rais'd by no Inclination to the Man, the passive Jade thinks of no Pleasure but the Money; and when he is as it were drunk in the Extasies of his wicked Pleasure, her Hands are in his Pockets searching for what she can find there; and of which he can be no more sensible in the Moment of his Folly, than he can fore-think of it when he goes about it.
>
> (pp. 227–8)

Moll is particularly eager to distance herself as much as possible from these 'passive Jades', and makes it seem as though the exploit which has prompted this reflection is unrepresentative and reluctant. However, what the whole narrative cumulatively does is complicate and confuse the sexual economy Moll inhabits. At times, it is seen as fundamentally exploitive of women, who have little legal protection in the face of sustained male aggressiveness and confidence. At others, it is a more complex game in which a few self-confident women may hold secret compensatory powers. As in the Hogarth series, these different perceptions are never fully reconciled or disciplined in the book, and Moll's eventual status as wife and mother, apparently returned to a comfortable legal existence once more, shows at least the possibilities of living the contradictions successfully.

A much more sombre presentation of the legal status of women appears throughout Defoe's later novel, *Roxana*. Whereas Moll's early connections with Newgate surround her with images of criminality from the very beginning, Roxana's privileged background has set her up for the life of a leisured gentlewoman:

> I was (*speaking of myself as about Fourteen Years of Age*) tall, and very well made; sharp as a Hawk in Matters of common Knowledge; quick and smart in Discourse; apt to be Satyrical; full of Repartee, and a little too forward in Conversation; or, as we call it in *English*, BOLD, tho' perfectly Modest in my Behaviour. Being *French* Born, I danc'd, *as some say*, naturally, lov'd it extremely, and sung well also, and so well, that, *as you shall hear*, it was Afterwards some Advantage to me: With all these Things, I wanted neither Wit, Beauty, or Money. In this Manner I set out into the World, having all the Advantages that any Young Woman cou'd desire, to recommend me to others, and form a Prospect of happy Living to myself.[53]

Despite this assembly of qualifications, Roxana is led into poverty and despair by the incompetence and desertion of her 'Thing call'd a Husband' (p. 7). Once she has been left impoverished, there seems to be no legally-recognised, acceptable way for her to survive unassisted. She cannot re-marry, as she does not know if her first husband is still alive, divorce seems out of the question, and there are no legitimate avenues of trade open to her. At this point in the narrative, she seems similar to the pathetic 'seduced maiden', only further disabled by having been married and encumbered with children.

Defoe then introduces a most interesting complication. Roxana's landlord makes a proposition of pseudo-marriage to Roxana, which she feels unable to accept. As far as she is concerned, any extra-marital liaison could only be described as whoring (as legally it would be), and she is not prepared to entertain the idea seriously, despite the absence of alternatives. Her maid Amy, however, is less fastidious, and, in a reversal of the mistress/maid relationship in *The Whore's Rhetorick* and other instructional dialogues, she successfully disabuses Roxana of her inappropriate idealism – '*Amy* had but too much Rhetorick in this Cause' (p. 39). Roxana eventually and reluctantly sleeps with the landlord, and puts Amy to bed with him as well, thus starting a career of whoring which takes her to the very highest levels of her society. For what she discovers is that the genteel training she has received, allegedly designed to make her the perfect wife, actually makes her the perfect mistress. Working within the authorised categories, Roxana feels that sleeping with the landlord has irretrievably branded her as a whore, and she feels that if that is indeed what she is, she ought to make the most of it.

Although the narrative is primarily an investigation of one woman's life, it also becomes a social anatomy, and the conclusion it offers about the world Roxana inhabits is a thoroughly bleak one. It is seen as a world where there are no fully successful marriages, where Roxana's lovers feel unembarrassed about ignoring their wives, and where the most successful path for a woman to pursue seems to be the career of the accomplished courtesan. Having seen the standard behaviour of husbands, Roxana remains 'obstinate against Matrimony' (p. 159), and defends the economic prowess of whoring over the subordinated position of wives. In discussion with Sir Robert Clayton (like the characters in Hogarth, a well-known public figure), Roxana analyses the conventions of marriage:

> I told him, I knew no State of Matrimony, but what was, at best, a State of Inferiority, if not of Bondage; that I had no notion of it; that I liv'd a Life of absolute Liberty now; was free as I was born, and having a plentiful Fortune, I did not understand what Coherence the Words *Honour* and *Obey* had with the Liberty of a *Free Woman*; that I knew no Reason the Men had to engross the whole Liberty of the Race, and make the women, notwithstanding any desparity of Fortune, be subject to the Laws of Marriage, of their own making; that it was my Misfortune to be a Woman, but I was resolv'd it should not be made worse by the Sex; and seeing Liberty seem'd to be the Men's Property, I wou'd be a *Man-Woman*; for as I was born free, I wou'd die so.
>
> (pp. 170–1)

Clayton is amused by this 'Amazonian' outburst, and suggests that very few women could live successfully by these principles – 'they wanted Resolution to go on with it' (p. 171). But what Defoe created in Roxana was a female figure who was capable of just this necessary resolution, and who suffered tragically as a result.

Defoe's narrative includes no persuasive counter-arguments to Roxana's words, and it seems as though her career is the most fulfilling one for any woman of spirit and resolve. However, her efforts are compromised by the vestiges of her brief marriage, when a daughter turns up and threatens to expose her. The ending of the book is unclear, but it looks as though Amy murders this daughter, and she and Roxana are left living miserably under the 'Blast of Heaven' (p. 330). The whole book then becomes a startlingly sombre account of the legal constraints on women, and the difficulties of living successfully outside them. Roxana's continual quest for an identity is defiant and painful to watch, leaving her caught between the contradictions that Moll Flanders can blithely surmount. Defoe's point seems to be that the legal circumscription of women was impractical and potentially destructive, both in its overt operations and in the way it made women internalise certain very restricted images of themselves. Though it is clear by the end of the book that Roxana has turned into some kind of monster, Defoe does not give us the stability of detesting her for it. The social anatomy of the book has been too disconcerting to let us see Roxana's grim fate as an idiosyncratic example of due punishment.

In contrast to the darkness of *Roxana*, it is suggestive to place the much jauntier success story of John Cleland's *Memoirs of a Woman of Pleasure*

(1748/9). Fanny Hill, Cleland's heroine, achieves a life of security and happiness at the age of 19 after a four-year period as a prostitute in a well-patronised brothel. As opposed to Richardson's Pamela, Fanny gets her reward after giving in to almost anyone who will pay for her, and the narrative may well belong alongside *Shamela* and some later novels by Eliza Haywood as part of the anti-Pamela vogue of the 1740s.[54] However, as it stands it is a pornographic exposé of sexual foibles and practices of all kinds, as meticulously delineated as anything in Grose's dictionary, designed to titillate or entertain a male audience rather than to disturb or disconcert them. As an attempt to engage imaginatively with the problems of the woman who lives outside the law, it is curiously compromised by its mixture of frankness and stylisation, and by Cleland's failure to entertain the full implications of his subject. Although the narrative offers an alternative formulation of female possibility, giving more room to women's sexuality than the law openly acknowledged, it remains fundamentally exploitive of its women. Like the court reports of 'criminal conversation' later in the century, Cleland's book simply appropriates the notion of the sexually-alive woman for the purposes of male titillation.[55]

Amidst the carnival of sexual congresses the book delights in mentioning, it insinuates a moral homily about Fanny's surprising emotional fidelity to her Charles, and the rewards of a certain kind of constancy. The powerful male, that is, still retains the power over his lover, who is true to him in her fashion. By the end of her tale, Fanny is surprisingly eager to cleanse herself of the taint of corruption:

> in the bosom of virtue, I gather'd the only uncorrupt sweets: where, looking back on the course of vice, I had run, and comparing its infamous blandishments with the infinitely superior joys of innocence, I could not help pitying, even in point of taste, those who, immers'd in a gross sensuality, are insensible to the so delicate charms of VIRTUE, than which even PLEASURE has not a greater friend, nor than VICE a greater enemy.
>
> (p. 187)

What Cleland's narrative suggests, then, is that there are benign and malign prostitutes, that sexual pleasure comes in all sorts of forms, that women entertain desire just as much as men, but that eventually a mutually loving relationship within the legally-prescribed limits of matrimony is the most satisfying way to live. The book thus becomes an orthodox love story, with a great deal of graphically-described sex in it. There is little sense of suffering or duress in the lives of the whores, and instead we see a series of cheerful couplings (and triplings) with only rare appearances of the notion of exploitation. All the whores in Mrs Cole's sexual emporium end up in comfortably stable relationships, and no one seems to be punished or to suffer unduly. It is true that Fanny has periods when things do not go well, but eventually romantic love triumphs, and the novel is only disquieting for the contemporary reader in the way it reveals the sophisticated organisation of the underworld. Despite the book's pornographic reputation, it does not protest loudly about the sexual or economic exploitation of women, or of men. In fact, it seems happy enough with the world as it is, since the laws interfering with sexuality are made to seem marginal and ineffective.

All these various depictions of whores are thus ways of investigating the law, and exploring the plausibility of the available roles for women it disseminated. The harlots in these extended narratives display a great range of emotions and adopt various attitudes, from the martyrdom of the seduced maiden to Roxana's resolution to Fanny Hill's cheerfulness. All these various possibilities, compiled and problematised in Hogarth's engravings, show little respect for the law, and, deliberately or not, serve to undermine its authority as the socially-privileged body of commentary on human affairs. The efforts by artists and readers to engage imaginatively with these extra-legal women inevitably lead to a protest against the unsubtle legal characterisation, and the whole chorus of commentary in the narratives shows an attempt to disrupt the complacency and confidence of the statute by infiltrating into the public domain a whole battery of contending images.

4 Satire's rough music

THE GRAMMAR OF PUNISHMENT

> Lay then the axe to the root, and teach governments humanity. It is
> their sanguinary punishments which corrupt mankind.[1]

One informative way of investigating the priorities, the internal tensions
and the hidden politics of any culture is to look at its grammar of
punishment, to anatomise what offences it recognises and punishes, how
it punishes them, the ways it attempts to justify punishment, the
legitimising philosophies with which it surrounds punishment, and the
complex rules governing who is allowed to punish whom. Such an
exploration can produce insights which are significant for the historian,
the political theorist, the legalist and the anthropologist. As an integral
part of the exploration of literature and crime, I want to argue in this
chapter that certain features of the grammar of punishment in Augustan
England, as well as being worth exploring for their own sake, can be of
service to the literary historian and critic by offering a context and
repository of meanings in which the singular attractiveness of satire for so
many oppositional writers of the day makes sense.

Investigating Augustan England through this perspective can confirm
the ideological and practical centrality of punishment as the approved
societal response to behaviour classified as immoral and more specifically
as 'criminal'. Official penal policy and practice thus assume a very
important place in the legitimising ideology of the state and in the day-to-
day lives of its subjects. However, such an enquiry can also reveal an
important change in procedures at this time, namely the state's gradual
abrogation of a number of time-honoured alternative forensic tribunals
throughout the period, and its replacement of them with its own
elaborately stylised and ritualised courtroom trial.

Throughout the seventeenth century and before, it is possible to detect
a range of very diverse punitive practices in Britain, with punishments
being legitimately meted out by individuals, institutions, community
groups and the locally powerful church courts, which had enormous
parochial authority in punishing moral offences like fornication or

drunkenness. At the same time, the established legal authorities retained the right to intervene in the most serious cases and administer the most severe sanctions. In all of these cultural practices, formal and informal, the law-breaker or offender was seen as someone for whom punishment of some kind was quite uncontroversially appropriate, and should the malefactor be subsequently reformed or rehabilitated, even if only in the next life, then so much the better.

The supporting ideologies for such practices articulate a very complex and nuanced assembly of ideas about religion, death, sin, hell, divine punishment, the need to make examples of miscreants and the need to make the state more awesome. On looking through the Augustan period, however, it becomes clear that these heterogeneous activities were gradually being centralised and standardised, and that the polyphony of social punishments was slowly being replaced by the virtually exclusive arbitration of the rule of law and its accredited agents. The legal trial itself became more clearly regulated, with the increasing prominence of lawyers in the courtroom, the professionalisation of legal advisers, the introduction of 'expert' witnesses like the doctor who gave evidence about the defendant's state of mind in the trial of Lord Ferrars in 1760, and the more elaborate extensions of established forensic procedures and protocols. Even by the end of the period, the official legal trial may still have had rivals, and may not have been the only forum in which punishment could be conferred, but it had become much more central and authoritative than previously.

The state, as it was assembled in post-revolution Augustan England, became increasingly assertive and intrusive in the legal circumscription of its subjects' lives, while simultaneously preaching a more *laissez-faire* attitude in most other spheres. One forceful way in which it established its authority and power was by its seizure of the sole claim to enforce its laws by legitimised violence, outlawing or stigmatising previously acceptable practices like revenge or duelling or other informal community or personal reprisals, while retaining for its own purposes much of the fire-and-brimstone sin-based rhetoric of the church courts. The arm of the state might not always be blatant in the enforcement of justice, and older patterns still persisted vestigially in various forms, but as the period unfolded, the centralised agency of law became much more confident. As J. A. Sharpe puts it, in the Augustan period 'we see the replacement of the local justice of the manor by a justice which, however flexible in relation to specific local circumstances, was essentially that of the gentry and, at one or two removes, of the state'.[2] In the courtroom, of course, the odd recalcitrant or obstructive jury could still interfere with the smooth process of gentrified command, by failing to come up with the directed verdict. Magistrates and judges, too, might give eccentric and idiosyncratic directions, or might simply misunderstand the statute. However, for defendants found guilty, there was only one response. Both before and after this demonstrable shift in legislative power, the notion of the appropriateness of punishment remained constant, ideologically central to the discussion of offences and offenders, and, by taking upon itself the exclusive authority to regulate and administer retribution, the state was stealthily reinforcing its own powers and enhancing its own authority.

At the beginning of the period, the unprivileged Briton was subject to punishment by various bodies, in various forms, and for various offences, throughout his or her life. Within the prevailing hierarchical understanding of society, members of the community held responsibility for the discipline of those below them, and they could quite legally inflict punishments of some severity on virtually anyone in their power. As we shall see, not only could the state punish those it identified as criminals, landlords could also evict miscreant tenants, employers could dismiss unsatisfactory apprentices and servants, husbands could beat or disinherit their offspring, or even have their wives committed to asylums, and, notoriously, schoolmasters could violently chastise ill-behaved or recalcitrant pupils. These rights were not, it almost goes without saying, reciprocal. Although there was a great deal of discussion of the most effective measures of punishment for particular offences, and although the whole pattern of official punitive policy began to change towards the end of the seventeenth century with the development of transportation and incarceration, there was still very little obvious or articulated doubt that punishment of some kind was the proper legal and societal response to misbehaviour.

When we come to the more forceful arguments for the reformation of the penal system later in the century, we can see that they are given inflections unheard in Augustan England. Jeremy Bentham's rousing claim that 'all punishment is mischief: all punishment in itself is evil', like the vociferous quotation from Thomas Paine with which this chapter begins, would have been incomprehensible and dangerously radical to earlier eighteenth-century authorities.[3] Although all the terms in Bentham's argument were conventional religious ones, and although the equation of punishment and evil could be found in a number of contemporary theological sources, such reforming zeal would have seemed very incongruous in the first half of the century. Similarly, the calls of the later reformers for what they saw as more humane and enlightened treatment of offenders would have seemed misguided and sentimentally soft-hearted to the hangers and floggers of the earlier period. Indeed, the move for penal reform instigated by Eden and Romilly and the others, charted so carefully by Sir Leon Radzinowicz, can be seen as an attempt to displace the ideological and practical centrality of punishment and retributive justice, and to introduce in their place some greater concern for the socially useful rehabilitation of the offender.

However, while it is possible to see the reformers as instigating a decisive and transforming break with precedent, it is just as interesting to see them as maintaining and developing the state's right to punish, albeit presented as the right to impose punishments which have more utilitarian justification. The societal response to crime was still to be fundamentally a punitive one, as indeed it still predominantly is. The reasons why criminals should be punished might change, and different punishments might be inflicted on them, but the validity of punishment itself remained secure. What many accounts of this progressivist reforming spirit overlook, however, is that the earlier practices of punishment which the reformers were arguing against were not simply atavistic reflexes, supported by inexplicable primitive superstitions. They were, instead, carefully established and defended positions, which were elaborately formulated and were seen to have a purpose. When the reformers were most effective, it was not when they argued that the law's severity was immoral, but when, following thinkers as diverse as Fielding and Beccaria, they demonstrated that it was not working very well.[4]

Although the Augustan state's reliance on the severe punishment of relatively minor offences through the 'Bloody Code' may now appear to be a flagrant attempt to retain and secure the power of the governing bodies and the social hierarchy by a legalised reign of terror, that was not how it was presented at the time. Instead, it was ideologically supported by the prevailing and biblically-sanctioned idea of human degeneracy and corruptibility. No-one with access to print seems to have doubted that punishment was a form of social control, but it was universally thought to be an essential form of control, a bastion against lawlessness and anarchy, correcting what was thought to be the inevitable human capacity for evil and destructiveness.[5] Indeed, as we have seen, while there were a few who protested loudly about the severity of the law, there were more voices raised in support of increased punishments for particularly awful crimes, like the aggravated forms of the death penalty employed elsewhere in contemporary Europe. And even those who proposed reforms during this period, like Mandeville or the Fieldings, still looked primarily for alternative punishments rather than for alternatives to punishment. Although the degree of authorised cruelty involved and the seemingly trivial nature of the offences so harshly punished were regularly contested in Augustan England, and made even Blackstone uneasy, very few commentators expressed scepticism about the validity of the notion of punishment itself.

The ideological basis of this widespread belief in making offenders suffer was a profound pessimism about human possibilities on earth, involving a refusal to take seriously the nascent Romantic ideas of progress or human perfectibility. Man would not be deterred from his post-lapsarian wicked ways by the prospect of distant rewards, or by having things carefully explained to him. Only the certain prospect of suffering or privation would dissuade him from evil or make him repent, and prepare him for the higher justice of heaven. In acting punitively, the punishers argued, the state was acting in the interests of society, protecting it from the baser instincts of its constituents, and thereby taking over and making even more awesome what had previously been seen as the church's power to censure. In this appropriation of the right to punish, the agents of the state were supported by the press's dissemination of the arguments of a surprisingly diverse range of divines, projectors and political theorists, who often agreed on little other than the social importance of punishment, and the need for it to be administered primarily by the state.

There was, of course, ample Old Testament support for the probity of punishing, from Cain onwards, although the biblical precedents suggest that the meting out of retributive justice and the administration of *lex talionis* should be primarily God's prerogative rather than man's. A civil or political authority wishing to justify its penal system on biblical or religious grounds must thus present itself as the earthly arm of the Lord, working in the service of divine justice, and the British state did not (and does not) feel embarrassed about so doing. And indeed in most of the recoverable arguments supporting punishment offered by magistrates, judges and ministers of religion, as Randall McGowan and John Addy have recently shown, there are undiscriminated traces of both temporal and spiritual rhetoric. Many Augustan commentators, including Locke and Blackstone, sanctioned the power of the temporal courts by emphasising the divine command in Genesis ix. 6, 'Whoso sheddeth man's blood, by man shall his blood be shed: for in the image of God made he man.' However, this ecclesiastical system of justification rarely stood alone and it was more often reinforced by the more intellectually elaborate defences of punishment created within the more secular bodies of philosophical commentary, in which the state's right to punish was assured by the implicit terms of the social contract undertaken between it and its citizens, and by the demonstrable utilitarian benefits to be derived from identifying and stigmatising criminality.

One of the most radical, but most powerful and influential defences of punishment and the state's role in administering it appeared in Thomas Hobbes's *Leviathan* (1651), a pre-Augustan text which remained the focus of much debate throughout the later period, as the many casual references to it in Swift's *Tale of a Tub* (1704), Mandeville's *Modest Defense of Publick Stews* (1724) and elsewhere suggest. Hobbes's unique combination of scepticism and conservatism clearly retained the power to arrest attention and shock Augustan readers in a way that the more sober contemporary counter-arguments by Robert Filmer and James Harrington did not. In Hobbes's account of the behaviour of a commonwealth, punishment was understood primarily in the context of the operations of the established state, which held sole authority to chastise its constituent members:

> A punishment, is an evil inflicted by public authority, on him that hath done, or omitted that which is judged by the same authority to be a transgression of the law; to the end that the will of men may thereby be disposed to obedience.

In this formulation, all the power of identifying crimes and punishing them is given to the 'public authority', and the function of punishment is to make submission to that authority more attractive, to demonstrate the expediency of passive obedience. That is to say, the commonwealth alone holds the power to decide what is right and wrong, as well as who is guilty or innocent, as well as what penalties to exact for specific offences. All anti-social or subversive behaviour becomes wrong in the eyes of the law, and the judicial public authority simply cannot make mistakes – whatever it does, is by definition right. Its laws are expressed as commands, and these commands have to be obeyed for the state to fulfil its purpose. For Hobbes, guilt or innocence thus seem to be socially-constructed categories rather than inherent qualities, whose limits are to be determined by the public authority alone. The consciences of individual members of the community, the right to resist, or any abstract notions of justice, simply do not figure in the whole enterprise.

However, Hobbes does not leave the matter there. In a piece of rather unconvincing equivocation he invokes supererogatory 'laws of nature' to get round some of the problems his formulation creates and to reintroduce some consideration of the rights of the innocent:

> All punishments of innocent subjects, be they great or little, are against the law of nature: for punishment is only for transgression of the law, and therefore there can be no punishment of the innocent. It is therefore a violation, first, of that law of nature, which forbiddeth all men, in their revenges, to look at anything but some future good: for there can arrive no good to the commonwealth, by punishing the innocent. Secondly, of that, which forbiddeth ingratitude: for seeing all sovereign power, is originally given by the consent of every one of the subjects, to the end they should, as long as they are obedient, be protected thereby; the punishment of the innocent, is a rendering of evil for good. And thirdly, of the law that commandeth equity: that is to say, an equal distribution of justice; which in punishing the innocent is not observed.[6]

In Hobbes's account, the state's authority to punish is derived eventually from an individual's right of reprisal in the state of nature, and from the individual's duty to honour the terms of the contract with authority. In a commonwealth, of course, the prevailing definition of what is harmful must be radically different from that in the 'state of nature', and, given the basic terms of reference of his argument, Hobbes has problems in finding effective ways to reintroduce considerations of equity or justice, to convince us that personal reprisal is fundamentally no different from the imposition of penalties by a superior body on its inferiors or persuade us that the state can only act in the best interests of its citizens.

Hobbes's deterministic and materialist account of human behaviour, where individuals can only act in their own interest, heedless of altruistic considerations, also sits oddly with his deterrence argument, where citizens must have the liberty to respond sensibly to the established system of penalties and rewards, to weigh up the consequences of particular decisions and deliberately choose approved courses of action. The account of punishment offered simply seems to leave no room for impartial considerations of justice, and Hobbes tried to effect a compromise between these contending emphases in *Of Liberty and Necessity* (1654), once again reinforcing the absolute authority of the legislative power:

> But you will say, how is it just to kill one man to amend another, if what were done were *necessary*? To this I answer, that men are justly killed, not for that their actions are not *necessitated*, but because they are *noxious*; and they are spared and preserved whose actions are not noxious . . . Men are not therefore put to death, or punished, for that their theft proceedeth from *election*, but because it was *noxious*, and contrary to men's preservation, and the punishment conducing to the preservation of the rest, in as much as to punish those that do voluntary hurt, and none else, frameth and maketh men's wills such as men would have them.[7]

The function of punishment is thus to deter others from behaving noxiously, by framing their wills in desirable ways, and at the same time to maintain the cohesiveness of the commonwealth. In this curious mixture of proto-utilitarian and retributivist theories, it is the state's sole prerogative to conduct such an apparently educational and therapeutic programme, and only the state can define the degree of 'noxiousness' in patterns of behaviour. With due concern for the enlightened self-interest of its subjects, the power of the state is thus greatly magnified and enhanced, and its exclusive authority to punish is assured. The individual citizen, of course, has no right of resistance or avenue for dissent, and is required to acknowledge the state's absolute authority to punish offenders in whatever ways it thinks fit, for whatever offences it might deem 'noxious'.[8]

Hobbes's argument thus clearly displays some of the tensions between the state's right to punish and the citizen's right to be protected. A similar endorsement of the state's prime right to identify offenders and to punish them can be found in John Locke's *Two Treatises of Government* (1690).

As part of Locke's great enterprise to legitimise the ideology of property, he confirms the state as the exclusive agent of punishment in political society, abrogating the more individualist and interpersonal retributions of the 'state of nature'. Throughout his argument, Locke seeks to demonstrate the felicity of surrendering the individual right of reprisal to the central agency of power, and he is much more loquacious on the justifiability of the state's power than on the definition of its limits. Like Blackstone, who is in many ways his most devoted follower, Locke gives the centralised authority the power to protect property and to manage its distribution, without in any way requiring it to rectify existing injustices. The law's main function is thus to protect the rights of the propertied from the depredations of the propertyless, and the main tool it uses in this project is punishment.

Although a very firm advocate of the rule of law, Locke is like so many Augustan commentators generally unsympathetic to the accompanying apparatus of lawyers, over-subtle interpreters of the law, and the labyrinthine intricacies of statute, and he is eager to see the uncluttered 'Law of Nature' as the foundation of the necessarily more elaborate penal code of civil society. As concerns the right to administer punishment, the Law of Nature is unambiguous:

> For in the State of Nature, to omit the liberty he has of innocent Delights, a man has two Powers.
>
> The first is to do whatsoever he thinks fit for the preservation of himself and others within the permission of the *Law of Nature*: by which Law common to them all, he and all the rest of *Mankind are one Community*, make up one Society distinct from all other Creatures. And were it not for the corruption, and vitiousness of degenerate Men, there would be no need of any other; no necessity that Men should separate from this great and natural Community, and by positive agreements combine into smaller and divided associations.
>
> The other Power a Man has in the State of Nature, is the *power to punish the Crimes* committed against that Law. Both these he gives up, when he joyns in a private, if I may so call it, or particular Political Society, and incorporates into any Commonwealth, separate from the rest of Mankind.[9]

The central principle in any political society is thus the legislature (or the judiciary), which, by articulating a comprehensible and consistent set of standing laws, acts to preserve the liberty and property of its honest citizens. Individual constituents thus voluntarily surrender their retributive powers, or transfer them to the legislature, in return for the promise that the governing body will carry out the general will dependably and consistently and advance the general benefit by prosecuting and punishing only the 'vitiousness of degenerate Men'.

Locke emphasises the exclusiveness of the legislature's authority on a number of occasions, and he is at pains to construct the central judicial body as a model of intelligent discrimination and painstaking fairness, fully protective of the rights of the propertied, much more collective in orientation and accountable to the citizenry than Hobbes's portrait of a despotic sovereignty:

> thus all private judgements of every particular Member being excluded, the Community comes to be Umpire, by settled standing Rules, indifferent, and the same to all Parties; and by Men having Authority from the Community, for the execution of those Rules, decides all the differences that may happen between any Members of that Society, concerning Matters of Right; and punishes those Offences, which any Member hath committed against the Society, with such Penalties as the Law has established . . . And this puts Men *out* of a State of Nature *into* that of a *Commonwealth*, by setting up a Judge on Earth, with Authority to determine the Controversies, and redress the Injuries, that may happen to any Member of the Commonwealth; which Judge is the Legislative, or Magistrates appointed by it.
>
> (§§ 87, 89)

This benign version of legislative and judicial behaviour seems very remote from the 'Bloody Code' as we have seen it in action, or from the severe punitive practices of the Augustan courts. However, as an attempt to legitimise the authority of the propertied class by disseminating the ideology of an impartial justice, Locke's argument was undoubtedly effective. The notion that magistrates were such disinterested arbiters, sanctioned and authorised by the community which they regulated, was a very powerful one, if one that is just as hard for the sceptical modern reader to swallow as it was for some contemporaries. Like Blackstone, and like the influential conservative philosopher Adam Smith in *The Theory of Moral Sentiments* (1759), Locke takes it for granted that there are certain acts which must naturally produce resentment in all impartial citizens, and that these are the ones to be properly punished by the courts. The legislature thus maintains its sole right to fulfil the terms of the social contract by its abilities to punish or stigmatise those deeds which offend the Law of Nature and arouse spontaneous abhorrence in citizens.

The justificatory basis for punishment in Hobbes, Locke, Blackstone and Smith, accepting the important differences of emphasis in each case, lies essentially in the anticipated beneficial social consequences of making wrongdoers suffer. Punishment, administered by a just and consistent authority, has the ability to help protect honest members of the community from the viciousness of their neighbours. State-enforced punishment enacts legitimate official retribution on criminals, encouraging good patterns of behaviour in others, and thereby maintaining the fabric of the commonwealth. The traditional problem with such consequentialist arguments, of course, is that they fail to establish a close connection between punishment and guilt, and that they give no basis for regulating the severity of the official reprisal in specific cases. If punishment is justified by its capacity to encourage others in good habits and discourage them from bad, there is no obvious reason only to punish the guilty, and no good reason to exercise reasonableness or clemency in sentencing. The salutary deterrent effect of a good hanging would be just as strong if the executed character happened to be innocent. Similarly, treating minor offences with the utmost severity should certainly create the appropriate amount of deterrent terror in potential offenders, bringing about the desired law-abiding consequences. Such patterns of thinking helped fuel the demands for increased severity in the implementation of the law, and, despite their declared intentions and their efforts to set acceptable limits on the exercise of power, Locke and the other consequentialists could be used to support calls for a more radically conservative reform of the penal system.

Other arguments in favour of centralised official retaliation in Augustan England relied less on the social utility of the suffering villain than on the offender's own need to be punished. More retributive and less consequentialist treatments of punishment, based, like the dwindling operations of the church courts, on the notion of 'sin', were given by many more orthodox religious thinkers. The eminent theologian Bishop Joseph Butler, for instance, in his widely-read *Dissertation of the Nature of Virtue* (1736), published as an appendix to his *Fifteen Sermons*, found the justificatory basis for punishment in the 'ill-desert' of the offender:

> every one speaks of such and such actions as deserving punishment; and it is not, I suppose, pretended that they have absolutely no meaning at all to the expression. Now the meaning plainly is not, that we conceive it for the good of society, that the doer of such actions should be made to suffer. For if unhappily it were resolved, that a man who, by some innocent action, was infested with the plague, should be left to perish, lest, by other people's coming near him, the infection should spread: no one would say, he deserved this treatment . . . The sight of a man in misery raises our compassion towards him; and, if this misery be inflicted on him by another, our indignation against the author of it. But when we are informed, that the sufferer is a villain, and is punished only for his treachery or cruelty; our compassion exceedingly lessens, and, in many instances, our indignation wholly subsides. Now what produces this effect, is the conception of that in the sufferer, which we call ill-desert. Upon considering then, or viewing together, our notion of vice and that of misery, there results a third, that of ill-desert. And thus there is in human creatures an association of the two ideas, natural and moral evil, wickedness and punishment. If

this association were merely artificial or accidental, it were nothing: but being most unquestionably natural, it greatly concerns us to attend to it, instead of endeavouring to explain it away.[10]

Although the argument in this passage is not entirely clear, Butler's basic proposition seems to be that our ideas of good and evil are 'natural' to us, and it is thus intrinsically right that wrongdoers, and only wrongdoers, should be made to suffer. By experiencing earthly justice, the offender is made ready for God's judgement, and observers are likewise reassured, chastened and prepared.

There is obviously some common ground here with the contemporary 'moral sense' arguments of the philosophers Francis Hutcheson and John Balguy and others, although Butler would certainly not have accepted the utilitarian and pragmatic drift of Hutcheson's proposals on punishment in his *System of Moral Philosophy* (1746). Also, Butler's apparent belief in the possibilities of effective innate moral perceptiveness is significantly different from the Hobbesian emphasis on man's natural self-interest. The bishop's justification of temporal institutions of punishment relies on the requirement that vice be treated, on earth as it is in heaven, with the proper collective disapproval. Temporal justice is thus seen by the theologian as analogous to the superior justice of the Lord. The fundamental point is that villains and miscreants are to be justly punished, not because others will benefit thereby (although Butler does not deny that they may), but more simply because these people deserve it and because it is demonstrably in keeping with the will of God that the wicked should be made to suffer.

The notion of innate ideas of justice, existing independently of the considerations of any subsequent social utility, appears in a number of other religiously-oriented commentaries obliquely concerned with punishment. Although these were motivated by a number of different considerations, they often explicitly argue against the secularised theories of social contract, and against the 'benevolist' tradition typified by the work of Lord Shaftesbury. To take just one example, in Richard Price's *Review of the Principal Questions and Difficulties in Morals* (1758), a much more retributivist critique of the alleged utility of punishment is offered:

'Shall it still be urged that, in cases of this kind, our disapprobation is owing to the idea of a plan or system of common utility established by custom in the mind with which these vices are apprehended to be inconsistent; or to a habit acquired of considering them as of general pernicious tendency, by which we are insensibly influenced, whenever, in any particular circumstances or instances, we contemplate them?' – But why must we have recourse to the influence of habits and associations in this case? This has been the refuge of those, who would resolve all our moral perceptions into views of private advantage, and may serve to evade almost any evidence which can be derived from the experience we have of the workings of our minds and the motives of our actions. In the cases which have been mentioned, we may remove entirely the idea of a public, and suppose no persons existing whose state they can at all influence; or, we may suppose all memory of the action to be for ever lost as soon as done, and the agent to foresee this; and yet, the same ideas of the ingratitude, injustice, or violation of truth will remain.[11]

Price's argument is not strictly concerned with the state's right to punish wrongdoers, but it has an important bearing upon that practice. His Kantian reliance on the moral force of a priori imperatives broadens the responsibility for punishment, making it everyone's duty, not just the state's, and Price offers the citizen more redress, greater possibilities of properly resisting the encroachments of an unjust state. In this respect, Price gives a summary of the earlier retributivist arguments, while anticipating the growing liberal tendencies of the 1770s and beyond, and he creates the possibility of the individual conscience rather than the official legislature being the forum in which the rightness of punishment is best considered.

It seems, then, as though amidst this very diverse discussion of the justificatory basis of the law in society there was little contestation of the fundamental idea of punishment. Also, until the development of the more elaborate Kantian arguments about conscience later in the century, there was little articulated doubt that the state was most often the proper agent of official retribution on offenders. As we shall see, the notion of conscience did infiltrate the writing of Shaftesbury, Fielding and others, but it seems to have had little place in the more influential discussions of state punishment. The various justifications of punitive practice which contended for supremacy were mixed versions of utilitarian and retributive theories, and there was much prolonged debate about what kinds of punishment were most appropriate, frequently ending with cries for increased severity. The debate was at times abstract and philosophical, but it had immediate practical relevance for the treatment of felons and the behaviour of the courts. For instance, at the beginning of the Augustan period, many convicted offenders were discharged through being able to claim benefit of clergy (a basic test of literacy), arousing the feeling that they were escaping due punishment. As a result, there was an urgent and highly-charged argument about the need to establish and justify some new kinds of punishment to ensure that justice be more reliably and consistently seen to be done, and this topical argument expressed itself through the language made available in sermons and the philosophical traditions mentioned above. The stimulus to debate was certainly a material change in policy, but the rhetoric in which it was articulated was philosophical or religious.

Penal policy was thus changing throughout the Augustan period, but changing in response to less easily detectable forces than the patterns of philosophical debate. Changes in penal practice were not really created by legalists or political theorists, but by long-term shifts in material and economic circumstances, dramatised by particular legislative moments. With the introduction of transportation in the 1660s, for example, magistrates were given greater powers of discretion in sentencing, and, even if they were not unduly concerned by the philosophical arguments surrounding the practice, they were able thereby to exact more severe and, as they thought, more appropriate punishments on those brought before them. But although the power of the authorised courts was being enhanced at this time, these courts still had to contend with other tribunals and agents of punishment, both formal and informal, all of which were surrounded by supportive and critical commentary. The state may have gradually and persistently taken over the role of the authorised punisher from the church and the community, but it never entirely eradicated a number of these other tribunals. The grammar of punishment in Augustan England had to accommodate a number of different voices and tones, and had to express itself through different institutions. Before seeing how literary satire operated as one of these informal or provisional tribunals, it is worth considering the range of other disciplinary structures discussed by contemporary commentators.

SHAME, SHAME, SHAME

As in all cultures, everyday life in Augustan England was conducted according to the rules. But in such a turbulent society, there were many different sets of rules in operation at any given moment, and many conflicting and contending interpretations of them. As a result, individual members of the community recognised overlapping and occasionally conflicting duties, points of contention and fissure which the emergent literature on the stage and in the novel did much to dramatise. According to the state, the dominant and supererogatory set of rules for all citizens was to be found in the statute book, which, in the hands of the officially-appointed wise and impartial judges, was to be the final arbiter in disputes. In theory, if by no means always in practice, everyone in Augustan England, of whatever rank or social status, was equally obliged to comply with the law and equally subject to its penalties. There were, however, other overlapping prescriptive systems which were often at least as important for particular citizens in specific areas of their existence, and the grammar of punishment could be articulated through many different lexicons and given many different inflections. For the more religious, the Holy Bible remained the unquestionable sole authority and source of everyday guidance, superior to the temporal and partisan claims of the state. For others, the recognised principles by which life should be lived were to be found in a number of less formalised or sacred sources, legitimised by local affiliations, tradition or longevity.

Alongside the church and the state, all the manifold institutions of Augustan England subjected their members to elaborate codes of discipline, and articulated more or less complex internal systems of sanction, reward and punishment in their organisation. Sometimes these codes of conduct coincided with the law; on other occasions, they conformed to the spirit of the law, without simply reproducing its expressions; while on a few others, like the frightening codes of the freemasons, they directly contested the authority of the law, and claimed greater legislative power. In some places, these rules were written down and established; in others, they could be understood and disseminated more obliquely, whether by oral transmission or customary practice; and in yet others, they might be so time-honoured as to be internalised. In any case, the various rules governing the day-to-day behaviour of Augustan citizens were open to widely differing interpretations, and the competing claims to exclusive authority might lead to conflict or might be contested by dissidents.

In many areas of Augustan culture, most obviously in the growth of the statute and the development of standards of commercial practice, the established rules of behaviour were visibly mutating in response to great changes in the economic base of eighteenth-century British society. One of the most interesting results of this transition was the way it created the possibility of conflicting allegiances, where different codes of practice would be thought proper by concurrent members of different generations, different denominations or different classes, or even by essentially similar people in the different parts of Britain. These changes in the superstructure of society, as Walter Benjamin argued, always lag some way behind the more fundamental and material economic changes in the base, and it is likely that more traditional codes of practice in domestic and public life exercised a surprisingly persistent hold over many citizens of early eighteenth-century England, despite the drastic underlying economic changes which were introducing the newer patterns.[12]

In the home, in schools, in the armed forces, in clubs, in the professions, in trades, and above all in church, the Augustan individual was acutely conscious of permissions and prohibitions, and of the penalties a breach of these acknowledged rules would bring. Once again, the press carried out both static and dynamic roles in its presentation of the practices of daily life. It helped in the maintenance and consolidation of the existing institutions, by producing conduct books and manuals and advisory pamphlets, and by offering a forum for public discussion of acceptable and unacceptable behaviour. In other ways, of course, the press helped increasingly to introduce and negotiate the emergent changes in codes of practice by its ability to destabilise or demystify these very institutions. In its various forms, literature was able to dramatise and intensify the nascent possibilities of social mobility and the personal consequences of the underlying changes in the economy in both enthusiastic and disparaging or admonitory ways, thereby creating a fascinating repository of highly-charged alternative and contending images of permissible behaviour.

The Augustan press's oscillation between confirming traditional practices and exploring more dynamic and subversive new possibilities can be seen in its complex treatment of the perpetually vexed question of domestic and familial discipline. Within the home, according to the most traditional and conservative versions, discipline was essential and was best maintained patriarchally, with the head of the household (usually the husband and father) having the incontestable right to discipline and, when necessary, chastise all those under his authority, throughout his life. Ideological support for this pattern came primarily from the scriptures, and from the tendentiously patriarchal writings of the seventeenth-century Royalist Robert Filmer and his followers, which still surfaced in various forms at this time. Although largely discredited as a piece of political analysis by the installation of William III in 1688, Filmer's arguments had not entirely disappeared. In 1705, Charles Leslie carried on Filmer's point of view in his periodical, *The Rehearsal*, and the patriarchal justification of political power was cited as a dangerous precedent during Sacheverell's trial in 1710.[13] Although it may have been dwindling in authority as a legitimisation of state and monarchical power, there can be no doubt that the patriarchal model of *domestic* discipline was a major constituent of the ideological fabric of the age. From the evidence of recent social historians, however, it is difficult to gauge the extent to which this backward-looking and reactionary model of family life was still enacted in the eighteenth century (assuming it ever had been faithfully followed at any time), and the extent to which it was understood as a crude antique caricature everyone recognised but virtually no-one tried to put into practice any longer.

Lawrence Stone has argued that although the patriarchal style of household management had been common throughout Britain in the sixteenth and seventeenth centuries, it rapidly fell into disrepute during the eighteenth century. As Stone sees it, the rather grim patriarchal model was being replaced by the growth of a more enlightened 'affective individualism', which allowed for greater and more open emotional expression between members of the household, and which required less reliance on a rigid code of discipline. He establishes this by looking at identifiable material differences in the management and transmission of property within families throughout the period, by isolating a number of expressions of a new view of relative matrimonial duties in conduct books and sermons, and by citing recorded examples of the way parents treated their children at this time. The main ideological support for this change of emphasis, Stone argues, came from the Lockean notion of marriage as a contract in which all parties had rights. To develop his argument, Stone draws on corroborative writing by Mary Astell and Mary Chudleigh on the new status of women, indicates the intense debate about obedience in Sir John Vanburgh's 1691 play *The Provok'd Wife* and similar debates in other works of drama and fiction, and refers to Mandeville's mockery of a tyrannical husband and father in *The Virgin Unmask'd* (1724). He also relies heavily on a little-known conduct book by Bishop Fleetwood, called *Relative Duties of Parents and Children, Husbands and Wives, Masters and Servants* (1716), in which parents' duties to love and care for their children are vociferously advocated.[14]

I have already said enough about the difficulties involved in Stone's habits of argument, amply in evidence here, where contemporary controversialist or tendentious writing is regularly (and often misleadingly) taken as conclusive evidence of actual behaviour or unanimous belief. However, in this particular case, Stone's views seem more persuasive, even if he does rather put his whole strategy in doubt once again by having as one of his key witnesses the egregious self-publicist and rascal John Dunton. In terms of Augustan thinking about discipline and punishment within the family, there is certainly reason to be sceptical about the progressivist tendency within Stone's argument, as there is to remain doubtful of his frightening portrait of loveless seventeenth-century parents. However, what he says in particular about a change in the enforcement of domestic discipline and a decline in the use of brutal corporal punishment of children within the home during the Augustan period may be plausible, and seems to be corroborated by more exhaustive complementary research.

According to the very extensive studies of eighteenth-century diaries and autobiographical writings by Linda A. Pollock, Augustan children were reared within a punitive disciplinary context, and they were indeed beaten, although perhaps irregularly and usually as a punishment for specific offences. In the maintenance of domestic discipline, and as part of the process of socialising their children, Augustan parents seem to have felt that they retained the right to punish their offspring in any way they thought fit, within certain acknowledged limits.[15] In Locke's argument in his 1693 essay on education, parents were encouraged to cajole children into the approved patterns of behaviour, by sensitive combinations of reward and punishment, until the children reached the age of independence in their teens, when parental authority was inevitably curtailed. In most conduct books, too, graded and discriminating punishments are recommended, although the parent's right to punish offspring remains largely unquestioned, and the child's fear of punishment is regularly cited as a valuable part of social training.[16] Even if Augustan parents or guardians did not habitually or indiscriminately beat their children, then, they could still legitimately punish them in various ways, retaining always the most powerful sanction of disinheriting or disowning them.

The extent and the precise limits of parental authority were thus clearly another regularly expressed point of ideological contention, with many recorded uncertainties about the best methods and the precise limits of legitimate domestic punishment. Few Augustan writers endorsed the most extreme patriarchal view, that the head of the household was in the position of absolute monarch over his dependents, but even fewer suggested that parents either had no authority to punish their offspring, or that they should not exercise such power when necessary. If contemporary writing can be seen as at all a reliable guide, eighteenth-century British children enjoyed very few independent rights, and the extensive body of commentary on their upbringing shows that the definition of such rights as they might have was by no means easy or unanimous. In the diverse literature of the Augustan period, incorporating the statute book as well as the private record of the diary and the pedagogic form of the conduct book, these tensions and uncertainties surrounding the proper treatment of children are prominent.

The static, conservative and didactic orientation of many conduct books sits alongside the more dynamic version of human experience in other contemporary literary forms, particularly in the early novel. For instance, to take a well-known example, the various writings of Daniel Defoe offer a vivid illustration of the dialectical tension between Puritan thinking and laissez-faire economics. Defoe's rather staid and fussy formalisation of filial duty and parental responsibility in *The Family Instructor* (1715) and the various 'Andrew Moreton' pamphlets is graphically contradicted by the less respectful attitudes and apparently unchecked irresponsible behaviour of the eponymous hero of *Robinson Crusoe* (1719). Having reached an age beyond the strict control of his family, and being drawn into the more self-assertive world of adulthood, adventure and commerce, Crusoe rejects all family ties, ignores well-meaning parental advice, and, despite even the threat of disinheritance, he drifts off to make his own way in the world. However much Crusoe's father may complain, cajole or command, he has no actual power to prevent Robinson or indeed any of his three sons from making their own decisions and suffering the possible consequences of their own impulsiveness.

Once he has reached a certain age, the youngest Crusoe, like his two elder brothers, is free of the encompassing constraints of domestic discipline, and is handed over, as it were, to the less paternalist and meticulous control of the legal system, his conscience and the vicissitudes of fortune. And, as we should always remember, Crusoe's independence of spirit is scarcely punished within the narrative. Although there are occasions when he sees his subsequent slavery and his imprisonment on the island as punishments for his filial impiety, most of his commercial ventures are remarkably successful, and he ends up much more prosperous than he would have been had he stayed at home. Defoe's narrator seems to represent a particularly tense point of ideological stress, an inconsistent, internally fraught combination of the penitent prodigal son and the boastful self-made man. As far as the present argument goes, Crusoe indicates through his contradictoriness and inconsistency great ideological uncertainties about the various rights and duties of parents and children, as well as deeper uncertainties about the relative merits of subservience and assertiveness.

What these literary examples suggest is not necessarily that the behaviour of parents or children was rapidly changing, but rather that there was an elaborate argument about the possible diversity in the methods of punishment in the home, and a more frequently articulated concern with the limits of parental control and authority. However, although uncertainties about the best procedures of punishment are obvious, it is difficult to find any real disquiet about the parent's established right to punish young children. Selective quotation from Defoe or from any other eighteenth-century controversialist cannot, of course, produce impartial or dependable evidence about how Augustans behaved, as all such writing requires careful interpretation and an awareness of context before it offers up its meanings. To take an obvious example, it would be quite misleading to assess the copious Augustan writing about flagellation as an accurate account of approved domestic or pedagogic practices, when it is so clearly a branch of pornographic fantasy.[17]

However, the existence of an extensive body of commentary, such as that about domestic and institutional discipline, can certainly indicate areas of ideological uncertainty and contention, and the silences in the Augustan press's repertoire might imply areas of untroubled consensus. In the absence of any radical protest about the subject, it is plausible to suggest that, however variously Augustan parents may have acted, they unanimously felt responsible for their children's behaviour, and consequently entitled to punish and discipline them, for the children's own good, up to the age of discretion, which could be variously defined. And the diverse body of commentary, as elsewhere, provided a forum where the limits of permissible strictness could be examined and reassessed, where newer ideas could be articulated, and where emergent shifts in emphasis could be negotiated.

In schools, too, it seems as if the teacher's right to punish pupils remained firmly in place, even if the press regularly agitated about the excessive savagery of particular punitive practices, and sometimes pornographically lingered over them. Indeed, while there are Augustan texts which reaffirm the teacher's right to treat pupils as original sinners and emphasise his duty to try to save their souls by regular bouts of judicious violence, like *The Christian School-Master* (1707) by James

Talbott D.D., there are many more powerful contesting presentations of school-masters as sadists and unenlightened authoritarians. Once again, the novelistic representations of Thwackum and Square in *Tom Jones* or young Rory's tutor in *Roderick Random* provide the most colourful portraits of authoritarian personalities in action. Without seeing these caricatures as anything other than the dramatised and deliberate misrepresentations they undoubtedly are, and without being taken in by pornography, it is still possible to use the press to identify systematic corporal punishment as one of the key components in Augustan educational practice, and as an area where the ideology of punishment was most keenly debated. As Dr Johnson put it in recounting his own schooling to Boswell:

> Mr [the Rev. John] Hunter, the head-master . . . according to his account, 'was very severe, and wrong-headedly severe. He used (said he) to beat us unmercifully; and he did not distinguish between ignorance and negligence; for he would beat a boy equally for not knowing a thing, as for neglecting to know it. He would ask a boy a question; and if he did not answer it, he would beat him, without considering whether he had an opportunity of knowing how to answer it.'

Taken purely as a piece of pedagogic practice, this indiscriminate behaviour of Hunter's greatly offends Johnson. However, and perhaps surprisingly, it does not lead him to be hostile to the use of institutionalised corporal punishment as an educational aid. Indeed, as the passage continues, he draws on his own unhappy experience and argues strongly for the effectiveness of more discerning, but equally severe punitive measures:

> Indeed Johnson was very sensible how much he owed to Mr Hunter. Mr [Bennet] Langton one day asked him how he had acquired so accurate a knowledge of Latin, in which, I believe, he was exceeded by no man of his time; he said, 'My master whipt me very well. Without that, Sir, I should have done nothing.' He told Mr Langton, that while Hunter was flogging his boys unmercifully, he used to say, 'And this I do to save you from the gallows.' Johnson, upon all occasions, expressed his approbation of enforcing instruction by means of the rod. 'I would rather (said he) have the rod to be the general terrour to all, to make them learn, than tell a child, if you do thus, or thus, you will be more esteemed than your brothers or sisters. The rod produces an effect which terminates in itself. A child is afraid of being whipped, and gets his task, and there's an end on't; whereas, by exciting comparisons of superiority, you lay the foundation of lasting mischief; you make brothers and sisters hate each other.'[18]

Johnson's argument acknowledges its context of contesting theories about suitable methods of punishment, suggesting that the subject was regularly debated, and that it was one on which most educated Augustans would be expected to have an opinion. The particular emphasis Johnson makes is to combine some Puritan thinking about the need to scourge young people early on to save them from damnation, with some proto-utilitarian thinking about the way comprehensible and consistent punishment encourages good habits in the young without causing them any lasting harm. Johnson's argument, of course, remains firmly within its pedagogic perspective, and entertains none of the sexual overtones or autobiographical uncertainties that dominate Jean-Jacques Rousseau's frank treatment of the same question in his *Confessions* (1781).

What Johnson gives here is an idiosyncratic and personalised version of one of the standard conservative defences of institutionalised pedagogic punishment, based on rank and authority, as well as on practicality and effectiveness. The school-master, acting *in loco parentis*, is entitled to chastise his charges by his hierarchical superiority over them and his innate status as pedagogue and custodian. Just as many contemporary educational treatises followed Roger Ascham and Richard Mulcaster in ennobling the dignified English school-master, so too many contemporary caricatures enjoyed the disconcerting spectacle of the frequently rather shabby and down-at-heel figure who actually carried out these elevated responsibilities, and there seems to have been room for discussion about the proper limits to set on the extent of the power which such possibly dubious characters could legitimately claim.[19] The elaborate revenge plot in Smollett's novel *Roderick Random* (1748), for instance, where the sadistic master is trapped by his abused pupils and flogged with his own rod, is a fantasised example of the poetically-just and humiliating punishment deserved by anyone who overstepped his authority. It remains a prank rather than a serious disruption of hierarchy, since the boys have the explicit approval of someone of higher authority than the school-master. It is thus obvious that there could be a disparity in individual cases between the status nominally conferred by rank and the baser motives of the individual who held that rank, which ironic commentary could elaborate and explore, but the ability to administer legitimate punishment was still maintained by rank, just as it was in the much more severe and formalised penal codes of the Augustan armies and navies.[20]

The penal codes of the military were officially-recognised, unmediated forms of hierarchical discipline, which the school, and, for some conservative thinkers, the family, reproduced in miniature. In all these cases, questions of guilt were assessed and punishment was administered by established authorities, through recognised forensic procedures. The right of these tribunals to behave as they did was conferred and legitimised by rank, which in turn was protected by the perceived social utility of the institution involved. In order for, say, a naval ship to operate efficiently, the authority of the captain had to be virtually unquestionable, making mutiny a capital offence and even insubordination a very serious one. At the same time, the necessary recruitment to the navy could only be kept up if the rights of the seamen were seen to be taken somehow into account. In this complex ordering of rights and duties, a formalised and comprehensible code of disciplinary practice and a recognised greivance procedure were considered essential. Punishments were thus not seen to be arbitrary or haphazard, but regulated and, it was thought by those administering if not those receiving, justifiable aids to maintain essential hierarchical discipline without the appearance of arbitrariness or tyranny.

Not all forms of punishment in Augustan England were so based on a recognised hierarchy, or so enshrined in the institutions of the state, or even so clearly established by law. Alongside the legally-stigmatised patterns of behaviour, there were various other ways of causing offence, of breaking less formalised rules, and there was a great deal of commentary about how it was possible to punish breaches of etiquette or decorum where the law was not directly involved. One interesting area of discussion surrounded duelling, the ritual combat engaged in by rakish gentlemen, settling offences against their honour which the law did not deign to recognise. Although the custom may more properly be associated with a slightly earlier and a slightly later period, it is clear that there were a number, if apparently a small number, of highly illegal duels fought between male members of the upper classes in Augustan England, and there is a more extensive attendant body of commentary in which duelling serves as a way in which the individual's right to engage in personal reprisal is open for consideration.

To begin with the court reports, there are some few recorded homicide trials throughout the Augustan period involving fatalities incurred during duels, although Beattie suggests that juries were lenient towards such defendants if it could be shown that the 'rules of honour' had been followed. In the contemporary press, the subject is more prominent – Swift included a scandalised report of one such combat in his *Journal to Stella* in 1711, and there are a great many references to duelling in the *Tatler* and the *Spectator* and the other widely-read papers of the day.[21] In Defoe's *Review* in 1704, Bishop Burnet's *History of My Own Time* in 1734, and in Richardson's *Sir Charles Grandison* in 1754, the duellists are derided, and in the 'Modern Glossary' Fielding incorporated into his *Covent-Garden Journal* in 1752, 'Honour' is mockingly defined as 'Duelling'.[22] The subject of interpersonal combat seems thus to have attracted literary attention more rigorously and rather more contemptuously than it attracted the attention of the courts. The reasons why such an intermittent and sporadic practice received such disproportionate attention are worth considering.

One of Richard Steele's most persistent subjects in his periodical writing between 1709 and 1711 was his attempt to encourage his middle-class readers to hold such swaggering practices in contempt, to be passively and industriously law-abiding rather than frivolously 'gallant'. Despite having actually fought such a combat in 1700 himself, Steele had already attacked duelling in *The Christian Hero: An Argument Proving that No Principles but Those of Religion are Sufficient to Make a Great Man* (1701), presenting it as part of an entirely inappropriate and archaic code of gallantry. Almost twenty years later, he reproduced this argument in the context of a rather ridiculous combat between two doctors in *The Antidote* (1719).[23] However, it is in the great bourgeois periodicals of the time that his main treatment of the issue occurs. In the *Tatler* in 1709, in papers written by Steele and Swift, there are a number of arguments put against the practice of duelling, and the only support offered for it comes, in an ironic version of the contemporary arguments about the antiquity of the English constitution, from its precedence in Saxon and 'Laplander' law, as reproduced in *The Grand Abridgement of the Common Law* (1516) by Sir Anthony Fitzherbert. As this distant precedent is cited by 'a very hopeful young Gentleman', with Scottish connections, who lives in the remote village of Llanbadarn Fawr near Aberystwyth, it is not to be taken very seriously by the middle-class English readers of the paper, and it is given no support whatsoever by Isaac Bickerstaffe. Duelling, it seems, may have been all very well for the Lapps, or the Celts, or even for the primitive Saxons, but it can have no place in the more advanced and developed bourgeois civilisations, like that of Augustan England.[24]

Elsewhere, 'Mr Spectator' makes the case against duelling more forcefully. In the *Spectator* #9 (10 March 1711), he recalled (or invented?) a duelling club said to have been active at the time of the Restoration:

> I cannot forbear mentioning a very mischievous one, that was erected in the Reign of King *Charles* the Second: I mean, the *Club of Duellists*, in which none was to be admitted that had not fought his Man. The President of it was said to have killed half a dozen in single Combat; and as for the other Members, they took their Seats according to the Number of their Slain. There was likewise a Side-Table, for such as had only drawn Blood, and shown a laudable Ambition of taking the first Opportunity to qualify themselves for the first Table. This Club, consisting only of Men of Honour, did not continue long, most of the Members of it being put to the Sword, or hanged, a little after its Institution.[25]

Steele is presenting this alleged club as a dimly remembered relic of the rough old days before the Revolution, as a rather quaint and charming antique which should have no parallels in Augustan England. The practice of duelling, his final words suggest, is futile and self-defeating, based on a code of honour which the bourgeois reader of the *Spectator* must think rather comic and absurd. The newer kind of sociable and civilised club Steele proposes immediately afterwards is thus presented as symptomatic of the great progress English society has made towards civilisation since those bad old days.

For Steele and Swift, then, the honourable duelling gentlemen are not romantic heroes, but preposterous fops. The notion of extra-legal reprisal, based on such stylised codes of personal honour, is offered to the middle-class reader of the periodical as old-fashioned and ridiculous, a custom which would be laughable if it were not potentially so deadly. Although Bernard Mandeville defended duelling, on the characteristically contrary grounds that the code of honour could act as a kind of Augustan *bushido* and produce splendidly uncaring and suicidal soldiers, his arguments were as usual not widely encouraged. As far as the more urbane writers were concerned, the enlightened and amicable modern gentleman should not respond to slights or challenges in this flamboyant way. Instead, his response to rivalry or competition should be to reach for his glass rather than his sword. As a correspondent from the 'Amorous Club' of Oxford told Mr Spectator in 1711, 'instead of duelling when we are Rivals, we drink together the Health of our Mistress'.[26]

Most interestingly and pertinently, there is a 1711 *Spectator* paper by Addison which continues and develops the argument. It applauds the efforts of Louis XIV to stamp out duelling in France, a custom which for Addison reveals a 'false Notion of Honour', then goes on to suggest suitable penalties for recidivist offenders:

> Death is not sufficient to deter Men, who make it their Glory to despise it, but if every one that fought a Duel were to stand in the Pillory it would quickly lessen the Number of these imaginary Men of Honour, and put an end to so absurd a Practice.[27]

The pillory, like the custom of 'charivari' or 'rough music' which still seems to have persisted in rural England, or like the 'drenching' of pick-pockets that Pope mentions in his *Epilogue to the Satires*, was a way of setting up offenders for humiliation by their peers, letting community pressures rather than official sanctions regulate and admonish the behaviour of miscreants.[28] Unlike the usual punishments of the temporal courts, the pillory was a forum in which shame, rather than guilt, was the prevailing factor, which Addison seems to find more effective in this case than the fear of death.

The pillory's humiliating display of its victims was interestingly similar to the plenary practice of the church courts in making offenders stand in public places proclaiming and doing penance for their sins. And it is the pillory, rather than any other form of Augustan punishment, which satirists felt drawn to, allowing the supporting ideology of shame-based punishments fascinatingly to infiltrate the reactionary defences of Augustan satire. As we shall now see, satire in the hands of Dryden and, later on, Swift and Pope and other oppositional authors was offered as a kind of alternative legal system, identifying and humiliating those who escaped official legal redress, and seeking to establish a punitive community superior to what they saw as the shabby and hopelessly inefficient judicial practices of contemporary bourgeois England. Although the satirists felt deprived of power, which was wielded only by the state, they saw their writing as a way to reclaim their rightful authority by orchestrating, and most importantly by directing, a chorus of disapproval.

A HYMN TO THE PILLORY

Although humiliating and shame-based punishments in and before the Augustan period were largely the prerogative of the church courts and the community outbursts of 'charivari', they were also intermittently and specifically employed by the official legal system. The public penances exacted by the ecclesiastical tribunals and the less formalised participatory community sanctions still had their equivalents in the authorised secular sphere. When convicted of certain offences, some criminals were not made to disappear, by incarceration or transportation, but were instead put on display, immobilised and annotated, in a public place, for the unconstrained attention of their peers. Such a publication of the criminal was part of the elaborate and popular ritual accompanying hangings, in the long procession from Newgate to the London gallows so forcefully described by Bernard Mandeville in his *Enquiry into the Causes of the Frequent Executions at Tyburn* (1725), as well as in the opportunities conventionally granted to the condemned to address their audience (penitently or defiantly) before the final sentence was carried out. The alleged beneficial effects of a combination of ignominious display and corporal suffering also figured prominently in the supportive ideology of public floggings and 'burning in the hand'. However, punishment by public humiliation was more regularly and less drastically imposed on felons by means of the most characteristic item of the Augustan penal apparatus, the pillory.

According to J. M. Beattie, this curious antique sanction was extensively used throughout Britain during the Augustan period. The offences which were most regularly punished by sentencing the convicted offender to stand shackled and labelled, sometimes nailed through the ears, for a fixed period (usually an hour) of display in the pillory in a popular meeting place were those where the public's indignation was most animated, such as child-molesting or sodomy or informing, or else those in which a public knowledge of the miscreant's identity would help prevent the perpetration of further crimes, like confidence trickery or importuning. The motivating idea behind the practice was clearly to identify and publicise dangerous characters, and simultaneously to exploit these paradigm cases of universal disapproval in order to demonstrate that the law was consonant with, rather than in opposition to, widespread public sentiment.

As a result, the pillory was normally reserved for recidivists or the perpetrators of particularly shabby or distasteful offences, male or female. The best-known and most elaborate case is that of Titus Oates, the traitor who was ordered to be exhibited annually throughout London, but most of those held up for scorn were more mundane offenders:

> Men and women were thus pilloried for various forms of fraudulence and cheating: pretending to tell a fortune; cheating at cards and other games; taking a watch as a pledge for a loan and not giving the full sum promised; offering to bury the body of a dead infant for ten pence and then not doing so; pretending to be a servant collecting for a master. Perjury occasionally brought offenders to the pillory, as did conspiracies to extort money by threatening a false accusation, especially when the mere accusation would have been very damaging, as in the case of a woman who threatened to accuse a clergyman of fathering her bastard child or a man accusing another of attempted sodomy. Women were occasionally pilloried for keeping bawdy houses.[29]

The treatment of these officially-stigmatised figures by the participatory audience varied extensively, and was not wholly predictable. At times, the crowd was so hostile and violent in its response that the pilloried character suffered severe injuries, or even died. At others, the sight of an alleged malefactor standing in the pillory led to the onlookers rallying round in support and protesting about the injustice of the sentence. Such demonstrations certainly took place on a number of well-documented occasions, as already indicated in the famous case of Defoe, for example, when that opportunistic entrepreneur seized the occasion to sell copies of a poem called *A Hymn to the Pillory*, but it would be wrong to over-emphasise them. More frequently, the spectacular punishment achieved its design and the terrified, helpless criminal was verbally abused and pelted with the most unpleasant items, to his or her great shame and humiliation, and no little pain.

In any of these cases, the pillory offered a focus for recognising and dramatising shared, community values, and it acted as a public forum in which citizens' attitudes towards crime and criminals could be actively expressed and directed. The relatively few occasions where the public's treatment of the characters so presented was significantly harsher or more lenient than usual are indicative of those points where the official legal system and the values of the local community differed substantially. Although the recoverable instances of direct rebellious challenge are only intermittent and occasional, the general rowdiness and volatility of the 'mob' around the pillory was clearly one of the most significant factors in the fall from favour of all spectacular punishments in the later part of the eighteenth century. More often than not, though, the state's incorporation of informal and communal sanctions into its own penal repertoire by means of the pillory was successful, and official stigmatisation was corroborated and reinforced by the derisive participation of the crowd. One important ideological effect of this was to establish the idea that the authorised legal bodies served to express the will of the people, another was to allow the punishers to monitor public feeling and assess the acceptability of particular judgements. The pillory was thus as much a communicative signifying practice as a penal practice; it offered a way of disseminating official ideas about criminality and the status of the law, monitoring the public response to them, and directing public attitudes, as well as a handy and inexpensive way to punish crooks.[30]

As the century wore on, more voices were raised in pointing out the flaws in the practice of the pillory as established. In his *Principles of Moral and Political Philosophy*, published in 1785, William Paley pointed out the difficulties in the use of 'infamous' punishments:

> *Infamous* punishments are mismanaged in this country, with respect both to the crimes and the criminals. In the first place, they ought to be confined to offences which are holden in undisputed and universal detestation . . . In the second place: the delinquents who receive this sentence, are for the most part such as have long ceased either to value reputation, or to fear shame . . . The pillory, or any other infamous distinction, might be employed rightly, and with effect, in the punishments of some offences of higher life.[31]

Paley's argument about the inefficacy of shame-based punishments for those on whom they were inflicted is one which has echoes in the discussions of the policy by many Augustan writers. As Henry Fielding put it in his *Charge Delivered to the Grand Jury* (1749), 'the Rod of the Law, Gentlemen, must restrain those within the Bounds of Decency and Sobriety, who are deaf to the Voice of Reason, and superior to the Fear of Shame'.[32] The link between shame and reputation, and the problems involved in dealing with the shameless, are particularly interesting in the context of the work of the satirists, whose attempts to create a rival forum for the administration of infamy were overlapping, but not by any means identical with the state's use of such punishments.

The public presentation of miscreants in the pillory and the boisterous scenes surrounding them may now look like a peculiarly violent and atavistic theatre of highly-charged shame and terror, a theatre intended to be didactic, but experienced as melodrama. It may be difficult for contemporary readers, familiarised to post-Freudian ideas about the centrality of guilt and internalisation, to recognise the lost potency of shame and public display as part of the authorised apparatus of correction. In Britain today, there are occasional disturbing scenes outside courtrooms, when those particularly outraged by an offence seek to take personal reprisals on the offender. There are also intermittent reactionary blusterings in the right-wing press calling for the reintroduction of the stocks or the pillory today, usually alongside corporal punishment, national service, the ducking stool, and probably the employment of delinquent children as chimney-sweeps. But in spite of these deeply-felt unauthorised outbursts, the official penal policy is to ostracise criminals, to isolate them from society by their incarceration and to institutionalise their punishment rather than to make them prominent by public display. And the generating principle of official penal policy is that the whole apparatus of punishment is based on the identification of guilt rather than on the arousal and implementation of shame.

As I say this, I am conscious of the need to be less insular and am aware that my considerations only apply to western cultures, since shame and shaming remain a large part of the penal system and informal punitive practices of some Eastern societies even today, particularly Japan. In those cultures, the main dissuasive tactic for wrongdoers is to make clear to them that in behaving badly they have lost the respect of others, particularly of others who are important to them, albeit temporarily. This procedure does still exist in western culture, mainly in the process of child-rearing and in the patriarchal exhortations of indignant magistrates, but the treatment of criminals is generally much more concerned with guilt-induction, with the creation of internal remorse and self-disparagement in wrongdoers. The differences between shame and guilt, and the different forms of shaming understood in eighteenth-century Britain, are worth exploring in this context, as they offer a very interesting way of investigating the alternative tribunals set up by Augustan writers, which often draw on the rhetoric of the pillory and of shaming in their self-legitimisation.

A recent criminologist, John Braithwaite, has studied existing shaming practices in various cultures in some detail.[33] In the course of his argument (the overall direction and validity of which is not relevant to the present enquiry) he distinguishes between two different kinds of shaming, which he calls 'reintegrative' and 'disintegrative':

> The crucial distinction is between shaming that is reintegrative and shaming that is disintegrative (stigmatization). Reintegrative shaming means that expressions of community disapproval, which may range from mild rebuke to degradation ceremonies, are followed by gestures of reacceptance into the community of law-abiding citizens. These gestures of reacceptance will vary from a simple smile expressing forgiveness and love to quite formal ceremonies to decertify the offender as deviant. Disintegrative shaming (stigmatization), in contrast, divides the community by creating a class of outcasts. Much effort

is directed at labeling deviance, while little attention is paid to de-labeling, to signifying forgiveness and reintegration, to ensure that the deviance label is applied to the behaviour rather than the person, and that it is done under the assumption that the disapproved behaviour is transient, performed by an essentially good person.

(p. 55)

In terms of this distinction, the Augustan pillory was clearly a vehicle for disintegrative shaming, even if the volatile spectators could occasionally disrupt the proceedings and ceremonially reintegrate the offender. The 'labelling' of deviance was in this case taken literally, with a paper detailing the offence being pinned above the offender's head, and there were no official ceremonies of reintegration. We should remember too that, in the context of the extensively-used punishment of branding by 'burning in the hand', to talk of the 'stigmatisation' of offenders is not always to deal in metaphor. As in the supportive ideologies of punishment explored earlier, the function of the pillory and other punishments by display was both retributive and deterrent, but in this context it also served primarily to label and stigmatise individuals rather than patterns of behaviour.

Braithwaite's language of disintegration and reintegration, and the whole technical apparatus of criminology, sit awkwardly alongside the more impressionistic nuances of orthodox literary criticism. However, this way of thinking about punishment becomes more recognisable if we think of it beside the legitimising language of the Augustan satirists. At the same time as the punishers were actualising the subsequent metaphors of criminologists, poets were metaphorically transforming writing into a vehicle of quasi-formal correction. As can easily be documented, the graver satirists of this period excused and justified their activities by emphasising the deterrent and judicial features of their art, drawing on the precedent of Juvenal rather than Horace. As Dryden put it in the preface to *Absalom and Achitophel*, 'The true end of *Satyre*, is the amendment of Vices by correction.'[34] By saying this, he was both excusing the violence of satire and giving it enhanced social status by dignifying its ability to correct. Satire thus takes its place alongside other tribunals of correction, such as the pillory, as part of the whole official project of identifying deviants and labelling deviance.

In Dryden's terminology, there remains some doubt here about whether 'correction' means primarily improvement or just chastisement, and these uncertainties were intensified in the debate surrounding Dryden's personalised portrait of Zimri in that poem, and in the obvious element of personal revenge in his other satires, *Mac Flecknoe* and *The Medall*. Did the pillorying of fools and rogues in satire help to amend those characters, settle a few scores for the author, or simply serve to offer patterns to be scorned by less deviant readers? Much of the discussion surrounding the acceptability of satire focused on the satirist's right to identify deviance and on the validity of his/her claims to provide correction. The suspicions of those unsympathetic to the project of satire, of whom there were many, were that it provided the opportunity for slanderous and personal revenge rather than high-minded stigmatisation, that it exhibited the anarchic power of 'wit' rather than the responsible force of official didactic coercion, and that it was a vigilante form of justice, beyond proper institutional control. Indeed, a great deal of the legitimising rhetoric of satire in this period responds to or anticipates these criticisms and seeks to reassure the unsympathetic that satiric writing is more than a personal literary retaliation for perceived offences against the satirist's honour, to distinguish the legitimate gravity of satire from the frivolous slander of a lampoon. In other words, the satirists and their supporters persistently claim that satire is a legitimate and proper form of punishment, derived from a high-minded desire to castigate vice, and not a source of reprisal or revenge.

The hostility to satire as a vehicle for personal retribution is best expressed in a 1711 *Spectator* essay by Addison. Just as Steele argued insistently against the wild justice of duelling in his periodical essays, so Addison sought to regulate the rampant extra-legal punitive practices of satiric writers:

There is nothing that more betrays a base, ungenerous Spirit, than the giving of secret Stabs to a Man's Reputation. Lampoons and Satyrs, that are written with Wit and Spirit, are like poison'd Darts, which not only inflict a Wound, but make it incurable. For this Reason I am very much troubled when I see the Talents of Humour and Ridicule in the Possession of an ill-natured Man. There cannot be a greater Gratification to a barbarous and inhuman Wit, than to stir up Sorrow in the Heart of a private Person, to raise Uneasiness among near Relations, and to expose whole Families to Derision, at the same time that he remains unseen and undiscovered. If, besides the Accomplishments of being Witty and Ill-natured, a Man is vicious into the bargain, he is one of the most mischievous Creatures that can enter into a Civil Society. His Satyr will then chiefly fall upon those who ought to be most exempt from it. Virtue, Merit, and everything that is Praise-worthy, will be made the Subject of Ridicule and Buffoonry. It is impossible to enumerate the Evils which arise from these Arrows that fly in the dark, and I know no other Excuse that is or can be made for them, than that the Wounds they give are only Imaginary, and produce nothing more than a secret Shame or Sorrow in the Mind of the suffering Person. It must indeed be confess'd, that a Lampoon or a Satyr do not carry in them Robbery or Murder; but at the same time, how many are there that would not rather lose a considerable Sum of Mony, or even Life itself, than be set up as a Mark of Infamy and

> Derision? And in this Case a Man should consider, that an Injury is not
> to be measured by the Notions of him that gives, but of him that
> receives it.[35]

In this very dextrous and pejorative analysis, which some contemporary
readers interpreted as a 'character' of Swift, satirists and lampooners are
rendered indistinguishable, and surrounded by an elaborate rhetoric of
criminality. Rather than being legitimate agents of the law, they are no
better than terrorists. They are obviously slanderers, but are also
represented as poisoners, home-wreckers, anarchists, cowards, worse
than murderers, more hurtful than robbers, lurking unseen in dark
corners. Addison's argument is conducted more by the insistence of his
catalogue than by its logic, and he moves slyly from discussing only ill-
natured satire to tainting the whole satiric enterprise with criminality.

Addison's presentation of the hostility to satire is one of the most
vehement, but it shares most of its terms of reference with similar
denunciations by John Tillotson, Lord Kames, Richard Allestree, Samuel
Richardson, Pierre Bayle, Joseph Glanvill and many others.[36] While it
may seem strange to us to discover that what is often presented as the
dominant literary form of the Augustan period attracted such contemporary hostility, there are ways to explain this intense resistance to satire.
When Addison returned to his attack in a number of later *Spectator*
papers, the recurrent theme is that satire is irresponsible, an illegitimate
and unjustifiable abrogation of the right to judge and punish which
properly belongs only to the official legal system:

> I cannot but look upon the finest strokes of satyr which are aimed at
> particular persons, and which are supported even with the appearance
> of truth, to be marks of an evil mind, and highly criminal in
> themselves. Infamy, like other punishments, is under the direction and
> distribution of the magistrate, and not of any private person.[37]

The basis of Addison's argument here is his usual complacency about the
civilisation of his society, specifically his resolute Whig confidence in the
probity and integrity of the appointed authorities, combined with his
combative suspicion of rivals. As he sees it, satire does not offer to
reinforce the workings of the legal system, or disseminate its ideas more
forcefully: satire undermines the authority of the official body, and as a
result it is both dangerous and distasteful.

In the face of this style of argument, the satirists themselves sought to
reclaim the integrity and dignity of their role as punishers, reiterating the
Juvenalian arguments of Dryden, and anticipating some of Paley's
notions of the suitability of infamy in the dismantling of reputation.
Alongside the quasi-medical justifications of satire as a useful purgative,
or the various physiognomic presentations of it as 'snarling' or 'smiling',
there were other supportive presentations of it as a necessary

punishment, justified both by the good it did to the sufferers and the general benefits a society gained from identifying and shaming its miscreants. For some writers, the satirist was an earnest pedagogic figure, who retained the right to correct errant subjects with all the righteous severity exercised by genuine teachers. At the beginning of *A Tale of a Tub*, Swift playfully imitated this style of legitimation:

> I have observ'd some Satyrists to use the Publick much at the Rate that Pedants do a naughty Boy ready Hors'd for Discipline: First expostulate the Case, then plead the Necessity of the Rod, from great Provocations, and conclude every Period with a Lash. Now, if I know anything of Mankind, these Gentlemen might very well spare their Reproof and Correction: For there is not, through all Nature, another so callous and insensible a Member as *the World's Posteriors*, whether you apply to it the *Toe* or the *Birch*.[38]

Swift here sports with the corrective pedagogic analysis of satire, but finds it rendered impotent by the world's inertia. Elsewhere, he gave further accounts of satire's inability to change things for the better, emphasising that shame was a very blunt instrument indeed, and that those in most need of reform were always insufficiently sensitive to it, a point made with more irritation and spleen by both Dryden and Pope.

However, when it suited him, Swift was quite prepared to assume the guise of the just and high-minded punisher, and vindicate satire through its ability to correct. This argument is central to his defence of *The Beggar's Opera*, and appears more amusingly elsewhere. One of the commentating voices in his *Verses on the Death of Dr. Swift* pays tribute to the Dean's satiric integrity:

> Yet Malice never was his Aim;
> He lash'd the Vice, but spared the Name;
> No individual could resent,
> Where thousands equally were meant.[39]

This defence is clearly rather absurd in the context of a poem which is unsparing of names and thoroughly malicious throughout. Also, the incorporation of 'thousands' of targets scarcely makes Swift seem discriminating and fastidious in his satirical practice, or benign and forgiving in his disposition. However, these are all very arch and deliberate jokes, and it is still interesting to see Swift's defensive tactic of reaching towards generality, appropriating the punitive rhetoric of flogging, and making the reintegrative shaming gestures of dissociating the stigmatised behaviour from the potentially reformable offender. While it looks as though he lashes because the victims deserve it rather than because it will do anybody much good, he still feels drawn to offer a consequentialist defence, and to see his procedure as partly judicial. At least in jest, he is prepared to envisage himself as operating a tribunal in which Vice is isolated and punished, a more noble and exalted role than that carried out by the earthly courts.

Although these vindications of satire by Swift are always at least partly playful, he did use the more exalted rhetoric of defence in a more serious way on several occasions. In an essay in *The Examiner* in 1711, published exactly one month after Addison's attack on ill-natured or personal satire, Swift gave a very interesting account of the overlapping and mutually supportive responsibilities of the satirist and the law:

> 'tis very plain, that considering the Defectiveness of our Laws, the variety of Cases, the weakness of the Prerogative, the Power or the Cunning of ill-designing Men, it is possible, that many great Abuses may be visibly committed, which cannot be legally Punish'd: Especially if we add to this, that some Enquiries might probably involve those, whom upon other Accounts, it is not thought convenient to disturb. Therefore, it is very false Reasoning, especially in the Management of Publick Affairs, to argue that Men are Innocent, because the Law hath not pronounc'd them Guilty.
>
> I am apt to think, it was to supply such Defects as these, that Satyr was first introduc'd into the World: whereby those whom neither Religion, nor natural Virtue, nor fear of Punishment, were able to keep within the Bounds of their Duty, might be withheld by the Shame of having their Crimes expos'd to open View in the strongest Colours, and themselves rendred odious to Mankind. Perhaps all this may be little regarded by such harden'd and abandoned Natures as I have to deal with; but, next to taming or binding a Savage-Animal, the best Service you can do the Neighbourhood, is to give them warning, either to Arm themselves, or not come in its way.[40]

Swift here articulates the fine distinction between guilt and shame quite clearly, and sees the former as the province of the law, the latter as the prerogative of disintegrative satire. The satirist, in this formulation, takes over in the many areas where the legal system is inept or impotent or insufficiently subtle, and the function of satire is either to induce a shame-based penitence in the offender or (more likely) to publicise wickedness and the wicked for the general benefit of the public. The connections between the functions of satire and the pillory as vehicles for public disapprobation are thus made obvious.

The way Swift puts the case here depends on his sense that general or categorical descriptions of human behaviour, such as that encoded in the statute, must inevitably be flawed. The human capacity for particularity applies as much to the meticulousness of iniquity as to any other feature of the human condition, and it is up to the satirist to identify and number the streaks of this particular tulip. In his refusal to be surprised by the imaginativeness and creativity of human beings in the performance of vice and folly, in his recognition of the human ability to find so many startling new ways to disappoint and frustrate expectations, Swift is clearly the most pessimistic of all the Augustan satirists – a distinction as remarkable and yet as insignificant as being the tallest man in the US Olympic basketball team. He is prepared to defend the usefulness and integrity of satire when the occasion demands it, but seems to offer little confidence in the possibilities of achieving any success in amending the world. As ever, he has much more faith in the ability of the satirist to detect iniquity than in the ability of the public to profit from these warnings, and the satirical pillory he offers is more of a theatre of cruelty and humiliation than a genuine project for reform.

Swift, then, exploits the high-minded defence of satire, but does not fully endorse it. Pope, on the other hand, seems to have taken the satirist's punitive and reformative duties more seriously, and his writing gives a much more sombre account of the social responsibilities of the writer. In the debate about the personal or general focus for satire, Pope took the position that the project of amendment could only be successful if it was conducted through a judicious mixture of naming names and identifying general traits. As he put it when vindicating some of the personalised portraits in his *Epistle to Burlington* in a letter to Gay in 1731, 'I am afraid that all such Writings and Discourses as touch no Man, will mend no Man.'[41] Pope's confidence in the reforming power of his version of satire was intermingled with his views of punishment in more developed arguments with Arbuthnot in 1734:

> I thank you dear Sir for making that your Request to me which I make my Pride, nay my Duty; 'that I should continue my Disdain & abhorrence of Vice, & manifest it still in my writings.' I would indeed do it with more restrictions, & less personally; it is more agreeable to my nature, which those who know it not are greatly mistaken in: But General Satire in Times of General Vice has no force, & is no Punishment: People have ceas'd to be ashamed of it when so many are joind with them; and tis only by hunting One or two from the Herd that any Examples can be made. If a man writ all his Life against the Collective Body of the Banditti, or against Lawyers, would it do the least Good, or lessen the Body? But if some are hung up, or pilloryed, it may prevent others. And in my low Station, with no other Power than this, I hope to deter, if not to reform.[42]

Pope's belief in the deterrent possibilities of satire is articulated through its metaphorical equivalence with the pillory. Selecting a few individuals to be 'hung up' may discourage the others, even if it does little else, and the satirist's power is seen as being a miniaturised and subtle version of the more awesome, if less discriminating power of the state. The satirist may have little power, but he can claim Juvenalian authority, and has the freedom to accuse those the law neglects to recognise.

Again and again in his writing, Pope claimed the authority to accuse, sentence, and punish. Like Paley fifty years later, he was particularly concerned to use the infamous punishment of satiric exposure on those who existed by reputation. He clearly felt able to use the press as an alternative judicial tribunal, articulating this view much more aggressively and solemnly than Swift or Gay. In his more public pronouncements (remembering, of course, that even his correspondence has its element of public display), he was at pains to legitimise his own practice by seeing it as analogous to the practices of the courts, valuably extending the range of their effectiveness and refining their judgements.

This procedure is most obvious in the later versions of *The Dunciad*, a poem imbued with copious legal references and citations. Indeed, the whole procedure of Pope's great mock-epic poem is forensic. Not only does the whole pageant which forms the fabric of the piece imitate and parody the procession of the condemned from Newgate to Tyburn, as well as the Lord Mayor's procession which forms its apparent opposite in Hogarth's *Industry and Idleness* sequence, the animating idea of the poem is similar to a legal indictment. Like so many oppositional Augustan writers, Pope was concerned that the legal system only apprehended and deterred the smallest of fry, and that many greater outrages were being flagrantly committed with impunity. His response is retaliatory, although at times he seems to get his retaliation in first. In part he was aiming to provide the grossest caricatures of those who had caricatured him, like Eliza Haywood, but his procedures were also informed by a judicial and admonitory desire to accuse and shame those he saw as the genuine villains of the day. In a much more intense and specific way than the portrait of 'Sir Balaam' in the *Epistle to Bathurst* or the other individualised sketches in the moral essays, the presentation of the participants in *The Dunciad* is a rogue's gallery and pillory rolled into one.

In the process of his later poems, Pope accuses and carries out judgement and administers punishment simultaneously, without recourse to a trial by jury. The way in which he presents his satirical targets renders them ludicrous and turns them into unpitiable objects of scorn, with no rights of reply, like the most unpopular figures in the pillory. In the portrait of 'Sporus' in the *Epistle to Dr. Arbuthnot*, he anticipates the objection that his procedure is over-strenuous and too severe, appropriating the extraordinary image of an aggravated form of the death penalty – 'Who breaks a butterfly upon a wheel?' – and his reply is that his victims deserve no better, and that as a satirist he is fully entitled to treat them as he does. More than that, he is required to behave as he does.

Elsewhere, Pope takes on reformative responsibility eagerly, and uses it to justify his savagery, which he presents as the good man's rightful contempt for vice and the vicious. In his *Epilogue to the Satires*, he defines his role in the most judicial of ways. Referring back to the controversy over the naming of names which he had addressed in the prefatory material to *The Dunciad* and in correspondence with Swift, he imagines a dialogue in which he has to defend his decision to identify his victims:

> *F.* Yet none but you by Name the Guilty lash;
> Ev'n *Guthry* saves half *Newgate* by a Dash.
> Spare then the Person, and expose the Vice.
>   *P.* How Sir! not damn the Sharper, but the Dice?
> Come on then Satire! gen'ral, unconfin'd,
> Spread thy broad wing, and sowze on all the Kind.
> Ye Statesmen, Priests, of one Religion all!
> Ye Tradesmen vile, in Army, Court, or Hall!
> Ye Rev'rend Atheists! – *F.* Scandal! name them, Who?
>   *P.* Why that's the thing you bid me not to do.[43]

Pope goes on to list a series of rogues beyond legal censure, yet within the compass of the high-minded satirist. In the course of this dialogue, he refuses to recognise legitimate restraints on those he might accuse, taking upon himself sole judicial and legislative responsibilities, from motives he insists are high-minded and disinterested:

> Ask you what Provocation I have had?
> The strong Antipathy of Good to Bad.
> When Truth or Virtue an Affront endures,
> Th'Affront is mine, my Friend, and should be yours.
> Mine, as a Foe profess'd to false Pretence,
> Who think a Coxcomb's Honour like his Sense;
> Mine, as a Friend to ev'ry worthy Mind;
> And mine as Man, who feel for all mankind.

(ll. 197–204)

In complete contrast to Swift, therefore, Pope is trying to make himself culturally central. He does not see himself as one of the mob at the pillory, but as the Lord Chancellor, the Lord Privy Seal and the Lord High Executioner in exile. As David Nokes puts it, 'where Swift is content to portray himself as a rueful, rather ridiculous pedagogue, aiming one last lash at the world's posteriors, Pope truly feels himself entrusted with a divine mission'.[44]

The ideology of Augustan satire thus established several positions in opposition to or in extension of Augustan legal practice. In Addison's view, satire should only corroborate and reformulate the judgements of the courts, avoiding any extraneous accusations. In Swift's, the possibility of any effective general system of acceptable prescription was made to seem so remote in the tangled world of human affairs that satire was just another impotent attempt to legislate and regulate things, although that was all the more reason to carry on with it. In Pope's version, as in Dryden's, satire was an infinitely superior form of judicial procedure to that shabbily carried out by the courts, offering a pillory in which the true villains might be displayed, and where public response could be more effectively controlled and directed. The sceptical temperaments of the ironic writers saw punishment as probably ineffective, but still necessary, the shaming process of satire being even more disintegrative than that of the pillory. Once Shadwell or Marlborough or Chetwood or Curll or any of the figures satirised by these writers appeared in their caricatured form in print, their new shape took on a permanence which an appearance in the pillory did not have, and no reintegrative gestures of forgiveness were offered.

The other project of the satirists, particularly Pope, was to create a community whose judgemental role would be more authoritative and less disruptive than that of the crowd, finding its victims in high life as well as in low life. Satire was designed to flatter the intelligence of its readers, even when, in Swift's case, it simultaneously disparaged them. It was attempting at this time to create a punitive community outside the vested-interest groups of rigid Tories or Whigs, drawing on like-minded people in a pseudo-egalitarian way, in the hope of exerting pressure on the actual courts, and redressing the misuses of legal power obvious to so many in Walpole's England. But to see the way an engagement with the issues of crime and legislation could be used to train discernment and encourage responsibility, we have to turn from the tendentious satirists and look at the riven and contesting anatomies of Fielding.

5 Fielding and the discipline of fiction

THE MAGISTRATE AND THE MOB

The study of literature and crime in Augustan England has by now revealed an extensive gallery of contending representations of criminal and legal activities. Some of these expressions are broadly conservative and some more subversive, articulated through writing which is supportive of the state's established legal practices as well as through writing which is intensely or obliquely critical of these very practices. In all the output of the Augustan press examined so far, ideological uncertainties created by or dramatised in the representations of crime and the recognised procedures of justice are prominent and remarkably diverse. As a fitting climax, we can see many of these inconsistent and contending possibilities and contradictions held together and displayed in the career of one astonishing figure who straddles both the Augustan legal and literary worlds: Henry Fielding.

Fielding's presence in our contemporary perception of Augustan literature and crime is formative and pervasive, and his appearances and disguises throughout the period are many. In the present context, his diverse writing can offer a rich repository of the contending and contradictory images and representations of crime and the law disseminated at the time, with Fielding in his different roles giving apparently inconsistent accounts of the main issues. It may eventually be discovered that the differences between Fielding's various formulations of the status of the legal system are only differences of emphasis or inflection, rather than fundamental shifts in allegiance, but these subtle variations in tone and attitude are still worth investigating, offering as they do a conspectus of many of the recoverable ideological uncertainties, an avenue of insight into the differing functions of the various parts of the Augustan press, and an indication of the range of critical and supportive possibilities available to its authors.

It may seem strange to talk of uncertainties and hesitations with so urbane and confident a figure as Henry Fielding, but his various identities produced conflicts of loyalty and purpose which lead to confusion. As dramatist, journalist, social critic, magistrate and, of course, as novelist, Fielding intersected with the structures of power in his society in a number of different ways, holding different status and authority in each case, and saying things which were not always obviously consistent with each other. In looking for images comprehensive enough to represent this dynamic and versatile figure in his widely differing roles, it is tempting to ransack the popular mythology of crime, and to present him alongside the legendary master-criminals or the great detectives. Like the notorious Jack Sheppard, he is exceptionally elusive, yet persistently present. Like Sherlock Holmes, his methods are well known, but almost impossible to articulate or convincingly reproduce. And above all like Raffles, he inhabits both the world of the righteous and that of the wicked, at once the benevolent and urbane English gentleman and the charming yet clear-headed thief.

In the course of his very various and successful literary career, Fielding's writing intermittently articulated most of the available ideological attitudes to the law, both hostile and supportive. As a popular dramatist in the first third of the century, he produced subversive and satiric theatrical pieces of the kind which provoked Walpole to introduce the repressive Stage Licensing Act in 1737. There have been often-repeated accusations, originally and most vehemently expressed in *An Apology for the Life of Mr Colley Cibber, Comedian* (1740), that Fielding alone was responsible for this measure, his plays being so peculiarly offensive to Walpole that the legislation was an act of personal reprisal. Although such individualised or mono-causal explanations of Augustan political behaviour are now largely discredited, there can be no doubt about Fielding's contemporary prominence or his prolificacy as a dramatist, and no questioning of the degree of political irritation his work caused. In plays like *Pasquin*, *The Historical Register for 1736*, *The Tragedy of Tragedies* and many others, Fielding offered his eager public a wittily critical and broadly burlesque vision of his corrupt society, reprimanding the misuses of power and the ineptitude of officialdom in a way reminiscent of the earlier work of Gay and Swift.

An even more extreme and vitriolic scepticism animates his sustained satire on criminals and 'Great Men', *The History of the Life of the Late Mr Jonathan Wild the Great* (1743). Amidst all the writing inspired by Wild's remarkable career, discussed earlier, Fielding's bizarre and curiously belated addition is the most disturbing and unsettling, much darker and more insistent than the jauntier tone of *The Beggar's Opera* or the allegedly factual version in Defoe's journalistic pamphlet, *The True and Genuine Account of the Life and Actions of the late Jonathan Wild*, both published soon after Wild's death in 1725. In his major comic novels, *Joseph Andrews* and *Tom Jones*, too, there are numerous cries of protest about specific legal practices, regular hostile and satiric presentations of lawyers and justices, and frequent authorised gestures of sympathy for their victims. The various forensic tribunals and their participants dramatised in the comic fictions are, as we shall see, at best incompetent and at worst malicious. And in his much more sombre and disconcerting last novel, *Amelia*, the inadequacies of the legal system and the miseries it predictably creates, are most fastidiously and relentlessly dissected.

This version of Fielding's career makes him seem persistently oppositional and resistant to the authorised version of eighteenth-century English life, placing him alongside Pope as another vigilante 'opposition laureate', in this case a Whig 'Patriot' activist who exploited the press in all its forms to disseminate ideas critical of those in power through the indirect forms of satire and irony. But this can only be a crude caricature of the man, based almost exclusively on the fictional and dramatic work, and much more of Fielding's writing seems accommodated to the demands of his society, deeply conservative in its attitudes, and defensive of reactionary social policies, than is extensively critical of them. Also, Fielding's eventual incorporation into contemporary political life as a prominent magistrate is very different from the self-proclaimed marginalisation of the Scriblerian writers. His supportive and personally rewarding relationships with the Duke of Bedford and with Henry Pelham's administration were significantly different from Pope's friendship with the exiled Bolingbroke, in that they established Fielding as a spokesman for a prevailing and powerful ideology, rather than for one which could present itself as oppositional, unheeded and powerless. And Fielding's closeness to powerful figures is also different from Defoe's association with Harley, in being less obviously a direct relationship of clientage, less like the employment of semi-official propagandists by politicians. Fielding's support for Pelham seems more autonomous and independent than either of these other relationships, allowing him space to be constructively critical, and both more rewarding for him and more supportive of the established authorities of his time.

Alongside the sly Fielding who infiltrates a sustained sceptical commentary into his fiction, then, there is another version of the man in which he seems just as persistently on the side of officialdom and its practices, seeming eager to increase rather than to diminish the effective power of the law and the state. Although he shared with Pope the elevated sense that writers might carry the conscience of their culture, articulating its highest values and its best version of itself, and although he certainly seems to have felt that writers might thus retain the right or even the duty to reprimand their governors when necessary, Fielding's writing after the fall of Walpole in 1742 often appears much more strenuous in the service of the official conservative ideology than in the creation of an alternative critical or oppositional one. There are, for example, a great many pamphlets on matters of social policy where Fielding's recognised habits of irony are rendered almost invisible or drastically restricted, and where a much fuller confidence in the authorised operations of the law than can be found anywhere in Swift or Pope is apparently displayed.

On becoming a magistrate for Middlesex in 1749 – an obviously political appointment given in return for his pro-government propaganda work in the *True Patriot* and the *Jacobite's Journal* – Fielding published *A Charge Delivered to the Grand Jury*, in which he mounted a ringing defence of the specific glories of English law:

> There is no Part in all the excellent Frame of our Constitution which an *Englishman* can, I think, contemplate with such Delight and Admiration; nothing which must fill him with such gratitude to our earliest Ancestors, as that Branch of *British* Liberty from which, Gentlemen, you derive your Authority of assembling here on this Day.[1]

The terms of this peroration are elevated and elaborate, as though the author might be deliberately misdirecting us and setting us up for an ironic deflation. In the carefully developed panegyric, where all the participants in this extravagant ritual performance are congratulated simply for being there, we might feel as though the gap between the utopian ideal of the legal system and the less elevated day-to-day pragmatism of the courtroom, so often explored in Fielding's fiction, is about to be revealed once more.

But, alas, it is not. Fielding writes this pamphlet as though greatly enjoying the enhanced status and authority his elevation to the magistracy gave him, performing his august new role with obvious theatrical relish and no little complacency. In what must have looked to those who knew him like a complete repudiation of his past, or a flagrant and grotesquely hypocritical attempt to re-write his personal history, the reformed Fielding unhesitatingly assumes the mantle of responsibility and respectability, and proceeds to disparage and censure those very freedoms of the press and sources of recreation which he had previously exploited to the full. In one particularly startling volte-face, which would be surprising even from Defoe, he denounces the public's excessive appetite for pleasure by castigating the theatre:

> But, Gentlemen, so immoderate are the Desires of many, so hungry is their Appetite for Pleasure, that they may be said to have a Fury after it; and Diversion is no longer the Recreation or Amusement, but the whole Business of their Lives. They are not content with three Theatres, they must have a fourth; where the Exhibitions are not only contrary to Law, but contrary to Good-Manners, and where the Stage is reduced back again to that Degree of Licentiousness which was too enormous for the corrupt State of *Athens* to bear.
>
> (pp. 23–4)

This surprisingly vitriolic attack on amusements is difficult to take from the retired playwright and dramatist. In this particular case, it might just be a way for Fielding to use his new role to exact officialised retaliation on the comedian Samuel Foote, with whom he had conducted an extended and rather unimportant quarrel in the pages of the *Jacobite's Journal* the previous year. Even that, however, makes Fielding's rhetoric look more like a heavy-handed exploitation of the privilege of office to settle some trivial personal points than like a suitably solemn and portentous magisterial pronouncement. From many points of view, the sudden transformation of Fielding the poacher into Fielding the game-keeper here looks remarkably and disconcertingly complete, and, as we might expect, it did not go unnoticed by a number of unsympathetic contemporary commentators.

In keeping with his newly-discovered *gravitas*, Fielding quotes his legal precedents from Coke and Fortescue and elsewhere with knowledgeable confidence and assurance, alluding to obscure texts with all the facility of Abraham Adams, wrapping his listeners in the folds of shared responsibility. As Fielding develops the argument, he and his jurors (and his implied readers) are all fortunate to be Englishmen together, able to live lives of skilfully orchestrated liberty and responsibility in an environment politically organised for their benefit. As a result of these happy circumstances, they are uniquely equipped to respond to 'the peculiar Licentiousness of the Age' (p. 30) with the appropriate resolve and integrity.

In other complementary pamphlets, Fielding the magistrate reiterated the peculiar felicities of English law and its intrinsic superiority to its continental counterparts in a way reminiscent of Blackstone:

> Is *English* Liberty, or is *French* Slavery so little known, that it is necessary to expatiate a Moment on either? Shall I even be permitted to remind you of the Security, with which the Freedom, the Life, the Property of *Englishmen* are guarded by the Law? Can the greatest Man among us, even the King himself, take one of these from the poorest? Can any Man be imprisoned wrongfully, without present Redress, and future Satisfaction? Can he be punish'd without a Trial, without an unanimous Conviction, by twelve Men of his Equals, having been first accus'd on the Oaths of a Grand Jury of the like Number? Is he then liable to any other Sentence, than that to which the express Letter of the Law adjudges him, a Sentence which the King can neither aggravate or alter?[2]

The persistent Lockean idea that it was liberty, judiciously articulated and regulated by the law and its authorised agents, which provided the distinguishing feature of the English constitution was common in a certain version of conservative polemic throughout the Augustan period. In this particular passage, written in the early part of 1745, Fielding was seeking to arouse public feeling against the immediately threatening claims of the

'Young Pretender', recently landed in Scotland from France, and the pamphlet was explicitly addressed to local issues of anti-Jacobite policy. However, the tone of grave public concern he adopts and the fervour of his patriotic conservatism are very characteristic of Fielding's writing in this vein, and could also be found elsewhere in his non-fictional work at this time.

For modern critics interested in reclaiming Fielding from the mire of eighteenth-century authoritarian conservatism, such insistent and apparently unambiguous reactionary statements can only be very disconcerting. Instead of placing Fielding's work alongside the elaborate and subtle social critiques of Hogarth, tolerating what may seem to be their unacceptable basic values in return for the redemptive critical powers of their irony, it looks as though we may have to move them next to the more comfortable apologetics of Blackstone, where they may languish unread except by those impending critics interested in retrieving the work of Sarah Fielding's little-known brother, and the dwindling band of votaries of the old-time religion of Formalism. However, at the risk of protesting too much, I believe there is a way around this problem (and I am aware that not all readers would even consider that a problem exists). By exploiting techniques of juxtaposition and misdirection much more like the sceptical engraver than the complacent legalist, Fielding's writing betrays deep inner tensions, points of ideological stress and uncertainty which disfigure many of those very passages where he most strenuously tries to maintain control. Though this certainly happens in Blackstone too, when he has to confront the violation of his gentlemanly discourse by the blatant savagery of the Augustan penal code, it is much more part of the rhetorical fabric of Fielding's work, and its consequences are much more dramatic.

Even at his most conservative, Fielding seems unable to provide a fully coherent single perspective, to maintain concentration on the one clear point at issue, and his prose remains always haunted by the ghosts of irony. At the moments when he seems to be offering the clearest panaceas for all social ills, his prose emits little signals of the incompetence or partiality of these plans, and momentary recognitions of their inevitable ineptitude. As Michael McKeon puts it in his stimulating discussion of *Jonathan Wild*: 'Like his epistemology, Fielding's ideology is the issue of a double critique: first of aristocratic ideology by progressive, then of progressive ideology by conservative.'[3] Although, like many others, I remain a little perplexed by McKeon's fusillade of descriptive terms – 'aristocratic', 'progressive' and 'conservative' all need more clarification than he gives them, and his rendering of 'ideology' is certainly idiosyncratic – I feel his identification of the 'double critique' in Fielding's writing is perfectly accurate, and worth developing in this context.

What makes Fielding's work so interesting and so characteristic of eighteenth-century representations of legal matters is the warring of impulses within it, the way the contesting rhetorics of the law, the opposing forces of order and disorder, fight it silently out on the page. This conflict is sometimes fully in the author's control, as we shall see, part of a deliberate strategy, but at other times it seems to be stealthy and inevitable, outwith Fielding's manipulative control, and it often leaves his prose struggling to regain its composure. Although the contest between these two ideologies, the 'progressive' and the 'conservative', to label them crudely for the moment, is at its most intense and sustained in the fiction, its terms of reference and the rules of engagement are established and elaborated upon in his various social pamphlets.

When writing about the legal system around 1750, Fielding found himself offering patriotic tribute to the superiority of the English constitution and calls for sweeping reform at the same time, twin rhetorics difficult for him to sustain simultaneously. In the *Charge Delivered to the Grand Jury*, for example, the ringing praise of English legal institutions was followed by a long list of vice, iniquity, crime, depravity and corruptions particularly favoured by the English, without any overt recognition that there was anything odd about the juxtaposition of such a splendid constitution and such awful constituents. That is only one brief example of an inner tension between panegyric and revisionist disparagement, but it is representative of some of the contradictions and dialectical tensions Fielding's rhetoric has to negotiate or disguise. Whereas the social pamphlets are addressed to specific issues, Fielding's more encyclopaedic works encompass so many positions, and have so many shadowy vestiges of their opposites contained within them, that they become a repository of confusions dressed in the guise of certainties, a pageant of paradoxes masquerading as homilies.

All the complexities of ideological contest are directly or indirectly confronted in Fielding's major fiction, which even in its most comic forms is interrogative and investigative. It is obvious that, say, *Jonathan Wild* is a dynamic and interrogative text, rather than a static one. It adopts a form in which the dialectical interplay of values between Wild and Heartfree is more complex and unsettling than in a simple mock-heroic reversal or parody, and there is a glimpse of apocalyptic nihilism at its heart. Yet even in the apparently more assured comic novels, and still more flagrantly in *Amelia*, the questioning or teasing of aspects of the prevailing ideology is insistent. Furthermore, even in his most polemical works of social policy, which strive to be so resolute and single-minded, Fielding was unable wholly to discard irony or disperse the tensions within his ideological framework. As a result, his arguments even at their most assertive or seemingly confident never fall to the level of complacency or satisfaction that can be found in so many parts of Blackstone's *Commentaries*, and a fugitive internal critique is always available to the inquisitive reader.

The most interesting of Fielding's polemical works in this context are his *Enquiry into the Causes of the Late Increase of Robbers* (1751) and *A Proposal for Making an Effectual Provision for the Poor* (1753).[4] In each of these long essays, Fielding puts forward elaborate, if mainly conventional, solutions to problems which had recently become central to political debate, solutions which he offers as conciliatory and conservative, many of which were later implemented by his brother, Sir John Fielding. As he presents it, poverty and crime are social and political problems which the government is empowered to manage, and an improvement in the implementation of the existing laws, coupled with an extensive revision of the statutes is the best managerial strategy available. Fielding's role as a commentator is to present possible solutions which are ideologically acceptable to those with the power to make them happen, and, just as important, practical. It is necessary for him to adopt this particular advisory role because of his recognition, as he complains in his *Journal of a Voyage to Lisbon*, that the

> political economy of this nation, which, as it concerns only the regulation of the mob, is below the notice of our great men; though on the due regulation of this order depend many emoluments, which the great men themselves, or at least many who tread close on their heels may enjoy.[5]

Given the obvious indifference of the legislators, Fielding is enabled to present his tracts simultaneously as positive contributions to debate and corrective analyses of negligence, encouraging that potent mixture of pragmatic concern for those below the writer and exasperated complaint about those above which distinguishes the tone of so much Augustan political writing. As he says later in the same passage, 'I will represent the case, as it appears to me, very fairly and impartially between the mob and their betters.'

Under the abstractions of 'poverty' and 'crime', of course, Fielding was referring to the poor and the criminal, or, as we have seen, to what he constructs as the 'mob'. His motives in addressing these questions may have been wholly altruistic, as he saw it, articulating a genuine concern for the moral and political well-being of his country and his class. They might also, of course, have been less nobly connected to an attempt to secure further preferment for himself.[6] In either case, the rhetoric he employs incorporates straightforwardly many of the central themes of contemporary conservative thinking about the law, consonant with the terms of reference of the official Commons Committee charged with investigating the causes of and remedies for the perceived recent increase in crime, which was established by Royal Decree in 1750, and which led eventually to the introduction of the rather ineffectual 'Murder Act' in 1752, incorporating only a few of Fielding's proposals.[7]

Throughout Fielding's legalistic social analysis, the most pressing problems to be solved are civic disorder and the methods of legislative control. In his contribution to the literature about public disturbances and the procedures of the courts which arose from the controversial Bosavern Penlez case in 1749, in which a very unfortunate sailor was hanged for his part in the looting of bawdy-houses in the Strand, Fielding combined a defence of his own behaviour with an analysis of the history of rioting in England. Stressing the antiquity of the Riot Act, and the seriousness with which riots and rioters had always (and, he suggests, quite properly) been treated by the English courts, Fielding constructs an account of the need to control crowds, who may always unleash at any time their inherent potential for committing outrages:

> I think it may very fairly be inferred, that the Mob, which had already carried on their riotous Proceedings during two successive Nights, and who during the whole Day on *Monday*, were in Motion all over the Town, had they not been alarmed and intimidated by the Care of the Magistrate, would have again repeated their Outrage, as they had threatened on *Monday* Night. And had such a Riot continued a little longer, no Man can, I think, foresee what it might have produced. The Cry against Bawdy-Houses might have been easily converted into an Out-cry of a very different Nature, and Goldsmiths might have been considered to be as great a Nuisance to the Public as Whores.
>
> (p. 57)

The case Fielding makes looks on the face of it to be an extreme and rather unconvincing one, too clearly self-serving and designed to deflect criticism of his own seemingly shabby part in the affair. It is certainly one that seems to have aroused little contemporary sympathy or support.[8] However, what makes it interesting here is the way it tries to remove our attention from the unfortunate individual at the centre of it all (Penlez, or, to read the pamphlet as primarily an exercise in exculpation, Fielding himself), replacing him with that dangerous irrational marauding beastie so long beloved of conservative ideologues, the 'Mob'.

The criminalisation of the 'mob' was one of the central sustaining ideas behind much of the Augustan concern for the behaviour of crowds. A surprising number of subsequent historians have accepted that the many riots and civic disturbances at the time were over-boisterous agglomerations of the dishonest poor, eager to cause trouble, looking for any excuse to run amok, although the more sympathetic recent work of George Rudé, Peter Linebaugh and E. P. Thompson has made any such assumption much less easy to support.[9] For orderly and law-abiding Augustans, however, the notion of the potentially violent 'mob' was both convenient and disconcerting. One of the paradoxes within Augustan criminal legislation was that, although it was widely believed that the 'mob' behaved differently from the way its constituent members would normally behave, punitive sanctions could only be administered to some of those individuals. Whereas the legalists and theorists dealt mainly with abstractions, the courts were confronted with characters, and often rather sorry ones like the unfortunate Penlez. To reverse the terms of a formulation more familiar elsewhere, they dealt not with manners, but with men, and not with the species, but with individuals.

Inevitably, in the court's treatment of indicted rioters, it could seem that the wrong characters had been singled out, or that those unhappy felons were treated with undue exemplary severity. Each individual surely would resent, though thousands equally were meant. The Bosavern Penlez case was one of a number which brought this difficulty into the open. Another, slightly different in emphasis, was the case of the accused Mary Squires, which Fielding discussed (and misinterpreted) in *A Clear State of the Case of Elizabeth Canning* (1753). The desire to avoid the minute and contentious circumstances of particular cases, and thus keep out of needless controversy, may have been one reason why Fielding's longer pamphlets, like his fiction, claim to tackle the subject of crime control in a more generalised and less individualised way.

Fielding's *Enquiry* may offer itself as a pragmatic solution to the topical problems of crime, but it is just as much an essay on the behaviour of the poor in Augustan England, an essay given urgency by a sense of immediate crisis. Time and again, Fielding makes it clear that the crime problem is really a problem about the failure of the poor to conduct themselves properly, and about the failure of the government to carry out its various paternalist social responsibilities intelligently, a twin perspective which allows him space to criticise all parties involved. One recent critic argues that Fielding had 'no new theories but a vivid wish for national prosperity, safety, and order, so that the citizens – labouring class to landed gentry – could be prepared and permitted to fulfil their capabilities'.[10] It is certainly true that many of the main points of his argument in the *Enquiry* were conventional ones, promoting safety and public order, but we need to hesitate over the very liberal notion that Fielding wanted to promote a society in which everyone could develop all their capabilities. It seems much more obvious throughout this essay and elsewhere that the only capabilities the poor can be allowed are to be honest or dishonest, industrious or idle. What the essay is designed to provide is a legal framework in which the punishments for the dishonest or idle poor are sufficiently predictable and effective to ensure that this paternal model of social organisation is not endangered by emergent social mobility. The solution to the problem of the poor lies not in making them any less poor, but in making them honestly and usefully poor. The encouragement of industry, and the clearly limited rewards for diligent labouring people which are central to Fielding's argument are laid out more systematically and rather chillingly in his *Proposal for Making*

Effectual Provision for the Poor (1753), where no such generous provisions for individual personal development or fulfilment are seriously entertained.

Fielding's case in the *Enquiry* is not personalised, and he avoids libellous or potentially controversial remarks about any specific court-cases. Rather, his analysis, like Colquhoun's later on, is based on the perceived behaviour of groups and classes, and on the legalist measures that might be taken to improve their regulation, which are different in each case. The poor, it seems, have been infected by the desire for luxury, and this has given them ideas above their station. Taking seriously the very argument that Mandeville ironically disrupts, Fielding makes a number of very censorious remarks about the universal human taste for luxury, and the political and social evils it provokes:

> the vast Torrent of Luxury which of late Years hath poured itself into this Nation, hath greatly contributed to produce, among many others, the Mischief I here complain of. I aim not here to satirize the Great, among whom Luxury is probably a moral than a political Evil. But Vices no more than Diseases will stop with them; for bad Habits are as infectious by Example, as the Plague itself by Contact. In free Countries, at least, it is a Branch of Liberty claimed by the People to be as wicked and as profligate as their Superiors. Thus while the Nobleman will emulate the grandeur of a Prince; and the Gentleman will aspire to the proper State of the Nobleman; the Tradesman steps from behind his Counter into the vacant Place of the Gentleman. Nor doth the Confusion end here: It reaches the very Dregs of the People, who aspiring still to a Degree beyond that which belongs to them, and not being able by the Fruits of honest Labour to support the State which they affect, they disdain the Wages to which their Industry would intitle them; and abandoning themselves to Idleness, the more simple and poor-spirited betake themselves to a State of Starving and Beggary, while those of more Art and Courage become Thieves, Sharpers and Robbers.
>
> (p. 77)

Within this very dismissive and repressive argument, there is a controlled yet highly-charged analysis of confusion and disorder, reaching towards a predictably authoritarian conclusion about the origins of criminality in the poor. The terms of reference are conventional enough, and the notion of vice as a disease or as part of a causal chain was expressed regularly at the time.[11] What is especially interesting about Fielding's version, however, is the passing acknowledgement of the way this argument might allow for a more far-reaching satirical critique of the manners of the mighty. Although the paternalistic drift of the argument naturally brings greater concentration to bear on the misbehaving lower orders, and reiterates Fielding's customary contempt for tradesmen, it also allows him to pass judgement on the failure of the upper classes to provide proper patterns of behaviour for the respectful emulation of their inferiors.

Frequently throughout this pamphlet, Fielding embarks on a recognisably conservative critique of the behaviour of the poor, castigating their deplorable propensities for drunkenness or idleness or vagrancy. As he does so, though, he also offers veiled glimpses of a simultaneous, barely compatible argument about the vices in higher ranks, and the ironies of a double perspective are certainly introduced, even if they remain largely undeveloped. The language of 'contagion', which is so central to his presentation of 'luxury', requires, after all, some initial carriers of the disease, and these are located in the upper ranks of society. It is this capacity for double vision, for the subtle infiltration of secondary references and contradictory meanings, which makes Fielding a commentator in the dynamic and critical style of Hogarth, whom he so obviously admired and to whom there are copious adulatory references throughout *Joseph Andrews* and *Tom Jones*, rather than an apologist in the linear and expository style of Blackstone.

One of the most obvious examples of this double perspective appears in Fielding's treatment of the pernicious and pervasive vice of 'gaming'. Just as the Augustan period was marked by the expansion of standardised business practices and commercial statutes, so too it was a period of extraordinary unauthorised gambling by all classes. Alongside the officially-sanctioned State lottery, which had been established in 1694, and which is given prominence in Mr Wilson's tale in *Joseph Andrews* and the tale of the Man of the Hill in *Tom Jones*, there were a host of public venues for betting and wagering, some legal and salubrious, like Newmarket, others definitely not. Between 1739 and 1752, four statutes were put forward to control the activities of the gaming houses, but there is little evidence that they were in any way successful. As Roy Porter entertainingly puts it,

> England was gripped by gambling fever. Men bet on political events, births and deaths – any future happenings. For a few pounds challengers galloped against the clock, gulped down pints of gin, or ate live cats. A common wager was to take out insurance policies on *other* people's lives. When George II led his troops against the French in 1743 you could get four to one against his being killed. Cards were the opium of the polite.[12]

The evidence seems to suggest that gambling was not confined to any particular group, and that all classes participated in their various styles, but the law and the commentators did not interpret the problem in this universal way. When Fielding addressed this matter in his *Enquiry*, he made it central to his analysis of the vices of the 'Vulgar':

I come now to the last great Evil which arises from the Luxury of the Vulgar; and this is Gaming: A School in which the most dangerous Highwaymen of great Eminence have been bred. This Vice is the more dangerous, as it is deceitful, and, contrary to every other Species of Luxury, flatters its Votaries with the Hopes of increasing their Wealth; so that Avarice itself is so far from securing us from its Temptations, that it often betrays the more thoughtless and giddy Part of Mankind into them; promising Riches without Bounds, and those to be acquired by the most sudden as well as easy and indeed pleasant means.

(p. 92)

So gambling is the breeding-ground for highwaymen (a point commonly included in popular criminal biographies) and the great temptation for 'the more thoughtless and giddy'. In this passage, Fielding accurately reproduces the official legal position, which was eager to suppress 'Gaming in the lower Classes of Life, so plainly tending to the Ruin of Tradesmen, the Destruction of Youth, and to the Multiplication of every Kind of Fraud and Violence'. In response to this disruption of hierarchical stabilities, 'the Legislature hath provided very wholesome Laws' (p. 94).

Taken in isolation, this passage shows Fielding at his most unpleasantly patrician and dismissive, sneering at tradesmen and those below them, applauding any laws which help keep the poor in their place and keep temptation away from the feeble-witted. High-minded concern seems to turn rather quickly into high-handed contempt. Yet it would be misleading to remove this extract from its context. Just as in the comparable representation in the fourth plate of Hogarth's *Rake's Progress*, Fielding's attack on gambling reaches beyond 'Tradesmen', although entirely different remedies are suggested for suppressing the vice in the different social classes. In a densely paradoxical passage, Fielding seeks to excuse himself from commenting on the vices of the wealthy, while proceeding to enumerate a detailed account of them:

And here I must again remind the Reader, that I have only the inferiour Part of Mankind under my Consideration. I am not so ill-bred as to disturb the Company at a polite Assembly; nor so ignorant of our Constitution as to imagine, that there is a sufficient Energy in the executive Part to controul the Oeconomy of the Great, who are beyond the Reach of any, unless capital Laws. Fashion, under whose Guidance they are, and which created the Evil, can alone cure it. With Patience therefore must we wait, till this notable Mistress of the Few shall, in her good time, accomplish so desirable a Change: In fact, till Great Men become wiser or better; till the Prevalence of some laudable Taste shall teach them a worthier Manner of employing their Time; till they have Sense enough to be reasoned, Modesty enough to be laughed, or Conscience enough to be frightened out of a silly, a shameful and a sinful Profligacy, attended with horrid Waste of Time, and the cruel Destruction of the Families of others, or of their own.

In the mean time we may, I think reasonably desire of these great Personages, that they would keep their favorite Vice to themselves, and not suffer others, whose Birth or Fortune gives them no Title to be above the Terrour of the Laws, or the Censure of their Betters, to share with them in this Privilege.

(pp. 92–3)

Suddenly, the attempt to suppress the poor is suspended, and the focus of attention turns upward. The way Fielding constructs the argument makes the prosperous gambler seem considerably worse than the humble one, being oblivious to recommendation, deaf to advice, and beyond the power of the law.

In this passage, Fielding seems to turn his back for a moment on his earlier statements – 'I aim not here to satirize the Great' – and he ironically disrupts the even, measured tone of his earlier proposals by the pessimistic intervention of the serious problem of wealthy gamblers for whom no such practical measures can be taken. A similarly ironic insinuation occurs when he discusses gambling in *The Covent-Garden Journal* in 1752:

Gaming, a Vice so universally condemned by the Lords and Commons, that these ten or twelve last Years have, I think, produced no less than four several Laws for its Punishment and Extirpation. These are indeed virtually to be considered as the Censures of the whole Nation; but they must be considered as positively and expressly the Sentiments of all the greatest Men in it. How singular and contemptible the Character of a Gamester would appear in such an Age as this, needs very little Argument or Illustration.[13]

Fielding here seems unable to ignore the evil of upper-class gambling, but equally unable to incorporate or assimilate it fully into his magisterial perspective. The vices of the wealthy seem to him to be more dangerous, more severe and more ingrained than the vices of the lower orders, but his pamphlets can really find no place to address this issue clearly. The consequent strain on the register he adopts, praising the wealthy as his patrons, and as those with the power to implement his suggestions, while seeking to identify and disparage their flagrant vices, produces not only the defensive resort to irony, but the odd and rather unpleasant spectacle of the author mumbling the hands that feed him.

Fielding's pamphlets and journalism thus for the most part enunciate a deeply conservative vision of a paternalist society concerned to keep its poor and its not-so-poor in their proper hierarchical places, using the terrors of the law to that end. In the *Enquiry*, Fielding offers suggestions for increasing the awfulness of the death penalty, by making hangings private and by giving the bodies of the executed over to the surgeons for anatomies, and for making the laws better deterrents. In the *Proposal*, similar repressive measures, like the establishment of workhouses, are encouraged. The overall tone is of an author subservient to the needs of those in power, and eager to be practical. At times, as in his *Charge*, Fielding just about manages to carry this off consistently. But more often, as in the *Enquiry* and the *Proposal*, his attempts to be austere and magisterial are put under constant pressure by his recognition of the iniquities and unreliability of his audience. His interim negotiating position as a pamphleteer enables him to be frank about those below him, but only allows him to address his superiors through the intermittent disguises and indirections of irony.

The most complex and sustained ironic analysis in his writing is clearly *Jonathan Wild*, where legal issues and the status of the legislature are confronted directly. However, the double critical vision which informs that book is almost as important in his other fiction. Faced with his inability to bring his contemporary world to order, surrounded by its indiscipline, Fielding created alternative, overlapping worlds, which he could regulate at will and in which he would be able to act as disinterested benevolent law-maker and despot, presiding over a disciplined and regulated structure. The issues of order and disorder, of regulation and anarchy, of the 'mob' and its constituent members, of crime and punishment, all of which are so close to the surface of so much Augustan pamphleteering, form the fabric of Fielding's fictions, and his novels become sustained interrogations of the prevailing and emergent ideologies of law, and investigations of judgement.

THE APPEAL OF COMEDY

> However the Glare of Riches, and Awe of Title, may dazzle and terrify the Vulgar; nay, however Hypocrisy may deceive the more Discerning, there is still a Judge in every Man's Breast, which none can cheat nor corrupt, tho' perhaps it is the only uncorrupt Thing about him.[14]

Fielding's social pamphlets and magistratical pronouncements show him trying assiduously to create a space for himself in which his personal and class allegiances and his avowals of disinterested concern for the well-being of his society do not come into obvious or violent conflict. As in the writing of so many other Augustan commentators, Fielding's rhetoric is designed to acknowledge yet also to suppress the potency of its class values, claiming for the author the authoritative appearance of a non-partisan, impartial and altruistic observer. At one and the same time, he was trying to hold down difficult positions as both an unembarrassed agent of the state's law, and a revisionist critic of the statute, making the most strenuous efforts to appear loyal to his principles (and his patrons) and simultaneously *déclassé*. The strains between these positions are obvious and they appear throughout his non-fictional writing, where the recognition of universal human failings is mitigated by the provision of repressive legal remedies which primarily attempt to discipline the 'mob'. Similarly, questions of allegiance and protestations of impartiality are both very prominent in Fielding's comic fiction, where some of the inevitable tensions are offered resolution by persistent appeals to the disinterested private tribunal which Fielding believed lay hidden in 'every Man's Breast'.

That Fielding's comic fiction is judicial and judgemental as well as festive and celebratory is unquestionable. Starting from his first lampooning extended narrative, *Shamela* (1742), it is obvious that his work has something in common with the disintegrative and admonitory work of the Augustan satirists. His sustained derisive parody of Samuel Richardson's *Pamela* (1740) is unrelenting in its intricate hostility to the earlier narrative, and, like the other anti-Richardson tales of the day, energetically sets that author up for public scorn. In an admittedly less intense manner than the earlier work of Dryden and Pope, *Shamela* is Fielding's own contribution to the correction of contemporary taste, to cultural diagnosis and to the routing of those he saw as barely literate *arrivistes*. Although it is quite reasonable to identify the epistolary technique of Richardson's novel as one target of Fielding's mockery, the real object of his scorn is what he understands to be the system of values which that technique articulates. His most significant trick is to turn Pamela's protestations of innocence and chastity into a campaign of guile and policy, but the exuberant fun he constructs around this simple idea is not wholly light-hearted or tolerant. As Margaret Anne Doody puts it:

> What really bothered Fielding about *Pamela* was that it was subversive. It overthrew classical literary decorum in making a low, ungrammatical female its heroine; it overthrew social barriers in presenting a misalliance as not only possible but in given circumstances desirable . . . *Shamela* shows what a revolutionary book *Pamela* could seem. Richardson's novel affronted the old Etonian in Fielding, and he registered the reaction of the Establishment.[15]

There had been similar confrontational gestures in Fielding's writing before 1740, most notably in his satiric exploitation of mock-heroic bombast in the *Tragedy of Tragedies*. However, by this later stage of his literary career, the direction and function of Fielding's wit had changed, and he was no longer regularly articulating ideological positions oppositional to those in power. Rather, he was using the resources of the press to activate hostility to potential and actual disruptions of what he saw as settled hierarchical patterns of behaviour, reinforcing the deeply conservative attitudes to gender and conduct which were established through the legal system, and investigating the possibilities of an integrated and just society in which true virtue would be rewarded and hypocrisies detected.

However, the insistent boisterousness and coarseness of *Shamela* is unrepresentative of Fielding's subsequent comic narratives, and it may instead represent the final fling of his scathing theatrical style. In his later fictional work, he sought (or pretended to seek) a gentler and more ruminative approach. While still clearly judgemental and designed to be corrective, as we shall see, the comic form of *Joseph Andrews* and *Tom Jones* is less aggressive and apparently more tolerant, worldly and compassionate, altogether more positive, than the dismissive tone of the earlier lampoon. Fielding's alignment in this enterprise is with the traditional discussions of stage comedy from Aristophanes and Plautus onwards rather than with the more recent definitions of satire. Whereas the Scriblerian discussions of satire had often been couched in the aggressive language of the pillory, talking of 'snarling' and 'biting' and 'lashing', and had sought to establish writing as an effective vehicle for the unauthorised humiliation and public chastisement of rascals, Fielding sought a form of ridicule which was less violent and which could be effectively administered in private. His acknowledged precedents for this enterprise lay, as he claimed, in the combination of mockery and sympathy that distinguishes Cervantes' *Don Quixote*, but there were also English writers of the immediately earlier period who had thought of comedy as a stylised and relatively unaggressive vehicle for correction.

Although, as Fielding himself enjoys pointing out in the preface to *Joseph Andrews*, the informed discussion of comedy in English writing had never been as intelligent or sustained as the comparable discussions of tragedy or epic, the lighter style had certainly not gone unnoticed. Aristotle's alleged treatise on comedy might have disappeared, and rumours of the existence of a comic companion-piece to the *Iliad* remained unfounded, but nonetheless there were still some recent indigenous efforts to legitimise the 'low' style of comedy which were worth citing. After all, the Restoration stage of Wycherley, Etherege and Congreve had been dominated by a certain kind of comic writing, even if it was one which the newly censorious Fielding might have felt obliged to deplore. Like Jeremy Collier, whose *Short View of the Prophaneness of the English Stage* (1698) had set the terms of reference for those hostile to an unhindered and unlicensed theatre, Fielding in the later part of his career ostensibly sought to cleanse comedy from its racier, more cynical, and less salubrious associations, however much he covertly recognised and admired the wit and intelligence of Wycherley and the others. At the same time, he was eager to appropriate what he saw as the previously stigmatised and 'low' literary form of the novel as a vehicle for *haut-bourgeois* discernment and refined judgement. For him, the comic novel (in the right hands) could become a restrained and disciplined form of corrective writing, the 'comic-epic poem in prose' as he flippantly and paradoxically defined it, exposing the ridiculous while avoiding the barely-controlled rancour or venom of satire, and presenting its cases before that wise 'Judge' to be found in the human breast.

The precedents available to him in this act of appropriation and exaltation are not always the most obvious or easily available ones. Fielding largely ignores, or belittles, the existing traditions of British prose fiction, as his various derisive comments about Behn, Manley and Defoe indicate, and the arguments he draws on are more informed by earlier and contemporary dramatic criticism. One important text was George Farquhar's *Discourse upon Comedy in Reference to the English Stage* (1702), partly a defence of theatrical practice against some of Jeremy Collier's arguments, incorporating the view that comedy need not be strictly limited by adherence to the unities, an argument that in turn can find authoritative precedent in the statements of Eugenius and Neander in Dryden's *Essay of Dramatic Poetry* (1666). Farquhar based his argument on the peculiar mixed constitution and variousness of the English character, which made the application of rigid foreign systems of rules inappropriate, and in this particular patriotic tribute to the possibilities of a native comic spirit he was developing a view forcefully put in Sir William Temple's essay, 'Of Poetry' (1690).[16] Other Augustan defences of the comic spirit and English comic writing available to Fielding came from diverse sources, including John Dennis in his *Defence of Sir Fopling Flutter* (1722), where comedy is seen as having the capacity 'to expose persons to our view whose views we may shun, and whose follies we may despise'.[17] Dennis's version is characteristically furious and emotive ('shun', 'despise') but it does provide a corrective and judicial function for the comic writer, who can thus be lined up alongside the even more savage satirist in the literary project of seeking to improve contemporary manners and morals.

Given the dismissive way Fielding talked about Dennis in the *Covent-Garden Journal* in 1752, it is likely that he shared the view of Swift and Pope that nothing which that writer said was to be taken seriously. However, Dennis's remarks on the censorious powers of comedy were not entirely idiosyncratic, appearing in less intense form in the works by Farquhar and Temple already mentioned, and they may represent a particularly energetic and impassioned inflection of the most conventional way of thinking about comic literature. They may be compared with another earlier pertinent example, where Dryden's most famous enemy, Thomas Shadwell, wrote a prefatory essay to his play *The Humorists* (1671), in which comedy's corrective function is articulated and defended most interestingly:

My design was in it, to reprehend some of the Vices and Follies of the

Age, which I take to be the most proper, and most useful way of writing Comedy . . . Here I must take leave to dissent from those, who seem to insinuate that the ultimate end of a Poet is to delight, without correction or instruction: Methinks a Poet should never acknowledge this, for it makes him as little use to Mankind as a Fidler, or Dancing-Master, who delights the fancy onely, without improving the Judgement . . . I confess, a Poet ought to do all that he can, decently to please, that so he may instruct. To adorn his Images of *Vertue* so delightfully to affect people with a secret veneration of it in others, and an emulation to practice it in themselves: And to render their figures of *Vice* and *Folly* so ugly and detestable, to make People hate and despise them, not only in others, but (if it be possible) in their dear selves. And in this latter, I think Comedy more useful than Tragedy; because the Vices and Follies in *Courts* (as they are too tender to be touch'd) so they concern but a few; whereas the Cheats, Villanies, and trouble-some Follies, in the common conversation of the World, are of concernment to all the Body of Mankind.[18]

Although this passage anticipated the preface to *Joseph Andrews* by more than seventy years, it contains many of the Horatian ideas of delight and instruction which were acknowledged rather unconvincingly by Swift, but which came into greater prominence in Fielding's own developed legitimisation of comedy. To begin with, Shadwell defines comedy as a gentler, more discrete tribunal than the savage Juvenalian scourging and name-calling of satire, best restricted to depicting general types and common 'low' vices. The great theme of comic writing, according to the prefatory chapter to Book I of *Joseph Andrews*, is the ridiculous, which arises predominantly from affectation, and disfigures characters in a way which an astute author can make entertaining and instructive. The whole enterprise of the comic novel thus offers itself as a tribunal in which these vices or follies of ridiculousness are, in Shadwell's terms, reprehended, without going so far as to make readers 'hate and despise' the individuals involved.

In opposition to the public performance of dramatic comedy, and the metaphorical search for public display in satire, the private perusal of prose fiction allows its author to speak directly to the reader's conscience, changing the status of the presentation of ridiculousness. Unlike the tribunal of satire, the disciplinary structure of comedy is fundamentally reintegrative, encouraging its readers to entertain the possibilities of forgiveness and resolution rather than the full disintegrative force of stigmatisation. There are exceptions to this even in *Joseph Andrews*, like the derisive satiric treatment of Colley Cibber, the continuing intermit-tent parody of Richardson, and the introduction of a more serious narrative in the tales of Leonora and Mr Wilson. Similar inconsistencies and breaches of the comic tone are obvious also in the treatment of Lady Bellaston and Lord Fellamar in *Tom Jones*. However, the books mingle these satiric and parodic and more sombre or vituperative touches with the dominant structure of comedy, where greater reintegration is made possible than the darker interpolated tales might lead us to expect. Central to the comic writer's concern with affectation is the separation of the reprehended behaviour from the reprehensible character, a separation which Fielding insists on most strongly, and which may lead to the possibilities of amendment and resolution through a plea to the potential for benevolence which he believed lies hidden in us all.

Amidst Fielding's famous remarks at the beginning of Book III of *Joseph Andrews* about the nature of comic fiction and biography, we may recall his account of his presentation of the lawyer in the stage-coach, and the way he uses it to elaborate upon his own procedures and obscure the distinction between comedy and satire:

> I question not but several of my Readers will know the Lawyer in the Stage-Coach, the Moment they hear his Voice . . . To prevent therefore any such malicious Applications, I declare here once and for all, I describe not Men, but Manners; not an Individual, but a Species. Perhaps it will be answered, Are not the Characters then taken from Life? To which I answer in the Affirmative; nay, I believe I might aver, that I have writ little more than I have seen. The Lawyer is not only alive, but hath been so these 4000 Years, and I hope G-- will indulge his Life as many yet to come. He hath not indeed confined himself to one Profession, one Religion, or one Country; but when the first mean selfish Creature appeared on the human Stage, who made Self the Centre of the whole Creation; would give himself no Pain, incur no Danger, advance no Money to assist, or preserve his Fellow-Creatures; then was our Lawyer born; and whilst such a Person as I have described, exists on Earth, so long shall he remain upon it. It is therefore doing him little Honour, to imagine he endeavours to mimick some little obscure Fellow, because he happens to resemble him in one particular Feature, or perhaps in his Profession; whereas his Appearance in the World is calculated for much more general and noble Purposes; not to expose one pitiful Wretch, to the small and contemptible Circle of his Acquaintance; but to hold the Glass to thousands in their Closets, that they may contemplate their Deformity, and endeavour to reduce it, and thus by suffering private Mortification may avoid public Shame. This places the Boundary between, and distinguishes the Satirist from the Libeller; for the former privately corrects the Fault for the Benefit of the Person, like a Parent; the latter publickly exposes the Person himself, as an Example to others, like an Executioner.[19]

In this passage, Fielding happily joins in the chorus of vilification of lawyers which echoed throughout Europe in the eighteenth century, and continued to emerge in British fiction even later, in such books as *Great Expectations* and *Bleak House*. But Fielding also takes the opportunity to dignify his own comic procedures, by generalising the objects of his ridicule, and taking on the status of a well-meaning, reintegrative punisher. His approach is, almost literally, paternalist, in that he sets himself up as the prime source of authority in the text, its only begetter, and takes on the Solomon-like role of the just arbitrator in disputes, the chastiser of the wicked, and the custodian of values. His seriousness in this endeavour can be measured by looking at the gravity and censoriousness of his magistratical pamphlets and his works on social policy. But of course, his awareness of his own capacity for pomposity or ridiculousness can just as easily be seen in the way he figures an equally confident pedagogue, author and chastiser in one narrative in the figure of Abraham Adams. The 'double critique' identified by McKeon is here worked out in the most ironic and splendidly self-referential of ways, with Fielding as the model of order and regulation being mirrored in the text by a figure who, from similarly altruistic motives, repeatedly provokes the greatest disorder and comic mayhem.

It is by this method of generalisation and regulated commentary that Fielding uses comic fiction as a procedure of discipline, both in the sense of the sustained literary skill he is required to exert, and which he claims for himself in the preface to Book I of *Joseph Andrews* and in many of the authorial performances of *Tom Jones*, and in terms of the punitive ends to which that skill is directed. He seems to be arguing in this passage from Book III of the earlier novel that comedy is a superior form to 'libel' (or personalised savage satire) as it goes on behind closed doors, and brings the ridiculousness of the characters home to their representatives in the reading public, who laugh and suffer 'private Mortifications' at the same time. Fielding claims he is not putting his victims in his comic pillory so that we may scorn or revile them, but rather so that they may be reprehended and may thereby scorn themselves. His victims suffer embarrassment, not contempt, except perhaps for those reptilian critics so severely berated throughout *Tom Jones*, and Colley Cibber. Unlike Dryden, Pope and Swift, the novelist is not trying to organise an independent and pitiless punitive community in which those offenders whom the law ignores can be more rightfully displayed. He may intermittently sport with that form, in his portraits of those too exalted to appear before the courts, and Colley Cibber, but his main impulse is to portray things so that they become self-evidently ridiculous, in a way that universalises the problems, and chastens gently.

All through *Joseph Andrews* and *Tom Jones*, Fielding draws our attention to the ineptitude of most tribunals of judgement and their officers, and implies thereby the superiority of the comic novel as conducted by himself as a forum in which truth might be discovered and follies might properly be reprehended. The comic novel becomes, as it were, a kind of moot, a hypothetical working out of test cases, or a forensic tribunal without the immediate pressure of individual judgement or the painful responsibility of sentencing, to which all the relevant evidence might be presented. The author offers the controlled and disciplined comic novel as a fantastic replacement for the existing tribunals of justice, and, in so doing, finds room for a sustained, slyly insinuated critique of those present institutions. The critique may be extensive and revisionist, but it is saved from anarchic or oppositional taint by the persistent orderly and controlling figure of the paternalist author.

Early in *Joseph Andrews*, he offers casual asides about the habitual ignorance of Justices of the Peace, and the conventional hypocrisy of magistrates:

> It was this Gentleman, who, having, as I said, observed the singular Devotion of young *Andrews*, had found means to question him, concerning several Particulars; as how many Books there were in the New Testament? which were they? how many Chapters they contained? and such like; to all which Mr. *Adams* privately said, he answer'd much better than Sir *Thomas*, or two other neighbouring Justices of the Peace could probably have done.
>
> (p. 23)

> Will Magistrates who punish Lewdness, or Parsons, who preach against it, make any scruple of committing it?
>
> (p. 41)

These small cries of protest, audible enough without being especially strident, are continued throughout the book, and are insinuated with even greater force into *Tom Jones*. However, though these remarks and incidents might individually be unimpressive, they gradually increase in volume and, by sheer force of numbers, they accumulate emphasis. As we begin to see, it is not only the individual officers of justice who are at fault. They are human, and thus inevitably misinformed or ignorant or hypocritical or corrupt most of the time. Human affairs are so complex, and so distorted by the pressure of unrevealed tensions, that even a magistrate as sympathetic as Squire Allworthy inevitably makes regular mistakes. Through his many portraits of lawyers and Justices, Fielding is certainly suggesting that there is room for improvement in the selection of legal officers, but he is also aware that there are greater structural problems to be recognised. As well as the perennial difficulties caused by the human inability to do anything properly, the greatest internal problem in the conduct of legal matters is the way the courts have to proceed. The whole system of institutionalised forensic inquiry, when in the hands of vain or unscrupulous lawyers and advocates, supervised by hypocritical or insufficiently astute magistrates, acts more as a forum for contending interests to engage in ritualised combat than for the disinterested pursuit of truth and justice. And even when most scrupulously conducted, in the hands of the high-minded and thoughtful, it still performs in a rough and ready way.

At various points in both novels, Fielding illustrates much more extensively than he was able to do in his pamphlets the ways in which class interests and allegiances, the pressures of hidden desires, and conflicts of personality, alongside the dynamic tensions of the courtroom and inefficiency of the institutions of law, could disfigure the implementation of justice and create the possibility that great injustices might unwittingly be performed. As part of his comic project, however, he emphasises more strongly the ways such impediments might actually serve to prevent the legal system from perpetrating injustices in the specific cases entailed in his plot, and shows how the complexity of legal proceedings eventually leads to the right decisions being taken, for whatever reasons. When the legal system becomes prominent in the earlier book, Fielding both identifies its obvious weaknesses, and renders them momentarily ineffective. The benign presence of the comic narrator allows the possibility of an extended critique, without the pessimism or oppositional fervour of Pope, suspending the inevitability of catastrophe. Instead of impressing the difficulties of justice upon us, he accommodates the problems within his comic world, leaving us to speculate on the harsher realities of the world outside his benevolently despotic control. At various points, as in the tale of Mr Wilson or the Man of the Hill in *Tom Jones*, we become more strongly aware of the differences between the world Fielding creates and the world he inhabits, and there are intermittent points of contact between these two which are deeply discomforting.

In the famous stage-coach episode, where various characters respond uncharitably to the ridiculous but pathetic figure of the naked Joseph, and display their hypocrisies in the process, all these combinations of critique and accommodation are offered. The traditional character of the unsympathetic lawyer is fully anatomised, and the point about the injustices of the existing legal apparatus is intensified when the narrator parenthetically remarks that the postillion, socially the lowest participant as well as the kindest, 'hath since been transported for robbing a Hen-roost' (p. 53). Fielding's sketches of injustice and hypocrisy are often understated in this style or hidden away in the corners of his text, but they are nonetheless pervasive and unsettling. At one point, the narrator embarks on an allegorical representation of Lady Booby's mind, after she has decided to dismiss Joseph, and that leads him on to a bitter and sardonic representation of the operations of courts:

She was a thousand times on the very Brink of revoking the Sentence she had passed against the poor Youth. Love became his Advocate, and whispered many things in his favour. Honour likewise endeavoured to vindicate his Crime, and Pity to mitigate his Punishment; on the other side, Pride and Revenge spoke as loudly against him: and thus the poor Lady was tortured with Perplexity; opposite Passions distracting and tearing her Mind different ways.

So have I seen, in the Hall of *Westminster*; where Serjeant *Bramble* hath been retained on the right Side, and Serjeant *Puzzle* on the left; the Balance of Opinion (so equal were their Fees) alternately incline to either Scale. Now *Bramble* throws in an Argument, and *Puzzle's* Scale strikes the Beam; again, Bramble shares the like Fate, overpowered by the Weight of *Puzzle*. Here *Bramble* hits, there *Puzzle* strikes; here one has you, there t'other has you; 'till at last all becomes one Scene of Confusion in the tortured Minds of the Hearers; equal Wagers are laid on the Success, and neither Judge not Jury can possibly make any thing of the Matter; all Things are so enveloped by the careful Serjeants in Doubt and Obscurity.

(p. 45)

The chaotic courtroom is here used as a fitting image for Lady Booby's mental turmoil and confusion, not in itself a very ennobling comparison for either party, presenting the authorised legal procedures as a kind of wrestling match between the highly-paid performers, which has no bearing on truth or justice. Rather than being a disinterested tribunal where evidence is carefully sifted through and assessed in an atmosphere of seriousness and orderly calm, the proceedings (and Lady Booby's mind) resemble a circus, where the performance is more important than the outcome. As the awful lawyer Scout explains later on, 'the utmost that was in the power of a Lawyer, was to prevent the Law's taking effect' (p. 284). And despite Blackstone's claims to the contrary, it seems as if torture is inscribed as part of the experience of the English legal system after all, although it is administered to the suffering magistrate and the jurors rather than to the offenders!

Fielding creates this image as one of his narrator's elaborate perorations, a baroque improvisation on his central ideas, yet it is fully corroborated by the legal proceedings which are more directly incorporated into the main body of the narrative. When Parson Adams and Fanny appear before a Justice of the Peace, Fielding orchestrates a farcical mismanagement of procedures. The Justice himself is full of levity and drink, and after much coarse taunting of the accused, and no real attention to their side of things, he prepares to consign them both to jail to await the assizes. However, on hearing of Adams's acquaintance with Lady Booby, he begins to soften:

'Nay,' says the Justice, 'if he is a Gentleman, and you are sure he is innocent, I don't desire to commit him, not I; I will commit the Woman by herself, and take your Bail for the Gentleman . . . and give the Gentleman a Glass to whet his Whistle before he begins. I know how to behave myself to Gentlemen as well as another. No body can say I have committed a Gentleman since I have been in the Commission.'

(p. 149)

The magistrate simply waives the proceedings against Adams as soon as he is assured of his gentlemanly status, and the charges against Fanny disappear in the ensuing confusion. The deposing witnesses are treated roughly, and it becomes apparent that their zeal in the pursuit of justice has been based solely on the expectation of a reward. The tribunal, in essence, has made no efforts to get to the bottom of things, but has instead shown itself to be a proceeding where the powerful are driven by snobbery and the others by greed and the prospect of personal gain. The guilt and innocence of the parties in question are made to seem remarkably remote from the whole business. And yet, in one of the controlled paradoxes that typify Fielding's comic art, the confusion creates rather than prevents the correct outcome. From the chaos of greed, snobbery and stupidity, justice of a sort eventually emerges, and from the riotous assembly that Fielding creates, the proper decision is unintentionally reached. The comic spirit once again allows Fielding to show the chastening potential for disaster inherent within the legal system, while more strongly encouraging him to exercise his authorial privileges to prevent those very disasters from happening.

Fielding returns to legal matters towards the climax of the novel. Joseph and Fanny appear before a magistrate, who intends to send them to Bridewell for 'a little Correction . . . a little Stripping and Whipping' (p. 289). Squire Booby asks about the nature of the crime, and is told that the accused have been identified as the villains who stole a twig ('of the value, as he believes, of 3 half pence') from the lawyer Scout:

'Jesu!' said the Squire, 'would you commit two Persons to *Bridwell* for a Twig?' 'Yes,' said the Lawyer, 'and with great Lenity too, for if we had called it a young Tree they would have been both hanged.'

(p. 290)

This outburst is comparable to the discussion of the 'Black Act' in Blackstone's *Commentaries*, where the awful severity of the law was acknowledged, criticised, but quickly dispersed. Fielding also finds a plot device for ignoring the potential for disaster he has deliberately included. Booby asks the Justice to deliver Joseph and Fanny over to his custody, and the Justice does so without hesitation. He explains his change of heart by claiming that the only reason he intended to treat them harshly was that Lady Booby wanted rid of them, and he was going to let them escape anyway. So the shades of the prison house which hang over the young people are simply blown away by the exercise of gentlemanly influence, and Fielding lets his characters escape even more easily than the Justice intended.

There is always something discomforting about such evident slickness, a sense that the comic triumph of innocence is a strategy of evasion, and that Fielding's deliberate introduction of these more disquieting elements is in itself a recognition of the unreality of comedy, which we may celebrate and feel chastened by at the same time. The gentlemanly restraint of the Justice's tribunal is mirrored by Fielding's similar tactful reluctance to pursue his investigations, and by the transfer of class status which ennobles both Joseph and Tom at the end of their narratives. Rather than offer a developed critique of the social institutions of legality, animated by a sense of injustice and the urgent need for reform, Fielding in both his extended comic novels is content to point out failings and leave any rectification of them to the consciences of his readers. His treatment of these legal issues is much more restrained and tactful than his analysis of other ills in the book, like the state of the clergy, or the hypocrisies of bourgeois London life. In this way, he both takes on responsibility for analysing the failings of the legal system, and avoids the consequent responsibility of having to do anything about them. Reform becomes a matter for the reader's conscience to decide, rather than for Fielding to direct.

The emphasis on the active judicial and veridical role of conscience is even more strongly developed in *Tom Jones*:

> To give a higher Idea of the Principle I mean, as well as one more familiar to the present Age; it may be considered as sitting on its Throne in the Mind, like the LORD HIGH CHANCELLOR of this Kingdom in his Court; where it presides, governs, directs, judges, acquits and condemns according to Merit and Justice; with a Knowledge which nothing escapes, a Penetration which nothing can deceive, and an Integrity which nothing can corrupt.
>
>   This active Principle may perhaps be said to constitute the most essential Barrier between us, and our Neighbours the Brutes; for if there be some in the human Shape, who are not under any such Dominion, I chuse rather to consider them as Deserters from us to our Neighbours; among whom they will have the Fate of Deserters, and not be placed in the first Rank.[20]

In the much longer and more discursive structure of the later novel, Fielding conducts a sustained enquiry '*in Foro Conscientiae*', the private tribunal of the reader's conscience, where misaccusations, travesties of justice, miscarriages and improper punishments are all revealed within an extraordinarily intricate, eventually reintegrative narrative structure. Once again, all the materials for a radical critique of the legal system are present, and, once again, Fielding exercises restraint in pressing his points home, preferring instead to demonstrate the more liberal and latitud-inarian possibilities of an innate sense of right and wrong, enabled by the benign and reintegrative structure of his comedy. Although there are numerous opportunities within the narrative for a more splenetic or rancorous castigation of incompetent legal proceedings and inept officers, Fielding does not regularly indulge them. On many occasions, of course, he fulminates against the unscrupulousness and incompetence of lawyers, particularly in his portrait of Dowling, or he demonstrates the regularity and inevitability of miscarriages of justice, but, like their parallels in *Joseph Andrews*, these are once again almost conventional comic devices – a way of making things go wrong so that they may eventually be put right – and they do not amount to a highly-charged satiric onslaught on the flawed institutions of legality. Instead, Fielding replaces the transparently fallible legal structure described within the tale with the superior discipline of comic fiction, where the magisterial author may overcome the obduracy of the world, and dispense justice, exercise restraint, or allocate and administer punishment and reward, as he thinks fit.[21]

That legal issues are made even more prominent in the later comic novel can be seen in the way its narrative is suspended between the activities of two local magistrates: Allworthy and Western. It would be a simple matter to contrast the characters of these two squires. Where one epitomises charity and active Christian concern, the other is choleric and hasty. Where one seems to embody many of Fielding's (and Blackstone's) ideals of high-mindedness, disinterest and informed compassion, the other is a self-interested roaring Country Tory caricature of everything Fielding thought ridiculous. One brief example will show the effect of these differences. When Allworthy hears that Tom is imprisoned and faces possible execution, he is acutely distressed. When the same news comes to Western's ears, his reaction is rather different, if no less deeply felt:

> 'What's that,' cries *Western*, 'Murder, hath he committed a Murder, and is there any Hopes of seeing him hanged? – Tol de rol, tol lol de rol.' Here he fell a singing and capering about the Room.
>
> (p. 885)

With all their apparent differences, the two magistrates seem to offer a stark and dramatic contrast between mercy and justice, reproducing the contrast which is embodied in a more extreme version in the diverse characters of Jones and Blifil, articulated through the differing political attitudes and responses to distress of these two locally-powerful individuals.

But that is not the whole story, and there is a very telling point of comparison between them. What Fielding contrives for us in the shaping of his plot is the opportunity to see both Allworthy and Western, from their remarkably different motives, regularly getting their judgements wrong. Paradoxical though it may seem, the parallel inadequacy of their tribunals is more striking than their vivid personal distinctions. When Allworthy tries the case of Jenny Jones, he is caring and compassionate, firm in his resolve to do the right thing, and fully informed of his legal rights and responsibilities. When Western tries to send Mrs Honour to Bridewell for allegedly insulting his sister, he is misinformed, ignorant of the law, and ridiculously hasty in his deliberations. The contrast between the two tribunals looks very graphic. But, in each case, the magistrate is attempting to pass sentence on the wrong person, and Allworthy's greater integrity only makes his misguided conviction more damaging, by provoking envy, spite and confusions.

Of course, it would be wrong to suggest that Fielding is being equally critical of both magistrates. Squire Allworthy is as good a judge as it is possible for a compassionate and unworldly provincial man to be. Greater discernment could only arise from greater scepticism and knowledge of the world, and that would be incompatible with Allworthy's basic decency and trustfulness. However, Allworthy misreads the Jenny Jones case, albeit blamelessly, consistently fails to see through the hypocrisies of Blifil, and misguidedly banishes Tom. There are doubts too about the trials of Black George and Partridge, and the way the compassionate Allworthy as legislator has to rely on the violent Thwackum as his executive is, to say the least, disquieting. Furthermore, Allworthy's well-intentioned incompetence has a wider sphere of operation, in his appearances on the 'Grand Jury' (p. 969), the very body that Fielding gave such a ringing tribute to in his first magistratical pamphlet in 1749. Given that Fielding represents Allworthy as untouched by the usual features of cynicism, hypocrisy, ignorance or self-interest, which distinguish most of the other legal officers in the novels, as being exactly the kind of responsible figure he wanted on his own Grand Juries, yet as still unable to come to the right decisions even when most fully informed, the prospects of an effective and discerning legal system are not made encouraging.

There are repeated problems raised about the legal system throughout this novel, culminating in the confusions surrounding Tom's imprisonment in the Gatehouse after his scrap with Fitzpatrick and the incest scare concerning Tom and Mrs Waters. Although the book moves predictably to its comic resolution, these difficulties are not simply made to disappear, and they indicate points of radical uncertainty in Fielding's ideological position. The most awkward area of confusion for him to negotiate concerns the status of villainy, and its recognisability or predictability. At various points in this novel, he can be seen to give inconsistent accounts of the human capacity for malice, and the appropriate way for the courts to proceed. At his most generous, he gives a reintegrative account of misbehaviour which is based on the human capacity to forgive and change, and on the separation of stigmatised behaviour from the potentially more noble character of the offender. In a conventional comparison of the world and the theatre, Fielding celebrates the human capacity for mixed, inconsistent behaviour:

> Now we, who are admitted behind the Scenes of this great Theatre of Nature, (and no Author ought to write any Thing besides Dictionaries and Spelling-Books who hath not this Privilege) can censure the Action, without conceiving any absolute Detestation of the Person, whom perhaps Nature may not have designed to act an ill Part in all her Dramas: For in this Instance, Life most exactly resembles the Stage, since it is often the same Person who represents the Villain and the Heroe; and he who engages your Admiration To-day, will probably attract your Contempt To-Morrow.
>
> (p. 327)

This tribute to human volatility and mutability is structurally important in the novel, allowing Tom to misbehave, particularly in his dalliance with Lady Bellaston, while retaining a basis of authorial respect. It also prepares the ground for the forgiving, integrative gestures at the end, where even the awful Blifil seems to be forgiven and accommodated, and the possibilities of renewal are acknowledged by this separation of action and character.

However, this principle of mutability is at odds with the knowability and rigidity of comic characters, and with the judgemental element in the book. On other occasions, the narrator of *Tom Jones* offers a much stricter version of human possibility:

> I shall add but one more, however unchristian it may be thought by some, I cannot help esteeming to be strictly justifiable; and this is a Suspicion that a Man is capable of doing what he hath done already, and that it is possible for one who hath been a Villain once, to act the same Part again.
>
> (p. 616)

Here we see the point of intersection between Fielding's idealism and his pragmatism, with the ideological contest being won by the more conservative sense of the predictability of human behaviour. There is, of course, room for interpretation of this passage, depending on whether 'possible' is taken to suggest 'not impossible' or 'likely', but my own view is that the more conservative and pragmatic version is the predominant one. That this is Fielding's more firmly held belief can be corroborated by citing a supportive passage from his earlier 'Essay on the Knowledge of the Characters of Men' (1743):

> I shall not here dispute the Doctrine of Repentance, any more than its

Tendency to the Good of Society; but as the Actions of Men are the best Index to their Thoughts, as they do, if well attended to and understood, with the utmost Certainty demonstrate the Character; and as we are not so certain of the Sincerity of the Repentance, I think we may with Justice suspect, at least as far as to deny him our Confidence, that a Man whom we once knew to be a Villain, remains a Villain still.[22]

This distrustful and wary attitude seems to be at odds with the flexibility and capacity to surprise that Fielding mentioned when comparing actions and acting. Its pertinence to the resolution of the novel is obvious, as Sophia challenges Tom in these very terms in the penultimate scene (p. 972). Angered and hurt by the evidence of his letter to Mrs Bellaston, she feels unable to take Tom's protestations of innocence at their face value, and forces him to prove that his character is better than his actions might suggest.

In the 'Essay', the relevance of this wariness to legal proceedings is further clarified:

Actions are their own best Expositors; and though Crimes may admit of alleviating Circumstances, which may properly induce a Judge to mitigate the Punishment; from the Motive, for Instance, as Necessity may lessen the Crime of Robbery, when compared to Wantonness or Vanity; or some other Circumstance attending the Fact itself, as robbing a Stranger, or an Enemy, compared with committing it on a Friend or Benefactor; yet the Crime is still Robbery, and the Person who commits it is a Robber; though he should pretend to have done it with a good Design, or the World should concur in calling him an honest Man.

(pp. 163–4)

The position articulated here is consistent with Fielding's role as magistrate, proceeding with due caution, exercising a concern for justice above all, and, according to Margaret Anne Doody, it is also 'consistent with the delineation of character found in Fielding's novels'.[23] There is something to be said for this, if the comic novels are seen as exercises in mitigation, revealing all the circumstances of any action in a much more detailed and interconnected way than would be available to a legally-constituted court. And it is a useful way to contrast Fielding's confidence about discovering the nature of character with Richardson's much more contested examinations of the human capacity for disguise and inscrutability.

Yet again, this consistency does not seem to be the whole story. Fielding uses the comic structure to put these two ideas about human knowability and inscrutability together, only arbitrating between them in the benign guise of the comic author. The reintegration that resolves his fiction is so persistently the result of mishap and accident that we are both reassured by the momentary achievement of justice and disconcerted by the structural pressures which make such accidents possible. Justice, in these novels, is a poetic and comic fiction, constructed and facilitated by the slick untying of ideological knots and tangles available to the prestidigitative narrator, who can simply reveal that Tom's good nature is, after all, the result of innate good breeding. The revelation about character at the end, appealing to the reader's conscience, enables the dissociation of personality and action which allows reintegration. The harder line put forward in the 'Essay' and in parts of *Tom Jones* remains in dialectical opposition to the ideology of comedy, where transformation is essential if a reintegrative ending is to be achieved. That the pressures on this ideological fissure were powerful and intense can be seen in the partial breakdown in reintegration in Fielding's last novel, *Amelia*, where the law is once again represented as a necessary, but deeply flawed description of human conduct and where the changeability or consistency of the human character is a deeply disturbing and contested issue.

LAW AND DISORDER

But without considering *Newgate* as no other than Human Nature with its Mask off, which some very shameless Writers have done, a Thought which no Price should purchase me to entertain, I think we may be excused for suspecting, that the splendid Palaces of the Great are often no other than *Newgate* with the Mask on. Nor do I know any thing which can raise an honest Man's Indignation higher than that the same Morals should be in one Place attended with all imaginable Misery and Infamy, and in the other, with the highest Luxury and Honour. Let any impartial Man in his Senses be asked, for which of these two Places a Composition of Cruelty, Lust, Avarice, Rapine, Insolence, Hypocrisy, Fraud and Treachery was best fitted, surely his Answer must be certain and immediate; and yet I am afraid all these Ingredients glossed over with Wealth and a Title, have been treated with the highest Respect and Veneration in the one, while one or two of them have been condemned to the Gallows in the other.[24]

As a pamphleteer, journalist and magistrate, Fielding attempted to address the questions of civic order and control which were raised by the operations of the contemporary English legal system. The solutions he offered were of a broadly conservative cast, emphasising the need for discipline and restraint, rarely showing the ironic vigour of the above quotation. Into his comic novels, too, Fielding insinuated a complementary critique of Augustan social justice which, although often understated or unemphatic, was nonetheless pervasive and sustained. With differing degrees of scepticism, exasperation, tolerance or mitigation, he anatomised the veridical incompetence of the law itself, its magistrates, its courts, and the various authorised and official forensic tribunals, contrasting them unfavourably with the firm and kindly authoritative supervision of the comic narrator. Under the tolerant jurisdiction of comedy, the inept operations of legal discrimination initially provoked, yet, by the controlling intrusions of the narrator, also eventually helped resolve the necessary comic confusions. In the face of these obvious institutional failures, Fielding sought to present his cases directly to that less partial and more reliable judge in chambers, the conscience of the good-natured reader. However, this pursuit of a universal and disinterested appeal was in some measure compromised by radical uncertainties in the novels about the nature of human villainy and the knowability of character, and by the possibilities of eventual forgiveness and reintegration required by comedy.

Amidst the confusions about human predictability and the stability or volatility of character in these novels, it remained unclear whether the law was best understood as a necessary, if flawed, bastion against inevitable human depravity, rather inefficiently protecting the essentially innocent from the essentially wicked, or as a rather crude mechanism designed to assist the promotion of social harmony by stigmatising vice and encouraging those transformations towards virtue which comedy invites. In other words, was the law valuable because it might occasionally intervene to make things better, or only because its existence could sometimes prevent things from getting worse? Although the comic novel, Fielding's own private forensic tribunal, allowed the author to indicate the failings of the authorised legal system and the manifest hypocrisies and affectations of upper-class life, his basic conservative allegiances, working together with the traditional gestures of acceptance in comedy, prevented him from offering radical or potentially disturbing solutions to these problems. His preferred strategy is instead to gloss them over and accommodate them within the plot by a slickly devised reversal of fortunes, climactically re-establishing hierarchical expectations by suddenly providing the honourable and previously humble central character with 'Wealth and a Title'.

As we have already seen, there are problems involved in identifying a fully coherent ideological position in Fielding's novels. The complex interactions of their announced moral values and their more covert class allegiances are difficult to disentangle. For most of the time, he assumes the uncontested acceptability of a comfortably hierarchical and conservative presentation of society, recognising that there might be internal problems in the alignment of rank and merit within it, but pleading that those at the top live up to the responsibilities conferred by their status and those at the bottom are not unnecessarily mistreated. More insistently, however, he seems to be advocating a more egalitarian analysis of moral worth, expressing profound scepticism about the standards of behaviour in those 'Palaces of the Great', showing that decency and integrity are at least as frequently to be found in the hearts of the humble as in the exploits of the privileged, and that consequently some redistribution of rewards might be appropriate, even if only within the fantasised and marginal instrumentality of comedy.

While it is obvious that Fielding expresses contempt for many of the vices and habits to be found exclusively in 'high life', he complicates matters by showing the virtual universality of the weaknesses of pride, vanity and envy. It is obvious in *Jonathan Wild* and elsewhere that he is prepared to redefine the prevailing moral vocabulary, becoming especially vehement about the social significance of the term 'Great', as misapplied to both Walpole and Wild. But he is not prepared simply to invert the established social hierarchy, and defend the lowly at the expense of the elevated. Instead, he attempts to adopt a moral perspective which does not restrict itself exclusively to questions of rank, based rather more on apparently classless ideas of 'benevolence', 'good-nature' and 'conscience', allowing him to stand apart from his strictest affiliations and assess the relative merit of individuals of whatever rank in a quasi-objective manner.

Within the discipline of fiction, rewards and punishments can momentarily be administered to the morally deserving, under the reliable jurisdiction of the presiding authority in the text. In the process, Fielding also engages in a social critique, which is not entirely straightforward. Sometimes he seems eager to demonstrate that the humble are just as good as the wealthy, while at other times he contrives to reveal that they are just as bad. These two ways of thinking about the organisation of society, the social and the moral, or, in terms of Fielding's own allegiances, the hierarchical and the latitudinarian, are mutually interrogative, offering a McKeonish 'double critique'. The tensions and disparities exposed between rank and merit within the fictions cannot be easily dismissed, and they create fissures and rifts in the comic structure. The narrative structures of the two comic novels might be extraordinarily regular and symmetrical, but the complex and inconsistent affiliations on which they are based create conceptual instabilities which no amount of rhetorical finesse or organisational dexterity can fully disperse.

On occasions like his brief and seemingly casual aside about the transported postillion in *Joseph Andrews*, whose rank might be humble but whose merit is paradoxically great, Fielding seems to be infiltrating hints of far-reaching disintegrative satire, after the fashion of *Jonathan Wild*, into a plot whose overall pattern is incompatibly reintegrative and hierarchical. It is unsettling to remember that some of the characters unable to participate in the festive comic ending, like the postillion, are the most decent and generous of spirit encountered anywhere in the whole tale On other occasions, like the derisive treatment of Lady Bellaston or Beau Didapper, Fielding seems to be using the exclusive moral authority and virtually complete discernment of his narrator within the world of the fictions to reassemble the hierarchical model of society, with which he still remains fundamentally in sympathy, along more evaluative lines.

This exercise in transvaluation is well exemplified when he redefines the 'Mob' in the early part of *Tom Jones* as 'Persons without Virtue, or Sense, in all Stations, and many of the highest Rank are often meant by it' (p. 59). Clearly, he is here entertaining a different agglomeration from the 'low' crowds of drunken sailors and their like who were defined as the sources of the problems dealt with in the magistratical pamphlets. However, although the comic novels are full of these satirical asides and rhetorical flourishes, they remain largely gestural, and the overall pattern of the narrative does not fully live up to the radical potential of this moralistic and socially subversive assessment. The oddity of Fielding's comic novels is that they seek to reproduce their society in a reintegrative way and while simultaneously exposing its flaws, exploit an ideological space in which the author can both accommodate himself to the defects he identifies, and feel free to criticise them.

These ideological complexities arise mostly from overlapping affiliations, from the conjunction of a class-based or rank-based political and legal system with a moral ideology which announces the equal worth of all citizens, and they furtively but persistently interrupt or disturb the leisurely progress of the comic fictions. The role of the comic narrator is to acknowledge these awkwardnesses and points of ideological pressure, but to ensure that they are contained as much as possible within the overall reintegrative structure of the fiction. As a result, the novels can more or less achieve a form of integrated resolution unavailable in society, slickly re-aligning most of the disparities of rank and merit which the machinery of the plot seemed designed to separate, making the wonderfully contrived justice of the ending a pleasing but, upon closer examination, a rather empty imaginative fiction. Poetic justice momentarily takes precedence over institutionalised justice, by an authorial process of selection, prestidigitation and omission. Again, Fielding seems prepared to acknowledge and incorporate, but not to develop, the social, moral and political problems of his culture, which its legal system and its inequitable allocation of justice encapsulate.

However, the tensions and difficulties created by the intersection of disguised or unpredictable individual behaviour with the more rigid categories and practices of the statute and the social hierarchy, which lurk in the shadows of the comic novels, are much more openly discussed and indeed form the central concern of Fielding's final novel, *Amelia* (1751). As is well known, this more sombre novel was felt by many contemporary readers to be disappointing, and a relatively dismissive attitude towards the book has only recently begun to be challenged. Although the usually unsympathetic Dr Johnson thought it Fielding's finest work, and William Cleland reviewed it with some qualified enthusiasm, most other Augustan commentators found little to please them in *Amelia*, and its inconsistencies, anachronisms and sobriety of tone even resulted in Fielding being treated to that same derisive parodic mockery to which he had earlier subjected Samuel Richardson.[25] In an appropriate form of reply, Fielding answered his critics (and anticipated further objections) through the mock trial of *Amelia* before 'the Court of Censorial Enquiry' in *The Covent-Garden Journal* in January 1752, seeking to defend his novel and dismiss resistance to its 'low' preoccupations and its unorthodox non-proboscidean heroine.[26] Once again, deliberately leaving these vexed questions of literary merit aside as largely irrelevant, there can be no doubt that this last novel is most interesting from my point of view, revealing as it does the various connections and misconnections between Fielding the conservative magistrate and pamphleteer and Fielding the imaginative novelist.

Unlike the comic novels, *Amelia* does not offer its readers the guarantee of safe conduct and fair dealing promised by a fully-realised presiding narrator, and its characters seem as a result much less assiduously protected from the vicissitudes of fortune. This final novel is a much starker recitation of adversities and impediments, of sustained injustice and hardship and misfortune, than either of the comic fictions. It is also much less even in tone, mingling bouts of Juvenalian invective, and apparently unrelated satiric episodes with intermittent sentimental disclosures of domestic life. Furthermore, it is perhaps the only novel in English in which a character dies by falling down a well with a tea-kettle. As Terry Castle puts it, '*Amelia* resists recuperation as a unified artistic whole; it has never been adduced as a New Critical heterocosm.'[27] Indeed, despite Fielding's earlier contemptuous treatment of *Pamela*, the didacticism of *Amelia* shows signs of its author having assimilated elements of the more developed Richardsonian version of domestic or connubial tragedy. In a comparable way, Richardson, in his final novel, *Sir Charles Grandison*, perhaps showed signs of having learnt from the reintegrative structures of Fielding's work.[28] While by no means directly imitating the extensiveness or intensity of *Clarissa*, or essaying its epistolary style, Fielding nonetheless uses the marriage-based plot of this novel in an analogous way to construct a dramatised debate about the role of fortune in human affairs and to identify the proper response to adversity, worked through the concerns of private life, a subject he returned to frequently in *The Covent-Garden Journal* and elsewhere. However, alongside these rather more abstract concerns, he also used the narrative to provide an imaginative enactment of his legalistic and magistratical positions, and to insinuate a vigorous embellishment of their motivations.

Without the elaborate perorations or the intricate introductions and preliminaries of the earlier comic works, this tale opens abruptly and unceremoniously in the courtroom of the lazy and corrupt 'trading justice' Jonathan Thrasher:

> The second Criminal was a poor Woman, who was taken up by the Watch as a Street-walker. It was alledged against her that she was found walking the streets after Twelve o'Clock, and the Watchman declared he believed her to be a common Strumpet. She pleaded in her Defence (as was really the Truth) that she was a Servant, and was sent by her Mistress, who was a little Shopkeeper, and upon the Point of Delivery, to fetch a Midwife; which she offered to prove by several of the Neighbours, if she was allowed to send for them. The Justice asked her why she had not done it before. To which she answered, she had no Money, and could get no Messenger. The Justice then called her several scurrilous Names; and declaring she was guilty within the Statute of Street-walking, ordered her to *Bridewell* for a Month.[29]

As well as proceeding with callously undue haste and a demeaning lack of dignity in the conduct of his tribunal, Justice Thrasher also flagrantly exceeds his authority, wholly misinterprets the law, and briskly mistreats the various other characters who appear before him at this session, including the novel's central figure of Captain Booth. Without the supportive reassurances and comforting presence of the comic narrator, the Justice can be seen to be acting throughout in a more unpleasantly capricious and inconsistent way than even the roaring Squire Western managed to do, and in a fashion which has more genuinely disturbing and damaging consequences.

It is interesting to notice that, by casually incorporating the parenthetical '(as was really the Truth)', Fielding's narrator tells readers how to interpret Thrasher's actions, and shows us unambiguously how despicable they are. We see the appointed officer of the law committing travesties and injustices, our responses supervised by the narrator's authoritative intervention, and our outrage and abhorrence are being solicited. The Justice's behaviour here would be reprehensible enough if the woman actually was guilty, but it is made doubly vile by our privileged knowledge of her innocence. Yet we are not encouraged to see this as a particularised attack on some thinly-disguised contemporary, for Thrasher is clearly meant to represent a species rather than an individual, typifying the polar opposite of the enlightened Justice Fielding. Indeed, the author uses this episode not only as an opportunity for the creation of a grotesque and a spot of generalised character assassination, but also as the starting point for a critique of the legal constitution of England, exemplified by the corrupt practices of the metropolis. The analysis offered is consistent with the dark view of London life seen in the tales of Mr Wilson and the Man of the Hill, but its installation in the main body of the narrative makes it seem more far-reaching and radical in its tone than anything in his comic writings:

> It will probably be objected, that the small Imperfections which I am about to produce, do not lie in the Laws themselves, but in the ill Execution of them; but, with Submission, this appears to me to be no less an Absurdity, than to say of any Machine that it is excellently made, tho' incapable of performing its Functions. Good Laws should execute themselves in a well regulated State; at least, if the same Legislature which provides the Laws, doth not provide for the Execution of them, they act as *Graham* would do, if he should form all the Parts of a Clock in the most exquisite Manner, yet put them so together that the Clock could not go. In this Case, surely we might say that there was a small Defect in the Constitution of the Clock.
>
> (p. 19)

Although there are undeveloped hints of similar constitutional defects in parts of the *Enquiry*, and an equally disenchanted tone throughout *Jonathan Wild* and the *Voyage to Lisbon*, Fielding's position is more usually that it is the defects in the execution of the laws and personal inadequacies in its officers which provoke the difficulties. By analogously pointing the finger of accusation at George Graham, a famous contemporary horologist, Fielding is daringly suggesting that there are fundamental constitutional problems embedded in and expressed by the legal system, which are exacerbated rather than created by the shabby individual performances of corrupt individuals like Thrasher.

So the scene may look set for a radical novel of social and political dissent, an anticipation of the later Jacobin stirrings of Godwin's *Caleb Williams* or Bage's *Hermsprong*. However, Fielding's grimmest novel depends much less on agitation and protest than it does on consolation, with the moralistic and pious (if rather joyless) statements of Dr Harrison providing its centre of gravity. A deeply flawed world is unsparingly revealed throughout the book, but the aim is to teach readers how best to cope with it, not how to correct it. The tone of address is always admonitory rather than revolutionary, more reminiscent of Johnson's *Rasselas* than anything else, although there are incongruously playful undertones which seem to disrupt the solemnity of the proceedings. As the narrator puts it, reversing the terms of reference of the comic ending, 'how capable the most insignificant Accident is of disturbing human Happiness, and of producing the most unexpected and dreadful Events' (p. 184). The consolatory aspect of *Amelia* means that overall it accepts the world more or less as it is, for want of an alternative, offering suggestions for improvement only within what Fielding sees as strictly realistic limits. For Fielding, it might be possible to appoint better Justices and draw up more intelligent laws, but human nature will remain just as subject to its essential imperfections whatever happens. This perspective is certainly not romantic or progressivist, and the assumptions the author starts from are still deeply conservative in orientation, providing opportunities for him to articulate the concerns of his social pamphlets in a dramatic and intensified form.

In his fictional discussion of the existing system of watchmen, for instance, he puts forward a recognisably conservative critique of the inadequacies of the practice, based partly on the perceived dangers from 'Gangs of young, bold, stout, desperate and well-armed Villains' (p. 20). This notion of organised crime was, as we have seen, a very important part of conservative ideology, a point of convergence which breached normal party divisions, although even in his magistratical pamphlets Fielding was unable to provide much concrete evidence of the existence of such groups of well-disciplined brigands. The 'low' concerns of his earlier works, dealing as they did with the adventures of footmen, bastard outcasts and thief-takers, to the disappointment of such commentators as Johnson, George Cheyne and Richardson, are here intensified by the extended examination of 'those (not improperly called infernal) regions' of Newgate and their criminal inhabitants. However, it must be remembered that the examination is conducted within clearly established conservative parameters, and at the same time the reformative social concerns remain subordinate to the more dramatic clash of personalities, the examination of contemporary sexual politics, and the overall aim of reconciliation or consolation.

Despite the consistent injustice of the sentences passed at Thrasher's tribunal, Newgate is not portrayed as a place where none but the wrongfully arrested and the innocent are confined, contrasting greatly with the pitiful scenes of apprehended debtors and their families in Bondum's sponging-house later on. Instead, Fielding presents the prison as an unmitigatedly vile place, full of impenitent genuine criminals and grotesques like 'Blear-Eyed Moll', frauds like Mr Robinson, some pathetic victims of circumstance, and only a very few displaced persons of any merit. It is a world where rewards and comforts are entirely determined by the availability of money. The behaviour of the inmates, and their keepers, reveals that 'Composition of Cruelty, Lust, Avarice, Rapine, Insolence, Hypocrisy, Fraud and Treachery' which Fielding described in the passage from the *Miscellanies* quoted earlier. Given the cold disdain of the narrative's presentation of the incarcerated, and its equal contempt for their imprisoners, there is no reason to suppose that Fielding was seeking to romanticise any of the parties involved in this enterprise, offer a protest about prison conditions, or revisit the more intense paradoxes of *Jonathan Wild*. In fact, although offering an opportunity for a radical revision of the social hierarchy and an uncovering of the legal system's role in maintaining it in its present inequitable state, the social criticism inherent in the tale is watered down once again to a plea for more compassionate treatment of debtors and a conventional call for clear-sightedness about the presence of both good and bad at most points in the scale.

There are many occasions within the tale where Fielding's disengagement from an institutional analysis, and his consequent reliance on the moral integrity of individuals, become obvious. When Miss Mathews expresses astonishment at the native generosity of a humble Serjeant in Booth's story, he points the moral for her:

> yet I know not, on a more strict Examination into the Matter, why we should be more surprised to see Greatness of Mind discover itself in one Degree, or Rank of Life, than in another. Love, Benevolence, or what you will please to call it, may be the reigning Passion in a Beggar as well as in a Prince; and wherever it is, its Energies will be the same.
>
> To confess the Truth, I am afraid, we often compliment what we call upper Life, with too much Injustice, at the Expence of the lower. As it is no rare thing to see Instances which degrade human Nature, in Persons of the highest Birth and Education; so I apprehend, that Examples of whatever is really great and good, have been sometimes found amongst those who have wanted all such Advantages. In Reality, Palaces, I make no Doubt, do sometimes contain nothing but Dreariness and Darkness, and the Sun of Righteousness hath shone forth with all its Glory in a Cottage.
>
> (pp. 123–4)

These noble sentiments lie at the heart of Fielding's ideology, exposing his commitment to a revitalised definition of honour and to the 'reigning Passion' in individuals which cuts across the categories of rank, without being used to disrupt these categories in any very sustained or damaging way. The mismatch of status and merit is articulated throughout the novel by the incongruity of the precise system of military rank and the relative merits of, say, Serjeant Atkinson and Colonel James, with Captain Booth seeming to take up an interim position between them in both title and decency. Yet Fielding clearly does not burn with revolutionary fervour. Despite the acknowledged disparities in merit, the inhabitants of these palaces and cottages are not being encouraged to change places, and readers are not being incited to effect any such change. Within the novel, such sceptical perceptions about rank are given space, but are surrounded by ironic confusions, such as the belief which the Keeper of Newgate expresses that a man as refined as the Captain must be a 'Gentleman of the Road', a highwayman after the fashion of Gay's MacHeath, or the contrast in personal codes of honour between Booth and the conventionally 'gallant' Colonel Bath, or the misunderstandings about the marriage of Serjeant Atkinson and Mrs Ellison.

At a later point in the tale, the disparity of rank and merit is rehearsed in such a way as to suggest that marriage is one way of reconciling these conflicts, and that the identification and rewarding of true merit is best done by enlightened and perceptive individuals in their private lives rather than by a public mechanism as clumsy as the statute:

> 'How monstrous then,' cries *Amelia*, 'is the Opinion of those, who consider our matching ourselves the least below us in Degree, as a Kind of Contamination!'
>
> 'A most absurd and preposterous Sentiment,' answered Mrs. *Bennet* warmly, 'how abhorrent from Justice, from common Sense, and from Humanity – but how extremely incongruous with a Religion, which professes to know no Difference of Degree; but ranks all Mankind on the footing of Brethren!'

(p. 305)

The conflict between rank and brotherhood indicated by Mrs Bennet and predictably endorsed later by Dr Harrison is dramatised in the novel by the conflict between public roles and private desires. So often throughout this tale, hidden motives are uncovered, or secrets are disclosed, leading us to suspect that the outward carriage and public status of individuals is at best a clumsy guide to their true character, and that behind the smiling mask there may lie a disfigured visage.

This concern repeats some of the hesitations over the inscrutability of character which were embedded in the comic fictions, particularly in Fielding's presentation of the hypocritical Blifil. However, the treatment of character in *Amelia* extends such uncertainties into the day-to-day business of society and married life, and articulates them through the very inconsistent personalities of most of the figures, like Mrs Bennet/Atkinson, who at various points in the tale is noble, pathetic, intermittently snobbish, frequently tipsy, helpful and an accessory to deception. Fielding seems to be creating a world in which the ordering of events is both encouraged and impeded by the hierarchy of social status, and in which it is up to the active discernment of individuals to assess the merit of contemporaries, in areas of deceptiveness and duplicity where the law does not intervene, without making the whole necessary system too unstable. Rather than seeking a drastic review of society and its accepted disciplines, Fielding is using the disciplinary tribunal of the novel to teach discernment and help readers make the best of things, without offering a very confident account of the possibilities of success. After all, if even a disciplined novel is full of inconsistencies, changes in perspective, and surprises, how much more unsettling must be the larger and less strictly supervised arena of real life.

Through the mixed character of the Captain, just as through the good-natured inconsistencies of Tom Jones, Fielding conducts an examination of the possibility that a basically good (though rather dull) man might be able to live a consistently good life in a corrupt and hostile world, wherein the systems of social and personal regulation are greatly and inevitably imperfect. The impediments to the morally successful life in this case are made obvious. Booth is not socially elevated, and in fact spends most of the narrative incarcerated or hiding from his creditors and being pursued by Murphy the corrupt attorney. Being an unlucky military officer, then a particularly incompetent farmer, he yet retains some vestiges of gentlemanly standards and responsibilities without the financial resources to live up to them. Once he has been made bankrupt, however, it becomes much more difficult for him to behave well, and he starts the novel entrapped in Newgate apparently without prospect of bail, not because of debt but through an unfortunate act of sudden generosity in trying to help an innocent man beat off some roughs who were attacking him.

After his surprisingly prolonged 'criminal Conversation' with Miss Mathews, Booth is metaphorically arraigned before the reader's court of conscience, a forensic tribunal held by the author to be more intelligent and compassionate than that run by Thrasher or his like. In his summing-up, Fielding infiltrates another quasi-legal defence of his character's conduct to help us assess culpability and reach what the author sees as the correct decision, later rather astonishingly endorsed by Amelia herself:

> We desire that the good-natured and candid Reader will be pleased to weigh attentively the several unlucky Circumstances which concurred so critically, that Fortune seemed to have used her utmost Endeavours to ensnare poor *Booth's* Constancy. Let the Reader set before his Eyes a fine young Woman, in a manner a first Love, conferring Obligations, and using every Art to soften, to allure, to win, and to enflame; let him consider the Time and Place; let him remember that Mr. *Booth* was a young Fellow, in the highest Vigour of Life; and lastly, let him add one single Circumstance, that the Parties were alone together; and then if he will not acquit the Defendant, he must be convicted; for I have nothing more to say in his Defence.
>
> (p. 154)

This is a splendidly worldly and ironic passage, but its engaging patrician frankness should not gloss over the disturbing features and sexual tensions within it. By Fielding's authorial advocacy, the combat between the alluring predatory Miss Mathews and the helpless Captain is made to seem very unequal, like the comparable encounters in Gay's *Trivia* or Boswell's journals, with the odds stacked against Booth to such an extent that he cannot really be held responsible for his unavoidable inconstancy.

The strategy of Fielding's defence is most interesting, and more complex than his narrator's defence of Tom Jones in the Molly Seagrim episode. Rather than relying on more orthodox extenuating circumstances, like drink or youthful lustiness, Fielding presents a defence based on a specific understanding of gender. Leaving Booth's responsibilities to Amelia (as yet unseen by readers) out of the considerations, he seeks acceptance of the Captain's conduct by soliciting the complicity of the (male) reader, inviting him to imagine the difficulties of resisting his own ideal (female) seducer. The irresistible temptress is presented as an agent of powerful (female) Fortune, who is clearly an exculpatory projection of the (male) author. Fielding may be sensibly addressing his imagined jurors as males, since in fact females were ineligible for this public office, but the plea for worldly tolerance and acceptance sits oddly alongside his tacit acceptance of these exclusions and gendered equivocations. The notion that licentious women were to blame for male sexual behaviour, also prominent in so many other Augustan texts, is in this case disquietingly given the full endorsement of the magisterial author, alerting us to the subtextual re-writing of Fielding's own personal marital history which seems to go on throughout the novel.[30] The main narrative seems to be based around the interaction of the worthy, naïve and constant woman, Amelia, and the much more knowing and predatory female figure, of whom there are many interspersed through the history. As Booth tells his wife, before the intrigues really begin, 'how little dost thou guess at the Art and Falsehood of Women!' (p. 241). As readers, we are assumed to have much greater awareness of these wiles.

But again this is not the whole story, and Fielding introduces a number of contesting versions of sexual politics and male duplicity, including the tale of Mrs Bennet's seduction by the womanising Lord, although this attempt to redress the balance is compromised by its reliance on the 'Art and Falsehood' of Mrs Ellison, and by the much greater misery her infidelity brings upon her than Booth's did upon him. Although marriage is occasionally seen in the tale as a private way of reconciling disparities of rank and merit, sexual desire seems virtually anarchic, disfiguring the hierarchical understanding of society while being beyond the reach of legislation. Fielding describes the power and the dangerousness of sexual attraction when he discusses the consequences of Colonel James's passion for Amelia:

> Thus the Object of the Colonel's Lust very plainly appears; but the Object of his Envy may be more difficult to discover. Nature and Fortune had seemed to strive with a kind of Rivalship, which should bestow most on the Colonel. The former had given him Person, Parts, and Constitution, in all which he was superior to almost every other Man. The latter had given him Rank in Life, and Riches, both in a very eminent Degree. Whom should this happy Man envy? Here, lest Ambition should mislead the Reader to search the Palaces of the Great, we will direct him at once to *Gray's-Inn-Lane*; where in a miserable Bed, in a miserable Room, he will see a miserable broken Lieutenant, in a miserable Condition, with several heavy debts on his Back, and without a Penny in his Pocket. This, and no other, was the Object of the Colonel's Envy. And why? because this Wretch was possessed of the Affections of a poor little Lamb; which all the vast

Flocks that were within the Power and Reach of the Colonel, could not prevent that Colonel's longing for. And sure this Image of the Lamb is not improperly adduced on this Occasion: For what was the Colonel's Desire but to lead this poor Lamb, as it were, to the Slaughter, in order to purchase a Feast of a few Days by her final Destruction, and to tear her away from the Arms of one where she was sure of being fondled and caressed all the Days of her Life.

(p. 339)

The almost allegorical figuring of Amelia as a helpless lamb is very far away from the representation of the alluring Miss Mathews, and shows again some of the ideological uncertainties surrounding female sexuality, and, in this instance, profound irrationalities in the human character which seem capable of undermining the stabilities of hierarchy. 'Lust' and 'Envy' seem not to respect rank, yet not to work towards brotherhood, and the inability of society to contain or redirect these forces positively is reflected in the way they create great tensions and turmoil in Fielding's narrative.

The author brings together at this point a number of images of the human capacity for villainy, and reveals even more forcefully than in *Tom Jones* the concomitant imperceptiveness and impotence of the decent. Neither Booth nor Dr Harrison unaided can detect the schemes of Colonel James or the rakish Peer, and, when such designs are revealed, they have no avenue of redress through the law. They could, of course, be entitled to avenge insults to gentlemanly honour by duelling, but Harrison dismisses this possibility as barbaric and quite properly illegal. Harrison, normally so respectful of the law, also makes many indignant noises about its failure to criminalise adultery, rehearsing arguments that Fielding himself articulated in *The Covent-Garden Journal* in May 1752, which again sit oddly alongside the more casual treatment of Booth's Newgate dalliance. Once more, the valorisation of the chaste and pure wife seems to be underpinning a sexual ideology tolerant of male misdemeanours, creating an area of turmoil and confusion through male jealousy and suspicion which is animated and occasionally contested throughout the book.

What happens as *Amelia* progresses is that the certainties and starkness of the opening, with its unambiguous portrait of Thrasher, gradually get overtaken by the developing confusions of character, sexual politics, the law and the various imperfect systems of regulation which are insistently revealed. The simple paradox of the unjust justice becomes beset by more complex formulations of order and disorder, represented in society, in its institutions and in its personalities, culminating in the authorised disruptions and subterfuges of the masquerade and the very briskly-contrived felicities of the ending. The scenes at Hay-Market clearly advance the plot in a complex and sometimes rather baffling way, but they also confuse the strict Harrisonian morality of the book, by showing human affairs as much less rational and orderly than he would wish. When Harrison's letter to Colonel James falls into the wrong hands, and is publicly performed, with mocking interjections, by some disguised bucks, Fielding seems to be engaging with the entertaining craziness of the world more seriously than elsewhere. The orthodox and solemn morality of Dr Harrison is made to seem absurd and out-of-touch in this madcap environment, reflecting 'the generalized topsy-turvydom of the fictionalised world'.[31]

Recklessness and volatility are much more forcefully incorporated in the plot of this book than in any other of Fielding's works. Games of cards, dreams, sudden attacks, fainting, illness and jealousy all figure in the progress of events, and the eventual impression is of a world almost beyond control, hardly to be kept in check by the pious moralising of Harrison, or the high-minded conservatism of Fielding himself. As the narrative unfolds, it seems to slip away from its overt didacticism, and to take on a much more paradoxical zest for confusion, uncertainty and hesitation. When Amelia expresses anxiety about her husband's freedom of thought, she might be speaking to the reader on Fielding's behalf: 'I have often wished . . . to hear you converse with Dr. *Harrison* on this Subject; for I am sure he would convince you, though I can't, that there really are such Things as Religion and Virtue' (p. 451). Time and again, Fielding strenuously claims the existence of 'Religion and Virtue', while the surrounding narrative offers very little support for the efficacy of these claims, other than in the saintly tolerance and forbearance of Amelia herself. Indeed, in the latter part of the book, the plot itself seems to break down, and collapse into a series of not very closely related stories, whose composite effect is of manifold injustices and exceptional social confusion, interspersed with strident calls for reform from Fielding. The story of Trent's dealings with the law is one example, the affair of Booth and Betty the servant another, but the point is most dramatically put towards the end of the book, when a distinguished Peer analyses the state of the nation for the benefit of Dr Harrison:

> in the Natural Body, I believe, you will allow there is the Season of Youth, the Season of Manhood, and the Season of Old Age; and that, when the last of these arrives, it will be an impossible Attempt by all the Means of Art to restore the Body again to its Youth, or to the vigour of its middle Age. The same Periods happen to every great Kingdom. In its Youth it rises by Arts and Arms to Power and Prosperity. This it enjoys and flourishes with a while; and then it may be said to be in the Vigour of its Age, enrich'd at home with all the Emoluments and Blessings of Peace, and formidable abroad with all the Terrors of War. At length this very Prosperity introduces Corruption; and then comes on its old Age. Virtue and Learning, Art

and Industry, decay by Degrees. The People sink into Sloth and Luxury, and Prostitution. It is enervated at home, becomes contemptible abroad; and such indeed is its Misery and Wretchedness, that it ressembles a Man in the last decrepid Stage of Life, who looks with Unconcern at his approaching Dissolution.

(p. 461)

Harrison sees this 'three ages of man' attitude as excessively melancholy, leading a man of spirit to think of suicide. But the Peer does not take such a fatalistic stance, and argues that such a picture should instead impel a man to action – 'Would it not be wiser, think you, to make the best of your time, and the most you can in such a Nation?'

There can be little doubt that this combination of resignation and practicality was close to Fielding's own views. In a comparable passage in the *Enquiry*, Fielding had quoted with approval Conyers Middleton's analogy between the decline of the Roman Empire and the state of Britain (pp. 73–4). In *Amelia*, he tries to anatomise everything that is wrong with his society, its injustices, its venality, its excessive fondness for disguise, intemperance and luxury, its confusions about sexual proprieties, and its inability to recognise and reward true merit. Although he makes some intermittent hints about improvement, the overall impression is of a world of confusions and cross-purposes, wherein Harrison's morality and the authorised practices of the legal system look suspiciously remote. But Fielding, in his characteristically conservative way, tries to make the best of it. The narrative, which looks impelled to run headlong into tragedy, is turned round to felicity by a tribunal run by a magistrate who looks very much like a self-projection. Rewards and punishments are duly and fairly allocated, with the whole benign ending looking as fantastical a transformation as the ending of *Our Mutual Friend*.

Once again, we see Fielding exerting magistratical authority over his fiction, using its internal discipline to replace the chaos of the world which its narrative has revealed. His engagement with the legal system has already covered most points, from a belief that it is basically sound, and in need only of tinkering, through greater calls for reform, through more agitated concern that the constitutional make-up might be seriously flawed. In *Amelia*, all these possibilities are still present, but they are articulated through a catalogue of injustice and mayhem. The final effect is to suggest that only figures as well-informed, enlightened and intelligent as the narrator can successfully run a tribunal, and even then the nearest to regulation that human affairs can achieve is managed through the fictions of literary structure and poetic justice.

Postscript: Buttock and File

The final section of Samuel Johnson's *Rasselas* is headed 'The Conclusion, in Which Nothing is Concluded'. Readers should prepare themselves for an equally unemphatic ending to the present volume. It is not that I see the preceding pages as inconsequential or insignificant, of course. The whole range of writing about Augustan crime examined so far has revealed itself to be extraordinarily diverse and various in its treatment of the central issue of law-breaking, and capable of supporting both the most optimistic and the most pessimistic views of social organisation and civilisation. Such a juxtaposition of opposites would in itself be worthy of commentary, and, when the texts under discussion also articulate and contest contemporary notions of human nature, gender, social mobility and the status of literature, it is obvious that the subject of how writers addressed questions of legality demands serious attention.

But the problem of conclusion remains. I have deliberately restricted the compass of my discussion in a way that may look arbitrary, leaving aside, say, the complementary representations of the figure of the pirate, or the odd treatment of gypsies in the eighteenth-century novel.[1] Similarly, the other side of the coin, the way the Augustan legal system responded to literature and the ways its courts treated authors and publishers, has not been given any developed analysis. But even with these regrettable omissions, the material offered seems to resist easy summing up. The difficulties are well expressed by Michel Foucault:

> Perhaps we should see this literature of crime, which proliferated around a few exemplary figures, neither as a spontaneous form of 'popular expression', nor as a concerted programme of propaganda and moralization from above; it was a locus in which two investments of penal practice met – a sort of battleground around the crime, its punishment and its memory. If these accounts were allowed to be printed and circulated, it was because they were expected to have the effect of an ideological control – the printing and distribution of these almanacs, broadsheets, etc. was in principle subject to strict control. But if these true stories of everyday history were received so avidly, if

they formed part of the basic reading of the lower classes, it was because people found in them not only memories, but also precedents; the interest of 'curiosity' is also a political interest. Thus these texts may be read as two-sided discourses, in the facts that they relate, in the effects they give to these facts and in the glory they confer on those 'illustrious' criminals.[2]

Foucault's identification of the 'two-sided discourse' seems to me to be very apt and provocative. Although a great many legalistic texts at this time were clearly at the service of the legislators, designed to facilitate and advance the creation of hegemony, many others were just as clearly designed to resist it. Furthermore, as we have seen, the same text might contain both the possibilities of collaboration and dissent in a dialectical tension, and a text designed to support the maintenance of established power might yet be exploited by readers in unexpected and contentious ways.

Whatever its overt aims and deepest conscious commitments, then, Augustan literature both disseminates and resists the official criminalisation of activities and individuals. The point of discontinuity between literature and law becomes clearer in the formulation of Antonio Gramsci:

If every State tends to create and maintain a certain type of civilisation and of citizen (and hence of collective life and of individual relations), and to eliminate certain customs and attitudes and to disseminate others, then the Law will be its instrument for this purpose (together with the school system, and other institutions and activities).[3]

In this version, the law is the central mechanism used by political society to impose its meanings on civil society. By extension, literature intermittently projects and stabilises these meanings, while also having the capacity intermittently to disrupt and problematise them.

Augustan writers thus found in the notion of 'crime' an essentially contested concept within whose meanings many different emphases could be found. The idea also provided authors with a way of exploring the pressure points of contemporary ideology, of examining in a whole range of nuanced forms the distributions of power in society. What we see in the confrontation of literature and the law is thus not a collaboration but a 'battleground', to use Foucault's term, a prolonged skirmish of ideologies in which the inner tensions and contradictions of Augustan society are replicated, intensified and made manifest. Literature's role in society is thus never simply passive, recording or documenting practices and procedures, but always interventionist, seeking to stabilise or destabilise the prevailing distribution of power and allocation of meanings.

As I write these inconclusive conclusions, I am conscious that this formulation is reminiscent of the terms set out at the beginning, and it may still sound like an article of faith rather than a demonstrable historical hypothesis. However, in the examination of the numerous writers and texts offered in the earlier chapters, I hope the plausibility and acceptability of this view has by now been adequately demonstrated. In short, if a swindle has been perpetrated by these pages, I hope that the pleasures of the text have made it seem like a case of Buttock and File rather than Buttock and Twang.

Notes

INTRODUCTION: BUTTOCK AND TWANG

1 Stanley Cohen, *Folk Devils and Moral Panics* (London, 1972), p. 16.
2 Raymond Williams, *Keywords: A Vocabulary of Culture and Society* (London, 1976), pp. 150–4.
3 A full discussion of the history and significance of this term will be found in Howard Erskine-Hill, *The Augustan Idea in English Literature* (London, 1983), *passim*. See especially the lengthy bibliography on pp. 235–6. See also David Nokes, *Raillery and Rage: A Study of Eighteenth Century Satire* (London, 1987), pp. 32–42.
4 See Paul Hair, *Before the Bawdy Court* (London, 1972), pp. 232–55; and John Addy, *Sin and Society in the Seventeenth Century* (London, 1989), *passim*. For a discussion of the decline of the church courts, see Christopher Hill, *Puritanism and Society in Pre-Revolutionary England* (London, 1964), pp. 315–20.
5 J. A. Sharpe, *Crime in Early Modern England 1550–1750* (London and New York, 1984), p. 4. Sharpe's definition is critically discussed by Clive Emsley, *Crime and Society in England 1750–1900* (London and New York, 1987), p. 2.

1 LITERATURE/CRIME/SOCIETY

1 Sir William Blackstone, *Commentaries on the Laws of England*, 4 vols (Oxford, 1766), i, 5–6. Further references to this edition will be incorporated in the text.
2 Adam Smith, *An Inquiry into the Nature and Causes of the Wealth of Nations* (1776), ed. R. H. Campbell, A. S. Skinner and W. B. Todd, 2 vols (Oxford, 1976), ii, 910.
3 The statutes referred to by Blackstone are 9 Geo I c.22, and 31 Geo II c.42.
4 J. M. Beattie, *Crime and the Courts in England 1660–1800* (Oxford, 1986), p. 622. See also Douglas Hay, 'Property, Authority and the Criminal Law', in D. Hay, P. Linebaugh, J. G. Rule, E. P. Thompson and C. Winslow (eds) *Albion's Fatal Tree: Crime and Society in Eighteenth-Century England* (London, 1975), pp. 17–65.
5 Beattie, *Crime and the Courts*, p. 621.
6 Sir Leon Radzinowicz, *A History of English Criminal Law and its Administration from 1750, Vol. 1: The Movement For Reform* (London, 1948), p. ix. A very different version of the developments in penal behaviour will be

found in Michael Ignatieff, 'State, Civil Society and Total Institutions: A Critique of Recent Social Histories of Punishment', in Stanley Cohen and Andrew Scull (eds) *Social Control and the State* (Oxford, 1985), pp. 75–105.

7 ibid.

8 Michael Ignatieff, *A Just Measure of Pain: The Penitentiary in the Industrial Revolution, 1750–1850* (London, 1978), p. 17. See the discussion of this argument in David Philips, '"A Just Measure of Crime, Authority, Hunters and Blue Locusts": The "Revisionist" History of Crime and the Law in Britain, 1780–1850', in Cohen and Scull, *Social Control and the State*, pp. 50–74.

9 E. P. Thompson, *Whigs and Hunters: The Origin of the Black Act* (London, 1975), p. 23.

10 David Hume, *A Treatise of Human Nature* (1739), ed. L. A. Selby Bigge, 2nd edn rev. P. H. Nidditch (Oxford, 1976), p. 579.

11 Michel Foucault, *Discipline and Punish: The Birth of the Prison* (1975), trans. A. Sheridan (London, 1977), p. 7.

12 *Hanging Not Punishment Enough For Murtherers, Highway-men and Housebreakers* (1701), quoted by J. M. Beattie, 'Towards a Study of Crime in Eighteenth Century England: A Note on Indictments', in P. Fritz and D. Williams (eds) *The Triumph of Culture: Eighteenth-Century Perspectives* (Toronto, 1972), pp. 299–300.

13 See especially Geoffrey Pearson, *Hooligan: A History of Respectable Fears* (London, 1983), pp. 183–202; and Raymond Williams, *The Country and the City* (London, 1973), *passim*.

14 Quoted by M. Dorothy George, *London Life in the Eighteenth Century* (London, 1925), pp. 10–11.

15 Henry Fielding, *An Enquiry into the Causes of the Late Increase of Robbers &c.* [1751], ed. Malvin R. Zirker (Oxford, 1988), p. 75. For a discussion of the importance of Fielding's argument, see Hugh Amory, 'Henry Fielding and the Criminal Legislation of 1751–2', *Philological Quarterly* 50 (1971), 189–90.

16 Jonas Hanway, *The Defects of Police, the Cause of Immorality, and the Continued Robberies committed, particularly in and about the Metropolis . . .* (London, 1775), p. 224, quoted in J. J. Tobias, *Crime and Industrial Society in the Nineteenth Century* (London, 1967), p. 24.

17 Patrick Colquhoun, *A Treatise on the Police of Metropolitan London* (London, 1796), pp. vii–xi, 5, 230. For a discussion of these figures, see George Rudé, *Criminal and Victim: Crime and Society in Early Nineteenth-Century England* (Oxford, 1985), p. 123. An accessible account of them, as well as a detailed table of the figures, will be found in Donald A. Low, *Thieves' Kitchen: The Regency Underworld* (London, 1982), pp. 23–32. Rudé attributes the sensationalism of Colquhoun's demonstration to his 'Gaelic imagination' (p. 123). The researches of the present writer have been unable to confirm that this fervour is an intrinsic part of the psychological make-up of the inhabitants of Dumbarton.

18 Basil Williams, *The Whig Supremacy 1714–1760* (1939), 2nd edn rev. C. H. Stuart (Oxford, 1962), pp. 132–3.

19 Thompson, *Whigs and Hunters*, p. 194.

20 J. A. Sharpe, *Crime in Early Modern England 1550–1750* (London and New York, 1984), pp. 119–20.

21 *The British Crime Survey: First Report*, ed. M. Pugh and P. Mayhew, Home Office Research Study no. 76, HMSO (London, 1983). For discussions of the 'dark figure', see Joel Samaha, *Law and Order in Historical Perspective* (London, 1974), pp. 13–24; J. A. Sharpe, *Crime in Early Modern England*, pp. 46–8; J. J. Tobias, *Crime and Industrial Society in the Nineteenth Century*,

pp. 10–21; Howard Zehr, *Crime and the Development of Modern Society* (London, 1976), pp. 14–19.

22 Thompson, *Whigs and Hunters*, p. 196.

23 See M. D. George, *London Life in the Eighteenth Century*, pp. 16–18. For an exactly opposite view, see George Rudé, *Hanoverian London, 1714–1808*, pp. 96–8.

24 Beattie, *Crime and the Courts*, p. 78.

25 Beattie, *Crime and the Courts*, pp. 199–200; Douglas Hay, 'War, Death and Theft in the Eighteenth Century: The Record of the English Courts', *Past and Present* 95 (1982), 117–60. For a summary of this discussion, see Sharpe, *Crime in Early Modern England*, pp. 41–8.

26 John Styles, 'The Criminal Past: Crime in Eighteenth-Century England', *History Today* (March 1988), p. 39.

27 Michael Harris and Alan Lee (eds) *The Press in English Society from the Seventeenth to the Nineteenth Centuries* (London and Toronto, 1986), p. 21.

28 J. A. Sharpe, *Crime in Early Modern England*, pp. 8–9.

29 James Heath, *Eighteenth Century Penal Theory* (Oxford, 1963), pp. 27, 39, 52.

30 T. B. Macaulay, *The History of England*, ed. Sir C. Firth, 6 vols (London, 1913), i, 310–13. See also the discussion of this point in W. A. Speck, *Society and Literature in England 1700–1760* (Dublin, 1983), pp. 3–13.

31 Alan Macfarlane, *The Justice and the Mare's Ale: Law and Disorder in Seventeenth-Century England* (Oxford, 1981), p. 24.

32 For a persuasive sceptical assessment of Smollett's version of the navy, see N. A. M. Rodger, *The Wooden World: An Anatomy of the Georgian Navy* (London, 1986), p. 14.

33 Samuel Johnson, *Preface to the Plays of William Shakespeare* (1765), in *Samuel Johnson*, ed. D. Greene (Oxford, 1984), p. 421.

34 R. W. Malcolmson, 'Infanticide in the Eighteenth Century', in J. S. Cockburn (ed.) *Crime in England 1550–1800* (London, 1977), pp. 187–210. Passage quoted from p. 188.

35 W. A. Speck, *Society and Literature in England 1700–1760* (Dublin, 1983), p. 12.

36 Lawrence Stone, *The Family, Sex and Marriage in England 1500–1800* (London, 1977), pp. 280–1.

37 ibid., p. 366 (my italics).

38 ibid., p. 294. The passage quoted comes from *Moll Flanders* (Everyman edn), pp. 57–8, 52.

39 ibid., p. 522. The author of *Fanny Hill* was, of course, *John* Cleland, not James Cleland.

40 Speck, *Society and Literature*, ch. 2; John Loftis, *Comedy and Society from Congreve to Fielding* (Stanford, 1959), *passim*.

41 Lawrence Stone and Jeanne C. Fawtier Stone, *An Open Elite? England 1540–1880*, abridged edn (Oxford, 1986), p. 19.

42 See Ian A. Bell, *Defoe's Fiction* (London, 1985), esp. ch. 3.

43 W. A. Speck, 'The Harlot's Progress in Eighteenth Century England', *British Journal for Eighteenth-Century Studies* 3 (1980), 127.

44 Fernand Braudel, *Civilisation and Capital 15th–18th Century: Vol. II The Wheels of Commerce* (1979), trans. S. Reynolds (London, 1982), p. 516.

45 See Derek Jarrett, *England in the Age of Hogarth* (London, 1974), pp. 51–2.

46 For the most recent account of this incident, see Paula R. Backschieder, 'No Defense: Defoe in 1703', *PMLA* 103 (1988), 274–84. Interesting examples of the approval and occasional violent disapproval of pilloried felons are given in Beattie, *Crime and the Courts*, pp. 464–8.

47 A different, but complementary analysis of this print may be found in P. Linebaugh, 'The Ordinary of Newgate and his *Account*', in J. S. Cockburn

Crime in England 1500–1800 (London, 1977), pp. 246–69. See also the comparable selective description of an execution in Henry Fielding, *The Covent-Garden Journal*, No. 25 (18 March 1752), in *The Covent-Garden Journal and A Plan of the Universal Register Office*, ed. Bertrand A. Goldgar (Oxford, 1988), p. 416.

48 George Lillo, *The London Merchant* (1731), ed. W. H. McBurney (London, 1965), p. 78.

49 See Ronald Paulson, *Hogarth: His Life, Art, and Times*, abridged edn (New Haven and London, 1974), p. 255. A fuller account of the ambiguities detected by Paulson can be found in his *Emblem and Expression: Meaning in English Art of the Eighteenth Century* (London, 1975), pp. 58–78. A complementary discussion of the incongruities in the structure and composition of the *Industry and Idleness* sequence, particularly in the banquet scene, can be found in David Dabydeen, *Hogarth's Blacks: Images of Blacks in Eighteenth Century English Art* (Manchester, 1987), pp. 61–2.

2 REPRESENTING THE CRIMINAL

1 Samuel Johnson, 'London', in *The Complete English Poems*, ed. J. D. Fleeman (Harmondsworth, 1971), p. 68. Further line references, incorporated in the text, will be to this edition.

2 See the relevant and stimulating discussion of this issue in Lincoln Faller, *Turned to Account: The Forms and Functions of Criminal Biography in Late Seventeenth- and Early Eighteenth-Century England* (Cambridge, 1987), pp. 2–4. Faller's book is the most developed consideration of this particular kind of Augustan criminal literature so far, and what I say in the following pages is obviously much indebted to it.

3 See the discussion of crime reports in the contemporary newspapers in Jeremy Black, *The English Press in the Eighteenth Century* (London, 1987), pp. 80–1.

4 The advertisements and other peripheral references to crime in the newspapers are discussed by John Styles, 'Sir John Fielding and the Problem of Criminal Investigation in Eighteenth-Century England', *Transactions of the Royal Historical Society*, 5th series, 33 (1983), pp. 127–49.

5 Quoted in Gerald Howson, *It Takes a Thief: The Life and Times of Jonathan Wild* (London, 1987), pp. 68–9.

6 *The Spectator*, III, 187.

7 Jonathan Swift, *Journal to Stella* ed. Harold Williams (Oxford, 1948), II, 511. Swift was sceptical about the existence of these villains, but nonetheless felt sufficiently anxious for his own safety to take chairs home after dark during the scare, and characteristically complained about the expense. The whole business of the Mohocks is interestingly discussed in *John Gay: Dramatic Works*, ed. John Fuller (Oxford, 1983), I, 3–7.

8 Claude Lévi-Strauss, 'The Structural Study of Myth' (1955), in *Structural Anthropology* (New York, 1963), p. 229.

9 For discussions of crime fiction as pastoral, see John G. Cawelti, *Adventure, Mystery, and Romance: Formula Stories as Art and Popular Culture* (Chicago and London, 1976), pp. 80–106; Stephen Knight, *Form and Ideology in Crime Fiction* (London, 1980), pp. 107–35; and Anna-Marie Taylor, 'Home is Where the Hearth Is: The Englishness of Agatha Christie's Marple Novels', in Ian A. Bell and Graham Daldry (eds) *Watching the Detectives: Essays on Crime Fiction* (London, 1990), pp. 134–52.

10 I am indebted to K. O. L. Burridge, 'Lévi-Strauss and Myth', in Edmund Leach (ed.) *The Structural Study of Myth and Totemism* (London, 1967), pp. 91–119.

11 See Paul Salzman, *English Prose Fiction 1558–1700: A Critical History* (Oxford, 1985), pp. 209–18. Faller, *Turned to Account*, discusses the various biographies of Hind in some detail, pp. 1–16, 118–27.

12 Richard Bjornson, *The Picaresque Hero in European Fiction* (Madison, 1977), p. 164.

13 Alexander A. Parker, *Literature and the Delinquent: The Picaresque Novel in Spain and Europe 1599–1753* (Edinburgh, 1967), p. 7.

14 Lennard J. Davis, *Factual Fictions: The Origins of the English Novel* (New York, 1983), p. 85.

15 John J. Richetti, *Popular Fiction Before Richardson: Narrative Patterns 1700–1739* (Oxford, 1969), pp. 23–60. Further page references will be incorporated in the text.

16 See the lengthy discussion of this issue in John L. McMullan, *The Canting Crew: London's Criminal Underworld 1550–1700* (New Brunswick, 1984).

17 John Gay, 'Newgate's Garland', in *John Gay: Poetry and Prose*, ed. Vinton A. Dearing, with Charles E. Beckwith (Oxford, 1974), I, 287.

18 See the discussion of these terms in Victor Turner, 'Social Dramas and Ritual Metaphors', in *Dramas, Fields, and Metaphors: Symbolic Action in Human Society* (Ithaca and London, 1974), pp. 23–60.

19 For discussions of the ritualised procedures of the courtroom, see J. M. Beattie, *Crime and the Courts in England 1660–1800* (Oxford, 1986), pp. 314–18; John Baker, 'Criminal Courts and Procedure at Common Law, 1550–1800', in J. S. Cockburn (ed.) *Crime in England 1500–1800* (London, 1977), pp. 15–48; Douglas Hay, 'Property, Authority and the Criminal Law', in D. Hay *et al.* (eds) *Albion's Fatal Tree*, (London, 1975), pp. 26–31; and two important articles by John H. Langbein, 'The Criminal Trial before the Lawyers', *University of Chicago Law Review* 45 (1978), 263–316 and 'Shaping the Eighteenth-Century Trial: A View from the Ryder Sources', *University of Chicago Law Review* 50 (1983), 1–136.

20 Daniel Defoe, *The History of the Remarkable life of John Sheppard, etc.* (1724), in *The Shakespeare Head Edition of the Novels and Selected Writings of Daniel Defoe: The Fortunate Mistress Vol. II* (Oxford, 1928), p. 166.

21 Daniel Defoe, *A True and Genuine Account of the Life and Actions of the Late Jonathan Wild, etc.*, in *Shakespeare Head Edition: Colonel Jacque*, II, 232–3.

22 Peter Linebaugh, 'The Ordinary of Newgate and his *Account*', in Cockburn (ed.) *Crime in England*, p. 248.

23 The Gaol Delivery Rolls, and other surviving documents like bail bonds, recognizances, depositions, coroners' reports, jury lists, etc., are discussed by Howson, *It Takes a Thief*, pp. 327–8.

24 John H. Langbein, 'The Criminal Trial before the Lawyers', p. 271. By contrast, see the discussion of 'fictitious elements' in indictments and reports in Beattie, *Crime and the Courts*, pp. 20–4.

25 See the argument in Robert Robson, *The Attorney in Eighteenth-Century England* (Cambridge, 1959) and the copious illustrations in J. A. Sharpe, *Crime and the Law in English Satirical Prints 1600–1832* (Cambridge, 1986).

26 John Gay, *The Beggar's Opera*, in *Dramatic Works*, ed. John Fuller (Oxford, 1983), II, 16–17.

27 Alexander Pope, *The Rape of the Lock* (1714), III, 19–23.

28 See J. A. Sharpe, '"Last Dying Speeches": Religion, Ideology and Public Execution in Seventeenth-Century England', *Past and Present* 107 (1985), 144–67. Full consideration of the circumstances of public execution will be found

in Peter Linebaugh, 'The Tyburn Riot Against the Surgeons', in D. Hay *et al.* (eds) *Albion's Fatal Tree*, pp. 65–119.

29 Sir Leon Radzinowicz, *A History of English Criminal Law and its Administration from 1750, Vol. 1: The Movement For Reform* (London, 1948), pp. 178–81.

30 Bernard Mandeville, *An Enquiry into the Causes of the Frequent Executions at Tyburn* (1725), ed. Malvin R. Zirker, Jr, Augustan Reprint Society #105 (Los Angeles, 1964), pp. 24–5.

31 Jonathan Swift, 'Clever Tom Clinch Going to be Hanged', in *The Complete Poems of Jonathan Swift*, ed. Pat Rogers (Harmondsworth, 1983), p. 316.

32 *The Prose Works of Jonathan Swift*, ed. Herbert Davis (Oxford, 1948), IX, 37. Further references will be incorporated in the text. This pamphlet has attracted little critical attention. The most developed account of the piece itself and the fascinating circumstances of its publication will be found in George P. Mayhew, 'Jonathan Swift's Hoax of 1722 upon Ebenezor Elliston', in A. Norman Jeffares (ed.) *Fair Liberty Was All His Cry: A Tercentenary Tribute to Jonathan Swift* (London, 1967), pp. 290–310.

33 Gay, *The Beggar's Opera*, ed. J. Fuller, II, 59. Further references will be incorporated in the text.

34 See the presentation of the play in Emmett L. Avery (ed.) *The London Stage, 1600–1800: A Calendar of Plays, etc., Part Two: 1700–1729* (Carbondale, Ill., 1960).

35 Michael Denning, 'Beggars and Thieves: *The Beggar's Opera* as Crime Drama', in Peter Humm, Paul Stigant and Peter Widdowson (eds) *Popular Fictions: Essays in Literature and History* (London, 1986), p. 29. See also the discussion of the pastoral elements in the play in William Empson, *Some Versions of the Pastoral* (London, 1935).

36 Peter Elfed Lewis, *John Gay: The Beggar's Opera* (London, 1976), p. 59.

37 *The Correspondence of Jonathan Swift*, ed. Harold Williams (Oxford, 1963), II, 215.

38 'Newgate's Garland', in *John Gay: Poetry and Prose*, ed. Vinton A. Dearing, with Charles E. Beckwith (Oxford, 1974), I, 288.

39 A full discussion of these matters will be found in B. A. Goldgar, *Walpole and the Wits: The Relation of Politics to Literature, 1722–1742* (New York, 1976); and J. A. Downie, 'Walpole, "The Poet's Foe"', in Jeremy Black (ed.) *Britain in the Age of Walpole* (London, 1984), pp. 171–89. Further 'criminalisation' can be seen in the contemporary prints collected in Paul Langford, *Walpole and the Robinocracy* (London, 1986).

40 I am indebted to the discussion of this picture in Ronald Paulson, *Hogarth: His Life, Art and Times*, abridged edn (New Haven, Conn., 1971), pp. 75–84.

41 *The Letters of John Gay*, ed. C. F. Burgess (Oxford, 1966), p. 45

42 These references and borrowings are described in William Eben Schultz, *Gay's Beggar's Opera, its Content, History and Influence* (New Haven, Conn., 1923), pp. 167–73.

43 See Fuller's introduction to *John Gay: Dramatic Works*, I, 46–8; and C. F. Burgess, 'Political Satire: John Gay's *The Beggar's Opera*', *Midwest Quarterly* 6 (1965), 265–76.

44 *The Correspondence of Jonathan Swift*, ed. Williams, III, 267.

45 *The Prose Works of Jonathan Swift*, ed. Herbert Davis (Oxford, 1955), XII, 34–5.

46 See John Loftis, *The Politics of Augustan Drama* (Oxford, 1963), pp. 94–8.

47 This contrast is developed in detail in William Empson's chapter on the play in *Some Versions of the Pastoral*.

48 See Douglas Hay, 'Property, Authority and the Criminal Law', in Hay *et al.* (eds) *Albion's Fatal Tree*, esp. pp. 40–9.

3 THE HARLOT'S PROGRESS

1 George Lillo, *The London Merchant* (1731), ed. W. H. McBurney (London, 1965), p. 66.
2 Bonamy Dobrée, *English Literature in the Early Eighteenth Century* (Oxford, 1959), p. 254.
3 James Boswell, *London Journal 1762–1763*, ed. F. A. Pottle (London, 1950), pp. 240–1.
4 ibid., p. 304.
5 James Boswell, *Boswell in Holland 1763–1764*, ed. F. A. Pottle (London, 1952), p. 279. The extravagant sexual career of James Boswell is discussed in detail in Lawrence Stone, *The Family, Sex and Marriage in England 1500–1800* (London, 1977), pp. 572–99.
6 William Alexander, *The History of Women* (London, 1779), I, 210. Quoted in Bridget Hill, *Eighteenth-Century Women: An Anthology* (London, 1984), p. 111.
7 *Boswell's Life of Johnson*, ed. G. B. Hill and L. F. Powell (Oxford, 1964), V, 208.
8 Quoted in Stone, *The Family, Sex and Marriage in England*, pp. 356–7.
9 Bridget Hill, *Eighteenth-Century Women: An Anthology* (London, 1984), p. 108.
10 J. M. Beattie, *Crime and the Courts in England 1660–1800* (Oxford, 1986) p.438. See also Beattie's more elaborate account of women and crime, showing that, despite the prominence of the whore in literature, the most persistent female crime was petty theft or larceny: J. M. Beattie, 'The Criminality of Women in Eighteenth-Century England', *Journal of Social History* 72 (1975), 80–116.
11 G. R. Elton, 'Introduction: Crime and the Historian', in J. S. Cockburn (ed.) *Crime in England 1550–1800* (London, 1977), p. 13.
12 Quoted in Sir Leon Radzinowicz, *A History of English Criminal Law and its Administration from 1750, Vol. 1: The Movement For Reform* (London, 1948) p. 307.
13 Particular cases of sexual assault are discussed in Beattie, *Crime and the Courts*, pp. 124–32. For further discussion of the issue of rape, and of the practice of eighteenth-century courts, see Anna Clark, *Women's Silence Men's Violence: Sexual Assault in England 1770–1845* (London, 1987), pp. 46–58, and Nazife Bashar, 'Rape in England between 1550–1700' in London Feminist History Group (ed.) *The Sexual Dynamics of History: Men's Power, Women's Resistance* (London, 1983), pp. 28–31.
14 See Radzinowicz, *A History of English Criminal Law*, p. 148.
15 This incident is discussed in its context in Derek Jarrett, *England in the Age of Hogarth* (London, 1976), pp. 112–13.
16 See the discussions of women writers in Jane Spencer, *The Rise of the Female Novelist: From Aphra Behn to Jane Austen* (Oxford, 1986); Bridget Hill, *The First English Feminist* (London, 1986); and Maureen Duffy, *The Passionate Shepherdess: Aphra Behn* (London, 1977). Defoe's pamphlets on women are discussed in detail in Shirlene Mason, *Daniel Defoe and the Status of Women* (Vermont and Montreal, 1978). The female prize-fighters are discussed in Jack Lindsay, *The Monster City: Defoe's London 1688–1730* (London, 1978), pp. 54–5.
17 John Duncombe, *The Feminiad* (1754), ed. Jocelyn Harris, Augustan Reprint

Society, #207 (Los Angeles, 1981), pp. 14–15. See also Mary Scott, *The Female Advocate* (1774), ed. Gae Holladay, Augustan Reprint Society, #224 (Los Angeles, 1984).

18 For examples of the alleged connection between wit and licentiousness in women, see Spencer, *The Rise of the Female Novelist*, pp. 4–6; and Myra Reynolds, *The Learned Lady in England, 1650–1760* (New York, 1920), pp. 372–419.

19 Quoted in Felicity A. Nussbaum, *The Brink of All We Hate: English Satires on Women 1660–1750* (Kentucky, 1984), pp. 148–9. Nussbaum discusses the ideological tensions in female confessional writing in 'Heteroclites: The Gender of Character in the Scandalous Memoirs', in Felicity A. Nussbaum and Laura Brown (eds) *The New Eighteenth Century* (New York and London, 1987), pp. 144–67.

20 Further examples of the more sympathetic treatment of fallen women in later eighteenth-century English fiction are provided in Susan Staves, 'British Seduced Maidens', *Eighteenth-Century Studies* 14 (1980–1), 109–34.

21 Capt. Francis Grose, *A Classical Dictionary of the Vulgar Tongue* (1796), ed. Eric Partridge (London, 1931), p. 104.

22 See David Foxon, *Libertine Literature in England 1660–1745* (New York, 1965), pp. 3–19; Roger Thompson, *Unfit For Modest Ears: A Study of Pornographic, Obscene and Bawdy Works Written or Published in England in the Second Half of the Seventeenth Century* (London, 1979), *passim*; and Margaret Spufford, *Small Books and Pleasant Histories: Popular Fiction and its Readership in Seventeenth-Century England* (Cambridge, 1981), pp. 156–93.

23 William Wycherley, *The Country-Wife* (1675), ed. David Cook and John Swannell (Manchester, 1975), p. 14. Pepys refers to *L'escolle de Filles* [*sic*] as 'the most bawdy, lewd book that ever I saw . . . so that I was ashamed of reading in it'. See *The Diary of Samuel Pepys*, ed. Robert Latham and William Matthews (London, 1976), IX, 21–2.

24 See *The Works of Thomas Otway*, ed. J. C. Ghosh (Oxford, 1932; repr. 1968), II, 202. In his notes, Ghosh cites a number of other references to Creswel/ Creswold, and describes her as 'too well known in Restoration literature to need introduction' (II, 510). That certain 'madams' could become prominent figures in popular culture can be seen in the off-hand dedication of Wycherley's *The Plain Dealer* (1676) to one such. No explanation is offered, so it may be safe to assume that contemporary readers and audiences were familiar with such figures and did not need to have the woman's identity or significance laboriously spelt out.

25 Anon., *The Whore's Rhetorick etc.* (1683; repr. London, 1960), p. 30. My italics. Further references will be incorporated in the text. I am very grateful to my colleague, James Ogden, for lending me his well-thumbed copy of this book, and for his advice.

26 Quoted in Philip Pinkus, *Grub St. Stripped Bare* (Hamden, Connecticut, 1968), p. 94.

27 Ned Ward, *The London-Spy* (1704), ed. Ralph Straus (London, 1924), p. 141.

28 Daniel Defoe, 'Reformation of Manners', in *Poems on Affairs of State: Augustan Satirical Verse, 1660–1714*, ed. F. H. Ellis (New Haven and London, 1970), VI, 404–5. For an account of the Zachary Crofton case, and the attendant literature, see Thompson, *Unfit for Modest Ears*, p. 43.

29 These pamphlets are discussed in John J. Richetti, *Popular Fiction Before Richardson 1700–1739* (Oxford, 1969), pp. 35–9; and W. A. Speck, 'The Harlot's Progress in Eighteenth-Century England', *British Journal for Eighteenth-Century Studies* 3 (1980), 127–39.

30 'A Beautiful Young Nymph Going to Bed', in *Jonathan Swift: The Complete*

Poems, ed. Pat Rogers (Harmondsworth, 1983), pp. 453–5. All further references to the poem will be to this edition.

31 See Claude Rawson, 'The Nightmares of Strephon: Nymphs of the City in the Poems of Swift, Baudelaire, Eliot', in *Order From Confusion Sprung* (London, 1985), p. 163.

32 John Gay, *Trivia; Or, The Art of Walking the Streets of London* (1716), in *John Gay: Poetry and Prose*, ed. Vinton A. Dearing, with Charles E. Beckwith (Oxford, 1974), I, 134–81. Line references to this edition of the poem will be incorporated in the text.

33 *A View of London and Westminster, or the Town Spy* (1725), pp. 13–14; quoted in W. A. Speck, 'The Harlot's Progress in Eighteenth-Century England', p. 128.

34 J. W. von Archenholz, *A Picture of England* (London, 1789), II, 75. See the comparable descriptions in William Hutton, *A Journey to London* (1785), pp. 47–8, and the discussion of London prostitution in Fernando Henriques, *Prostitution in Europe and the New World* (London, 1963), II, 143–91.

35 Patrick Colquhoun, *A Treatise on the Police of Metropolitan London*, (London, 1796) p. 320. See Donald A. Low, *Thieves' Kitchen: The Regency Underworld* (London, 1982), pp. 23–32.

36 *The Spectator*, ed. Donald F. Bond (Oxford, 1965), II, 534–5. Further references will be to this edition, and will be incorporated in the text.

37 *The Rambler*, #170 and #171 (1751), in *The Yale Edition of the Works of Samuel Johnson*, ed. W. J. Bate and Albrecht B. Strauss (New Haven and London, 1969), V, 135–45.

38 *Boswell's Life of Johnson*, ed. Hill and Powell, I, 457. See also IV, 321–2.

39 Sir John Fielding, *A Plan for a Preservatory and Reformatory, etc.* (1758), pp. 5–6.

40 See W. A. Speck, 'The Harlot's Progress', and Roy Porter, *English Society in the Eighteenth Century* (Harmondsworth, 1982), p. 315.

41 See Russell P. Dobash, R. Emerson Dobash and Sue Gutteridge, *The Imprisonment of Women* (Oxford, 1986), pp. 73–4.

42 'Andrew Moreton' [Daniel Defoe], *Augusta Triumphans* (1728), in *The Versatile Defoe: An Anthology of Uncollected Writings*, ed. Laura Ann Curtis (London, 1979), pp. 409–13.

43 Bernard Mandeville, *The Fable of the Bees* (1714, 1725), ed. Phillip Harth (Harmondsworth, 1970), pp. 126–8.

44 Bernard Mandeville, *A Modest Defence of Publick Stews* (1724), ed. Richard I. Cook, Augustan Reprint Society, #162 (Los Angeles, 1972), iii. Further references will be to this edition, and will be incorporated in the text.

45 My discussion of this sequence is indebted to David Dabydeen, *Hogarth's Blacks: Images of Blacks in Eighteenth Century English Art* (Manchester, 1987), pp. 101–23. For the identification of the figures, see Ronald Paulson, *Hogarth: His Life, Art, and Times*, abridged edn (New Haven and London, 1971), pp. 104–14.

46 Speck, 'The Harlot's Progress', p. 131.

47 The story of Charlot is in Mary de la Rivière Manley, *Secret Memoirs and Manners of several Persons of Quality, of Both Sexes from the New Atalantis* (1709), I, 50–84. It is included in *The Novels of Mary de la Rivière Manley*, ed. Patricia Koster (Gainesville, Florida, 1971), I, 322–56. References will be to the 1709 pagination, and will be incorporated in the text. See the discussions of Manley in Spencer, *The Rise of the Female Novelist*, pp. 113–16; and Richetti, *Popular Fiction Before Richardson*, pp. 132–52.

48 Spencer, *The Rise of the Female Novelist*, p. 116.

49 See the discussions of Haywood in Richetti, *Popular Fiction Before Richardson*, pp. 168–210, and in Mary Anne Schofield, 'Exposé of the Popular Heroine: The Female Protagonists of Eliza Haywood', in *Studies in Eighteenth-Century Culture* 12 (1983), 93–103.
50 Schofield, 'Exposé of the Popular Heroine', p. 102.
51 I have dealt with these narratives in more detail in my *Defoe's Fiction* (London, 1985), Chs 5 and 6.
52 Daniel Defoe, *The Fortunes and Misfortunes of the Famous Moll Flanders etc.* (1722), ed. G. A. Starr (Oxford, 1971), p. 29. Further references will be to this edition, and will be incorporated in the text.
53 Daniel Defoe, *Roxana: The Fortunate Mistress etc.* (1724), ed. Jane Jack (Oxford, 1964), pp. 6–7. Further references will be to this edition, and will be incorporated in the text.
54 See John Cleland, *Memoirs of a Woman of Pleasure* (1748–9), ed. Peter Sabor (Oxford, 1985), pp. xxii–xxiii. Further references will be to this edition, and will be incorporated in the text.
55 See Peter Wagner, 'The Pornographer in the Courtroom: Trial Reports About Cases of Sexual Crimes and Delinquencies as a Genre of Eighteenth-Century Erotica', in Paul-Gabriel Boucé (ed.) *Sexuality in Eighteenth-Century Britain* (Manchester, 1982), pp. 120–41

4 SATIRE'S ROUGH MUSIC

1 Thomas Paine, *The Rights of Man* (1791), ed. Arthur Seldon (London, 1915), p. 32.
2 J. A. Sharpe, *Crime in Early Modern England 1550–1750* (London and New York, 1984), p. 93. Sharpe's findings are confirmed in a number of other studies, such as Alfred Soman, 'Deviance and Criminal Justice in Western Europe, 1300–1800', *Criminal Justice History*, 1 (1980); B. Lenman and G. Parker, 'The State, the Community and the Criminal Law in Early Modern Europe', in V. A. C. Gatrell, B. Lenman and G. Parker (eds) *Crime and the Law: The Social History of Crime in Western Europe Since 1500* (London, 1980); and Michael R. Weisser, *Crime and Punishment in Early Modern Europe* (Brighton, 1979).
3 Jeremy Bentham, *An Introduction to the Principles of Morals and Legislation (1789)*, ed. J. H. Burns and H. L. A. Hart (London, 1970), p. 158.
4 The contemporary justifications for punishment are discussed and assessed in Randall McGowan, 'The Changing Face of God's Justice: The Debates Over Divine and Human Punishment in Eighteenth-Century England', *Criminal Justice History* 9 (1988), 63–99.
5 See the discussion of this point in Douglas Hay, 'Property, Authority and the Criminal Law', in D. Hay *et al.* (eds) *Albion's Fatal Tree* (London, 1975), pp. 19–20.
6 Thomas Hobbes, *Leviathan: or, The Matter, Form and Power of a Commonwealth, Ecclesiastical and Civil* (1651), ed. John Plamenatz (London, 1962), pp. 277, 282. See the discussion of this point in James Heath, *Eighteenth Century Penal Theory* (Oxford, 1963), pp. 8–10, 59–65; and in Howard Warrender, *The Political Philosophy of Hobbes* (Oxford, 1957), pp. 200–21.
7 Thomas Hobbes, *Of Liberty and Necessity* (1654), in D. D. Raphael (ed.) *British Moralists 1650–1800* (Oxford, 1969), I, 63–4. There is a more elaborate discussion of these points in Hobbes's *Dialogue Between a Philosopher and a Student of the Common Laws of England* (1681), ed. Joseph

Cropsey (Chicago and London, 1971). I have not included it here, as there are some doubts about its authorship, and little evidence that it was widely-read. However, it adopts a stance firmly in opposition to the Whig position of the legalist Sir Edward Coke, which claimed that English common law was the embodiment of traditional Anglo-Saxon liberties. In Hobbes's interpretation, the common law simply ensured the maintenance of power, by expressing the will of the conqueror.

8 The diverse utilitarian and retributive theories of punishment are discussed in C. L. Ten, *Crime, Guilt, and Punishment: A Philosophical Introduction* (Oxford, 1987), pp. 7–52; Nicola Lacey, *State Punishment: Political Principles and Community Values* (London and New York, 1988), pp. 16–56, 153–9; and Christopher Harding and Richard W. Ireland, *Punishment: Rhetoric, Rule, and Practice* (London and New York, 1989), pp. 110–17. I am particularly grateful to Harding and Ireland, the human faces of the Law Department, UCW Aberystwyth, for helping me through this material.

9 John Locke, *Second Treatise of Government*, §128, in *Two Treatises of Government*, ed. Peter Laslett (2nd edn, Cambridge, 1967), p. 370. Further references will be to this edition, and paragraph references will be incorporated in the text.

10 Joseph Butler, *Dissertation of the Nature of Virtue* (1736), in *Butler's Fifteen Sermons*, ed. T. A. Roberts (London, 1970), pp. 148–9.

11 Richard Price, *A Review of the Principal Questions and Difficulties in Morals* (1758), ed. D. D. Raphael (Oxford, 1974), pp. 134–5.

12 See Walter Benjamin, 'The Work of Art in the Age of Mechanical Reproduction', in *Illuminations*, ed. Hannah Arendt, trans. Harry Zohn (London, 1970), pp. 219–20.

13 This issue is discussed in J. P. Kenyon, *Revolution Principles: The Politics of Party 1689–1720* (Cambridge, 1977), pp. 63–4; and Gordon J. Schochet, *Patriarchalism in Political Thought* (Oxford, 1975), pp. 192–225. The most wide-ranging treatment of the inheritance of the constitutional debate of the seventeenth century is J. G. A. Pocock, *The Ancient Constitution and the Feudal Law* (Cambridge, 1957), *passim*.

14 See Lawrence Stone, *The Family, Sex and Marriage in England 1500–1800* (London, 1977), pp. 239–45.

15 See Linda A. Pollock, *Forgotten Children: Parent–Child Relations From 1500 to 1900* (Cambridge, 1983), *passim*.

16 Locke's essay, along with other relevant pieces, can be found in *The Educational Writings of John Locke*, ed. J. Axtell (Cambridge, 1968). See the discussion of this point in Peter Earle, *The Making of the English Middle Class* (London, 1989), pp. 230–7.

17 See the extensive catalogue of eighteenth-century flagellation literature in Henry Spencer Ashbee ('Pisanus Fraxi'), *Index of Forbidden Books* (n.d.; reprinted, London, 1969).

18 *Boswell's Life of Johnson*, ed. G. B. Hill and L. F. Powell (Oxford, 1964), i, 45–6. For a discussion of the changes in scholastic discipline throughout Europe in the seventeenth century, see Philippe Ariès, *Centuries of Childhood* (1960; Harmondsworth, 1986), pp. 247–51.

19 See the discussion of the status of the Augustan school-master in Geoffrey Holmes, *Augustan England: Professions, State and Society 1680–1730* (London, 1982), pp. 43–80.

20 For developed accounts of Augustan military and naval discipline, see Christopher Duffy, *The Military Experience in the Age of Reason* (London, 1987), pp. 98–104; and N. A. M. Rodger, *The Wooden World: An Anatomy of the Georgian Navy* (London, 1986), pp. 205–14.

21 Jonathan Swift, *Journal to Stella* (1710–13), ed. Harold Williams (Oxford, 1948), I, 164–265. See also J. M. Beattie, *Crime and the Courts in England 1660–1800* (Oxford, 1986), pp. 97–8.

22 Henry Fielding, *The Covent-Garden Journal and A Plan of the Universal Register-Office*, ed. Bertrand A. Goldgar (Oxford, 1988), p. 37.

23 See *Tracts and Pamphlets by Richard Steele*, ed. Rae Blanchard (Baltimore, 1944), pp. 513–17.

24 *The Tatler*, #31, in *Selections from The Tatler and The Spectator of Steele and Addison*, ed. Angus Ross (Harmondsworth, 1982), pp. 93–4.

25 *The Spectator*, ed. Donald F. Bond (Oxford, 1965), I, 41. Further discussion of duelling will be found in I, 8, 358–60, 387–8, 410–12, 418–19. See also the broader context indicated by Donna T. Andrew, 'The Code of Honour and its Critics: The Opposition to Duelling in England 1700–1850', *Social History* 5 (1980), 409–34.

26 *The Spectator*, I, 126.

27 *The Spectator*, I, 418–19.

28 See the discussion of 'charivari' in Edward Shorter, *The Making of the Modern Family* (1975; pbk edn, Glasgow, 1977), pp. 216–24.

29 The pillory is discussed in detail in Beattie, *Crime and the Courts*, pp. 133–4, 464–8, 614–16. The passage quoted comes from pp. 464–5.

30 See the discussion of the pillory as theatre in Clive Emsley, *Crime and Society in England 1750–1900* (London, 1987), pp. 214–15; and the consideration of public punishment in Peter Linebaugh, 'The Tyburn Riot Against the Surgeons', in D. Hay *et al.* (eds), *Albion's Fatal Tree* (London, 1975), p. 67. The most stimulating treatment of the public's role in these proceedings is E. P. Thompson, 'The Moral Economy of the Eighteenth Century Crowd', *Past and Present* 50 (1971), pp. 76–136.

31 William Paley, *The Principles of Moral and Political Philosophy* (1785), Bk VI, Ch. 9, §4; quoted in James Heath, *Eighteenth Century Penal Theory* (Oxford, 1963), p. 261.

32 Henry Fielding, *A Charge Delivered to the Grand Jury* (1749), in *An Enquiry into the Causes of the Late Increase of Robbers and Related Writings*, ed. Malvin R. Zirker (London, 1988), p. 25.

33 John Braithwaite, *Crime, Shame and Reintegration* (Cambridge, 1989). Page references will be incorporated in the text.

34 John Dryden, *The Poems and Fables of John Dryden*, ed. James Kinsley (Oxford, 1970), p. 189.

35 *The Spectator*, I, 97. The contemporary arguments surrounding satire are identified and developed in P. K. Elkin, *The Augustan Defence of Satire* (Oxford, 1973).

36 See Elkin, *The Augustan Defence of Satire*, pp. 44–71.

37 *The Spectator*, IV, 88. See the discussion of 'real names' in Augustan writing in David Nokes, *Raillery and Rage: A Study of Eighteenth Century Satire* (Brighton, 1987), pp. 50–5.

38 Jonathan Swift, Preface to *A Tale of a Tub*, ed. A. C. Guthkelch and D. Nichol Smith, 2nd edn (Oxford, 1958), p. 48.

39 Jonathan Swift, 'Verses on the Death of Dr. Swift', in *The Complete Poems of Jonathan Swift*, ed. Pat Rogers (Harmondsworth, 1983), p. 497.

40 Jonathan Swift, *The Examiner*, No. 39 (26 April 1711), in Frank H. Ellis (ed.) *Swift vs Mainwaring: The Examiner and The Medley* (Oxford, 1985), p. 391.

41 Alexander Pope, *Correspondence*, ed. George Sherburn (Oxford, 1956), iii, 255.

42 Pope, *Correspondence*, iii, 423.

43 There is a more elaborate version of this argument in the 'William Cleland'

letter, in Pope, *The Dunciad*, ed. James Sutherland (London and New Haven, 1943), p. 14. The passage quoted here comes from Pope, *Imitations of Horace etc.*, ed. John Butt (London and New Haven, 1939), pp. 313–14.

44 David Nokes, *Raillery and Rage*, p. 120.

5 FIELDING AND THE DISCIPLINE OF FICTION

1 Henry Fielding, *A Charge Delivered to the Grand Jury* (1749), in *An Enquiry into the Causes of the Late Increase of Robbers and Related Writings*, ed. Malvin R. Zirker (Oxford, 1988), p. 3. Further references will be incorporated in the text. For the politics of Fielding's appointment, see M. C. and R. R. Battestin, 'Fielding, Bedford, and the Westminster Election of 1749', *Eighteenth-Century Studies* 11 (1977–8), 143–85.

2 Henry Fielding, *A Serious Address to the People of Great Britain* (1745), in *The True Patriot and Related Writings*, ed. W. B. Coley (Oxford, 1987), p. 13.

3 Michael McKeon, *The Origins of the English Novel 1600–1740* (Baltimore and London, 1987), p. 385.

4 These two pamphlets are included in *An Enquiry into the Causes of the Late Increase of Robbers and Related Writings*, ed. Zirker, along with *A Charge Delivered to the Grand Jury*, *A True State of the Case of Bosavern Penlez* (1749) and *A Clear State of the Case of Elizabeth Canning* (1753). Further references to all these pamphlets will be to Zirker's edition, and will be incorporated in the text.

5 Henry Fielding, *A Journal of a Voyage to Lisbon* (1755), ed. A. R. Humphreys (London and New York, 1973), p. 238.

6 See Zirker's introduction, p. xviii. Zirker gives a fuller account of the conservative orientation of these pamphlets in his book, *Fielding's Social Pamphlets* (Berkeley and Los Angeles, 1966), *passim*.

7 For a discussion of the 1750 Committee, and the role of Fielding's proposals, see Sir Leon Radzinowicz, *A History of English Criminal Law and its Administration from 1750 Vol. 1: The Movement For Reform* (London 1948), pp. 399–424; and, expressing a contrary view, Hugh Amory, 'Henry Fielding and the Criminal Legislation of 1751–2', *Philological Quarterly* 50 (1971), 189–90.

8 For a discussion of the Bosavern Penlez case, and an analysis of rioting as it was understood at this time, see Peter Linebaugh, 'The Tyburn Riot Against the Surgeons', in D. Hay *et al.* (eds) *Albion's Fatal Tree* (London, 1975), pp. 65–119; and Nicholas Rogers, 'Aristocratic Clientage, Trade and Independency: Popular Politics in Pre-Radical Westminster', *Past and Present* 61 (1973), 70–106.

9 See especially George Rudé, *The Crowd in History: A Study of Popular Disturbances in France and England 1730–1848* (New York, 1964), pp. 198–204.

10 Morris Golden, 'Fielding's Politics', in K. G. Simpson (ed.) *Henry Fielding: Justice Observed* (London and Totowa, N.J., 1985), p. 43.

11 Zirker quotes a number of comparable passages from contemporary pamphlets, pp. lxi–lxii. The issue is provocatively discussed in John Sekora, *Luxury: The Concept in Western Thought, Eden to Smollett* (Baltimore and London, 1977), *passim*

12 Roy Porter, *English Society in the Eighteenth Century* (Harmondsworth, 1982), p. 255. See also Paul Langford, *A Polite and Commercial People: England 1727–1783* (Oxford, 1989), pp. 296–7, 571–4. The statutes against gaming were 12 Geo II c.28 (1739); 13 Geo II c.19 (1740); 18 Geo II c.34 (1745); and 25 Geo II c.36 (1752).

13 Henry Fielding, *The Covent-Garden Journal and A Plan of the Universal Register-Office*, ed. Bertrand A. Goldgar (Oxford, 1988), p. 350.

14 Henry Fielding, 'Preface' to *Miscellanies, vol. 1*, ed. Henry Knight Miller (Oxford, 1972), p. 10.

15 Margaret Anne Doody, *A Natural Passion*: *A Study of the Novels of Samuel Richardson* (Oxford, 1974), p. 74.

16 See Irène Simon, *Neo-Classical Criticism 1660–1800* (London, 1971), pp. 96–7, 153–4.

17 John Dennis, *A Defence of Sir Fopling Flutter* (1722), in *Critical Works*, ed. E. N. Hooker (Baltimore, 1964), II, 245.

18 Thomas Shadwell, Preface to *The Humorists* (1671), in *The Complete Works of Thomas Shadwell*, ed. Montague Summers (1927, New York, 1968), I, 183–4.

19 Henry Fielding, *The History of the Adventures of Joseph Andrews* (1742), ed. Martin C. Battestin (Oxford, 1967), p. 189. Further references will be incoparated in the text.

20 Henry Fielding, *The History of Tom Jones, A Foundling* (1749), ed. Fredson Bowers, intro. Martin C. Battestin (Oxford, 1974), I, 172–3. Further references will be incorporated in the text.

21 See the comparison of Swift and Fielding in this light in Patrick Reilly, 'Fielding's Magisterial Art', in K. G. Simpson (ed.) *Henry Fielding*: *Justice Observed* (London and Totowa, N.J., 1985), pp. 75–101.

22 Henry Fielding, 'An Essay of the Knowledge of the Characters of Men', in *Miscellanies*, ed. Miller, p. 176.

23 Margaret Anne Doody, 'Identity and Character in *Sir Charles Grandison*', in M. A. Doody and Peter Sabor (eds) *Samuel Richardson*: *Tercentenary Essays* (Cambridge, 1989), p. 115.

24 Henry Fielding, 'Preface', to *Miscellanies*, ed. Miller, p. 10.

25 See *Henry Fielding*: *The Critical Heritage*, ed. Ronald Paulson and Thomas Lockwood (London and New York, 1969), pp. 15–16, 304–9, 321–5, 333. For a more recent version of the case against *Amelia*, see J. Paul Hunter, *Occasional Form*: *Henry Fielding and the Chain of Circumstance* (Baltimore, 1975), esp. p. 214.

26 Henry Fielding, *The Covent-Garden Journal*, ed. Goldgar, pp. 57–60, 65–6.

27 Terry Castle, *Masquerade and Civilization*: *The Carnivalesque in Eighteenth-Century English Culture and Fiction* (Stanford, California, 1986), p. 186.

28 See the discussion of this point in Peter Sabor, '*Amelia* and *Sir Charles Grandison*: The Convergence of Fielding and Richardson', *Wascana Review* 17 (1982), 3–18; but see also McKeon, *The Origins of the English Novel*, pp. 415–17. Further discussion of the relationship between Fielding and Richardson will be found in C. J. Rawson, 'Nature, Cruel Circumstance and the Rage for Order: *Amelia*, with Reflections on Defoe, Smollett and Orwell', in *Henry Fielding and the Augustan Ideal Under Stress* (London and Boston, 1972), pp. 88–93.

29 Henry Fielding, *Amelia*, ed. Martin C. Battestin (Oxford, 1983), pp. 22–3. Further references will be incorporated in the text.

30 For the autobiographical elements, see Battestin's 'General Introduction' to *Amelia*, pp. xvi–xxi.

31 Castle, *Masquerade and Civilization*, p. 206

POSTSCRIPT: BUTTOCK AND FILE

1 For a very stimulating discussion of adjacent issues to those I have sought to cover, see Joel H. Baer, '"The Complicated Plot of Piracy": Aspects of

English Criminal Law and the Image of the Pirate in Defoe', *Studies in Eighteenth-Century Culture* 14 (1985), 3–29.

2 Michel Foucault, *Discipline and Punish: The Birth of the Prison* (1975), trans. A. Sheridan (London, 1977), pp. 67–8.

3 Antonio Gramsci, *Selections From Prison Notebooks*, ed. and trans. Quintin Hoare and Geoffrey Nowell Smith (London, 1971), p. 246

Index